More!
Secrets
of
America's
Best Bass Pros

By Tim Tucker

BOOKS BY TIM TUCKER

Roland Martin's One-Hundred-and-One
Bass-Catching Secrets

Advanced Shiner Fishing Techniques

Secrets of America's Best Bass Pros

More! Secrets of America's Best Bass Pros

Bass Fishing's Trophy Hunters,
Volume Three of the Bass Pro Series
(available in spring of 1992)

To my late father-in-law Bill Palanko who passed on without ever knowing exactly what I did for a living. We miss him still.

Copyright 1991 by Tim Tucker

First Printing 1991

Printed in the United States of America by
Atlantic Publishing Company
P.O. Box 67
Tabor City, N.C. 28463

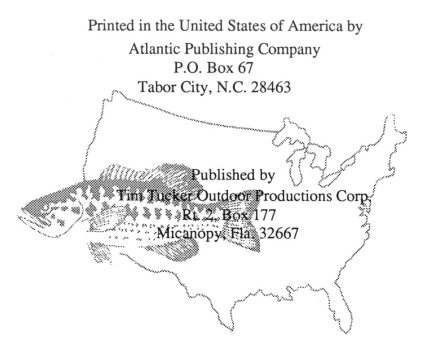

Published by
Tim Tucker Outdoor Productions Corp.
Rt. 2, Box 177
Micanopy, Fla. 32667

Library of Congress Card Number 91-091141
ISBN Number 0-937866-26-1

Photos and cover design by the author

About The Author

Tim Tucker, one of the country's most published outdoor writers, specializes in bass fishing. In addition to being a senior writer for *Bassmaster Magazine, Southern Outdoors* and *B.A.S.S. Times,* Tucker's work has appeared in *Field & Stream, Petersen's Fishing, Fishing Tackle Retailer, Southern Saltwater, Florida Sportsman, Florida Wildlife, Bass Fishing, Bassin'* and *Fishing Facts.*

Winner of more than 56 national, regional and state awards for his writing and photography, Tucker has four books on bass fishing to his credit. He also publishes *Tim Tucker's Florida Bass Update,* a unique monthly insider's newsletter on Florida fishing, and produces the Bass Sessions series of instructional audio cassettes.

In addition, Tucker is co-host of the Bass Radio Network, a national weekly radio show that focuses exclusively on bass fishing and is scheduled to begin broadcasting in the spring of 1992.

An outdoor columnist for the *Palm Beach Post* newspaper for more than a decade, Tucker, 34, lives in Micanopy, Florida, with wife Darlene.

Table of Contents

SECTION ONE
Tools of the Trade

SECTION TWO
Techniques & Tips

SECTION THREE
Patterns & Conditions

Special Bonus

SECTION FOUR
Rick Clunn's
Seasonal System
For Locating Bass

One Man's Plea

The wonderful aspect of our sport is that size limits apply only to the fish. To introduce a youngster to bass fishing is to provide him or her with a lifetime of pleasure in a sport that knows no age, physical or gender boundaries.

Acknowledgements

More! Secrets of America's Best Bass Pros, Volume Two of the Bass Pro Series, is a collection of information accrued by more than a decade of covering the Bassmaster Tournament Trail for *BASSMASTER Magazine*® and *B.A.S.S. Times*®. Like the highly successful *Secrets of America's Best Bass Pros,* this book utilizes the collective talents and wisdom of an amazing group of men.

From past experience dealing with professional athletes in other sports, I can tell you that these guys are a fascinating breed of down-to-earth men who truly enjoy their sport and respect its resources. They willingly share their secrets of catching more and bigger bass, despite the threat that such information could come back to haunt them in a future tournament.

These athletes do something that is, in my opinion, every bit as tough as hitting a major-league fastball — catching a limit of bass day-in and day-out under every condition imaginable. As a group, they have my utmost respect.

Individually, there are several people who deserve a public thanks for their efforts and friendships through the years.

To super-photographer Gerald Crawford, who provided some of the photos for this book, and publicity director Ann Lewis of B.A.S.S., thanks for making my job so much easier.

To editors Dave Precht and Matt Vincent, my appreciation for many years of friendship and direction. They are both journalists who share the same sincere appreciation for the tournament scene and its characters that I do.

To Gary Giudice and Mary Shelsby, fine friends, fishing companions and business partners.

To Horace Carter, good friend and source of constant encouragement. In him, the pioneer spirit has always been alive and well.

The greatest aspect of this profession is the solid people you associate with and the litany of lifelong friends you make. I appreciate such friends as Mark Thomas, Mike Walker, Rick Clunn, Roland Martin, Shaw Grigsby, Guido Hibdon, Bernie Schultz, Doug Hannon, Richard Bowles, Larry Lazoen, Lance Ramer, Cliff Shelby, Wade Bourne, John Phillips, Bobby Hulslander, Bill Dance and Bill Phillips — just to name a few.

Outside of the profession, I am grateful for the limitless friendships of Tom Mulligan, Carol Boger-Doyle, Nichole Bernhardt, Polly Grigsby, George Benchimol and Byron Terwillegar.

To Steve Moore, longtime sports editor of the *Palm Beach Post* newspaper, who convinced me to take the outdoors beat in 1981. I had no way of knowing how much impact his decision would have on my life, both professionally and personally.

Special thanks for my administrative assistant Emily Walker for her assistance on this manuscript and her effort throughout the year.

Thanks to Bernie Schultz and BASSMASTER® Magazine for permission to use the illustrations that accompany the Rick Clunn Seasonal System for Locating Bass. Bernie is a rare find — a talented artist as well as one of the country's top pros.

To Bob and Doris Tucker, I hope I've made you proud in some way.

And, finally, the most important person in my life for the last 16 years or so. Darlene is my wife, best friend and a source of inspiration. She is also the nicest person in this world. I look forward to growing old together.

Tim Tucker
Micanopy, Fla.
July 1, 1991

Foreward

The water is the color of day-old tea and its rippled surface reflects the sun's late-afternoon rays back into the angler's eyes like a hundred tiny strobe lights. Still, the fisherman sees through the intermittent flashes and into the dark water. He likes what he sees. With a smooth and effortless flick of the wrist, he sends a 1/16-ounce tube jig sailing toward his target, 20 paces away.

The fisherman's companion, finally spotting the whitish outline of a bass' spawning bed, silently notes that the bait has overshot its mark. It has not, of course; light refraction through the water only makes it appear that way. With a mixture of surprise and awe at the perfect cast, he watches the bait settle directly into the dark center of the "donut."

A few moments later, the tiny, tentacle-tailed lure disappears. The line twitches. The angler sweeps the rod sharply to the side, simultaneously cranking the reel handle three quick turns. Then he settles down to play the fish, instinctively applying just enough force to subdue the 8-pound bass without over-stressing the 6-pound-test line.

When the bass is ready to give up, the fisherman clamps its lower lip between his thumb and fingers, removes the tiny hook and lets the fish slide back into the water. It has been a flawless performance. But not an unexpected one. The angler is, after all, a pro.

Sight-fishing for spawning bass may seem easy to the uninitiated, but consider: Most of us weekend anglers would have (A) failed to spot the bed, (B) chosen the wrong lure, (C) missed the target on the all-important first cast, (D) set the hook too soon or too late, or (E) lost the bass by applying too much pressure. Or all of the preceding.

That's the main difference between a person who makes his living from bass fishing and those of us who make a living so we can go bass fishing — the pro executes every step with skill and precision. The professional knows where bass live and how they behave and which lure and technique are required to make fish bite under almost any condition.

Over years of fishing as often as 300 out of 365 days, the pro has widened the knowledge gap between himself and the part-time angler. Fortunately for the rest of us, most of these fishing aces are willing (eager, some of them) to share their hard-won expertise with readers of magazines like *BASSMASTER®* and books like Tim Tucker's *More! Secrets Of America's Best Bass Pros.*

Through years of following the Bassmaster Tournament Trail to top lakes and rivers across the country, Tucker has developed a rapport with some of the world's very best fishermen, and he has earned a reputation as a thorough, enterprising reporter of trends and techniques in bass fishing. By writing "Pro's Pointers" and numerous other how-to features in *BASSMASTER*, he has helped the pro fishermen educate hundreds of thousands of weekend anglers in the art of finding and catching bass.

Many of his best articles on productive bass-fishing techniques were compiled into *Secrets Of America's Best Bass Pros*, Volume One of the Bass Pro Series. But this latest volume is ample proof that the pros haven't run out of valuable lessons to share, and Tim hasn't exhausted his stock of how-to stories.

Whether you're a beginner in this wonderful sport of bass fishing or the perennial angler of the year in your B.A.S.S. club, this book should help improve your success — and your enjoyment — in catching bass.

Dave Precht
Editor
BASSMASTER Magazine
July 1, 1991

Introduction

The weigh-in for the second round of the Bassmaster Florida Invitational had just finished when I climbed into the boat of Arizona pro Greg Hines to go back out on the water for a photo session. It was at that point that Scott Secules approached the boat and quietly shook his head. "Man," he said, "you've got THE job."

This came from a man who is the back-up quarterback to the Miami Dolphins' superstar Dan Marino, a man who had participated in a playoff game a couple of weeks earlier, a man who, as a professional athlete, is a hero to thousands. I would trade a limb to play a single down in the National Football League. And he is telling me that I have THE job. But you know, he's right.

I have been fortunate to spend a great deal of my adult life outdoors and on the water with most of the brightest minds in professional fishing. Those countless hours have produced some wonderful, poignant, funny, embarrassing, breathtaking moments that will be with me always. Detailed below are just a few of those moments from more than a decade of covering the tournament trail. I hope they provide a glimpse of what this level of the sport — and its participants — are all about.

Many of my fondest memories involve Roland Martin. Roland was the first bass pro I ever met and the guy who introduced me to writing for outdoors-oriented magazines. Since that first fishing trip in 1981, we have collaborated on a couple of hundred newspaper and magazine stories, along with a book that we are both extremely proud of. And in the process we have developed the greatest of friendships.

I'll never forget that stifling hot summer morning on Lake Okeechobee when we fished so hard to catch a bass for a photo session. After several hours of failure, Roland laid his flipping rod down and said "Forget this. Let's go have some fun." And we did. We went "Okeechobee bonefishing," a joking reference to sight-casting to spawning bluegill in clear water. In less than three hours, we caught more than 140 fish and it became clear just how much this man enjoys the pure act of fishing. At one point, Roland was working on a string of 14 consecutive successful casts and if you closed your eyes and listened, you would have thought the BASS Masters Classic title was on the line.

I'll always remember spending the final round of the 1990 MegaBucks tournament as Roland's press observer. He staged a magnificent performance on that day, executing with the machine-like precision of the Roland Martin of old. It was so easy to get caught up in that excitement as Martin made one of his patented charges in the final hours. *The Bassmasters* television show director Bob Cobb, who is the former editor of *BASSMASTER® Magazine* and one of the pioneers of this sport, watched from a nearby camera boat and remarked that he had not been this excited in 20 years of covering the tournament circuit.

Although he would finish second to Larry Nixon, one part of that day stands out in my memory. Under the MegaBucks format, the competitors fish in designated areas or "holes" for a little less than an hour before rotating to the next. On one particular hole, Roland stopped next to a small open-water island in the middle of Little Lake Harris. Taking full advantage of the benefits of a good friendship, I remarked to him that in the four-year history of the MegaBucks event, the shoreline of this island had not produced a single fish (the observers chart the catches of each pro throughout the day).

"Sounds like the kind of place I like to fish," Roland replied as he picked up a spinnerbait rod. In the next 50 minutes, he proceeded to catch 17 bass off of this island wasteland. Never once did he pause to ridicule my comments. As the time arrived to move to another area, a sly grin crept across Roland's face. "Got anymore bad spots?" he asked as he cranked the outboard.

I sometimes have to remind him that I kicked his butt the first time we ever fished together. He does not, however, have to remind me that it was sheer luck.

●

Memories of the last decade flood my mind as I write this. I'll never forget watching Shaw Grigsby work a bedding bass in the Perrier-like waters of a spring-fed Florida river. I remember being captivated by the masterful way he manipulated the tiny finesse baits, as well as his ability to predict exactly when the strike would come.

I'll always remember a Grigsby deed in the 1990 Classic, the kind of sportsmanship and teamwork that is so often missing from other sports. I was a press observer in the boat of good friend Larry Lazoen, who had entered the final day in fifth place. With only minutes remaining in the fishing day, Grigsby stopped by to check on Lazoen's success, which included a small limit with one bass that might not measure.

Grigsby followed Lazoen's boat into the rear of a small creek, where a mini-drama was about to unfold. Lazoen hooked a bass that dove into an underwater tangle where it refused to budge. With time running out, a disappointed Lazoen was about to break the line when his friend intervened. From a prone position, Grigsby began working his way down the line until he felt the fish, which was solidly hooked. "I can feel it. I've got it," he exclaimed before pulling it to the surface. There was just enough time for Lazoen to bite the line, drop the keeper bass into the livewell and make a full-charged run back to the launch site. But the pair did take the time to shake hands.

•

I'll never forget a fishing trip with top pros Rick Clunn, Shaw Grigsby and Pete Thliveros (all Classic qualifiers) when I caught the largest bass of the day — a 6- or 7-pounder. Come to think of it, I've never let them forget it, either ... Or the pre-dawn greeting of ex-surfer and top western pro Rich Tauber as we were about to spend a hilarious practice day together — "Hey you big surf dog!" It's true what you've heard about Californians...Or a laugh-filled practice day on Alabama's Lake Guntersville with former Classic champion Charlie Reed, one of the nicest human beings on this planet ... Or the sheer enthusiasm and friendly nature of living legend Bill Dance as we spent a rainy morning in his Memphis home just talking fishing.

I'll always remember a day spent with Larry Nixon when he won his first MegaBucks title. How can I forget it — B.A.S.S. photographer Gerald Crawford captured me at my best — asleep in the boat — as Nixon attempts to doodle a plastic worm in my mouth. That photo rests on my office wall... And night-fishing on Pickwick Reservoir for *big* smallmouth with Tennessee pro Charlie Ingram. The quality of the fishing was only surpassed by the company... And accepting a last-minute invitation to join Florida pro Russ Bringger to fish an exclusive Florida Power & Light Co. lake to compete against several dozen media types and top bass fishermen. Relentless, 30-m.p.h. winds made fishing difficult, but the resourceful Bringger put out a pair of sea anchors and suggested working a buzzbait over an expanse of submerged peppergrass. His strategy produced bass weighing 4, 5 and 6 pounds for me. My 6-pound, 4-ounce largemouth won the event, but Russ deserves all of the credit.

I'll never forget fishing with former Classic qualifier and longtime friend Jimmy Rogers in a Florida Outdoor Writers Association mini-tournament. Rogers proved to be an excellent guide that day. The morning began with Rogers casting to one side of a log and catching a 4-pounder on his first attempt. My first cast to the other side of the log produced a 5-pounder. With Roger's help, the only four strikes I had that day weighed 17 pounds (including a 7-pounder), which was more than enough to win the event. The only credit I deserve in this sport is being smart enough to choose good fishing partners. (As an aside, Jimmy Rogers recently became the recepient of a new heart after fighting a heroic battle for survival. I've never known anyone who appreciates life as much as Jimmy. Welcome back!).

I'll always remember a crazy spring day spent in the boat with a pair of fine anglers and fun guys — Woo Daves and Greg South — on the James River. We cracked considerably more jokes than we caught bass, but it was one of the finest days I've ever spent on the water... And catching magnum-sized spotted bass on Lake Lanier with spot master Tom Mann, Jr.... And learning a great deal about catching open water bass and crappie with top pro Steve Daniel on

Lake Okeechobee, of all places... Getting to know Guido Hibdon, who represents all that is right about our sport... In this book, you will find a chapter entitled Last Secret Bait of the Pros. The chapter details the allure of the Rebel Pop-R and the lengths that a handful of pros went to keep it their own personal secret. What the chapter doesn't discuss how word of the Pop-R got out. You might find it interesting. When Zell Rowland won a B.A.S.S. event on Tennessee's Lake Chickamauga in 1987, he refused to identify the winning lure, except to say that it was a "small chugger." This secrecy immediately peaked my interest because the pros' are usually extremely open with such information. So I took the steps that any good reporter would take — I rooted around in his rod box, found the lure and then described it to another pro who identified it. I then took this information to Rowland and Rick Clunn, who realized that the secret was out and freely discussed the subject. Rebel went on to sell more than a million Pop-Rs.

●

Many of my fondest memories were created while observing as a press angler in the annual BASS Masters Classic. Here are just a few such memories:

... I'll never forget the day I spent with fellow Floridian Jim Bitter, who seemed on the verge of solidifying his career. He entered the final round of the 1990 Classic on the James River with a sizeable lead and seemed to have the victory in hand when it, er, slipped from his grasp.

Bitter had caught his fourth bass of the day around noon and as he headed toward the livewell, I asked if it was of legal length. He took out a measuring board, which was placed atop a large Plano tackle box. It measured 13 1/4 inches, which was plenty legal, but as he began to carry the small bass to the livewell, it somehow slipped out of his hand, landed on either the tackle box or the boat's windshield and escaped back into the waters of the James.

With the composure that I would never have been able to muster, Bitter handled the situation like a gentleman. Later at the Richmond Coliseum weigh-in before 10,000 screaming fishing fans, Bitter would come up just 2 ounces short of winner Hank Parker. Although the realization that the escaped bass would have given him the biggest victory of his career immediately set in, Bitter was gracious in painful defeat. My admiration and respect for him soared.

... My first Classic was the 1982 event on the Alabama River. My first pro partner was North Carolina's Jerry Rhyne, one of the genuinely nice guys on the tournament trail. Although Jerry has done a good job of keeping it a secret, I'm about to admit an embarrassing start to my career as a Classic press angler. Early that morning, I somehow tossed a new baitcasting outfit into the waters of the Alabama River. Don't ask me how it happened. But what I remember is that Rhyne spent an hour of his valuable time dredging the bottom for that rod-

and-reel. Although that outfit is still out there somewhere, I have always appreciated that gesture. Four years later, I watched from the back of Rhyne's boat as he lost the Classic lead on the final day of the event on Tennessee's Chickamauga. I was pulling for you, Jerry!

●

... One of my favorites on the tournament trail is Missouri pro Denny Brauer. We were partnered during the 1990 Classic on the James River and it proved to be a disastrous day. It was one of those days when absolutely nothing goes right. And I had a front-row seat to witness it.

Although he caught a few fish, Brauer struggled throughout the day. The normal precision flipping and pitching style that have become his trademark disappeared that day. He seemed to stay hung up or cut up by the barnacle-laden objects in the James. Equipment malfunctioned. His best spots were uncooperative. Everything that could go wrong did...

At about 1 p.m., Brauer lost a nice bass — 4 pounds or so — at the side of the boat. He then sat down on the front deck of the boat and bemoaned "What else could go wrong?" I had a ready answer. "There's only two things left that could go wrong," I replied. "You could lose a bigger fish and you could hit me with that bullet weight." I had been dodging a 1/2-ounce bullet weight throughout the day as Brauer freed his lure from various entrapments.

I should have known that my time was coming. With less than 10 minutes remaining before making the long run back to the launch ramp, Brauer hooked and maneuvered a 7-pound-plus bass from a submerged woodpile, but it then came "unbuttoned" as it reached the surface. Doing a war dance that would make most native Americans proud, Brauer took out his frustration in brisk circles on the casting deck of the boat. In the process, the bullet weight somehow circled behind me and made contact with my back. Perfection.

I was wrong about one thing, though. There was more that could go wrong. Brauer was late returning to the dock and was penalized most of the weight he had caught.

... I'll never forget seeing Rick Clunn on the weigh-in stand at the conclusion of the 1984 Classic, in which he destroyed the record book to the tune of 75 pounds. With then Vice President George Bush on hand to help with the weigh-in, Clunn paused to reflect on boyhood days spent wading the creeks behind his father, who now lay comatose in a Houston hospital. Holmes Clunn had taken seriously ill during his son's brightest moment and Rick had struggled with the possibility that if he stayed for the tournament, he might not get to see his father alive again. And his emotions took over as he accepted fishing's most coveted trophy. And mine overwhelmed me as I watched.

Rick, you became my hero that day.

SECTION ONE
Tools of the Trade

Larry Lazoen's speed-worming technique produced the largest bass of the 1988 B.A.S.S. event on Texas's Rayburn Reservoir.

Chapter 1

Speed Up
To Catch More Bass

It is a typical Okeechobee summer day, complete with the normal combination of relentless heat and flying insects. But this day has not been typical in the respect that the bass population in this famous southern-Florida hot-spot just isn't cooperating.

As a guide, Larry Lazoen knows the 730-square-mile lake as well as most people know their back yard. As a tournament competitor, he has the credentials qualifying him for the prestigious BASS Masters Classic on three occasions.

Yet, the shallow, weedy waters of Okeechobee have held him hostage on this bright, muggy morning, refusing to yield any of its aquatic bounty despite the repeated offerings of a plastic worm, weedless spoon and crankbait.

Grumbling to himself, Lazoen reties his worm and makes what by now must be his 500th cast of the day. But, strangely, he begins to work the worm differently — the way most anglers fish a crankbait. Instead of methodically hopping it through the vegetation, Lazoen begins bringing it back to the boat with a steady retrieve and without using the rod to create action. He is fishing at 45 rpm's when he should be at 33.

PROfile

Three-time BASS Masters Classic qualifier Larry Lazoen is a much-publicized bass and saltwater guide. He is also a two-time runner-up on the B.A.S.S. Tournament Trail.

The thought occurs — this guy has spent too much time in the sun. After all, this is Florida, land of the "dead-worming" technique, where the bass have to be finessed with these slinky pieces of plastic to be fooled into biting them. And this guy thinks he is fishing some type of plastic buzzbait.

Just as I'm giving serious consideration to checking his pulse, Lazoen suddenly snaps the rod skyward and quickly boats the first bass. It weighs about 4 1/2 pounds. After releasing it, Lazoen makes another cast and his super-fast worm retrieve again gets interrupted — this time by a 2-pounder.

In the next 30 casts, Lazoen fills out a 10-bass daily limit. Releasing each fish, he remains solemn, concentrating entirely on making long casts across the immense peppergrass bed and this unorthodox retrieve. Finally he speaks, answering some unspoken skepticism that, by now, has waned significantly.

"Most people think I'm crazy, fishing a worm that way," Lazoen says, only to be greeted by my enthusiastic denial. "You've just seen something that has worked for me in tournaments all over the country. From New York to Texas to Nevada, speed-worming has saved many a day for me."

Speed-worming is about as unconventional as plastic worm fishing can get. The rage the last couple of years has been the dead-worming technique, where the worm is regularly paused and then inched across the bottom. In fact, the gospel according to many pros, is that average angler simply fishes a plastic worm too fast.

Then there is Lazoen's method, which has produced well enough on the "Big O" to make him one of the lake's most renowned guides, and consistently enough on the national tournament circuit to pave the way to three Classic appearances.

Speed-worming involves making long casts and covering considerable amounts of water with a steady, almost lazy retrieve. Lazoen keeps the worm moving the entire time it is in the water, without shaking or hopping it. The built-in action of the plastic does the rest. The result is a worm technique that is considerably more potent for locating bass, which also has a surprising ability to attract strikes.

"I realize that slow-fishing a worm is the normal way to do it," says Lazoen. "All of the magazine articles tell you to fish it slower and slower until you can't stand it. And then slow down even more.

"Although I fish the worm slow at times, my overall philosophy is different from most anglers, particularly other tournament fishermen. A lot of my partners are amazed that you can get bit working a worm at this speed. My theory is that the more times you cast, the more water you can cover and the more chances you have of attracting aggressive bass.

"With this technique you take advantage of two main reasons bass strike — hunger and reflex action. You'll get some hunger bites, but you'll also get a reaction strike like you do when using a spinnerbait or crankbait. It comes by the bass and he snaps at it! It puts the odds a little more in your favor."

Although the speed-worming technique is most effective in the spring and summer, Lazoen has proven it will consistently produce throughout the year in bass waters as diverse as Nevada's Lake Mead, New York's Hudson River and Texas' Sam Rayburn Reservoir. It is especially effective on spawning bass. Lazoen has enjoyed remarkable success by throwing the worm well past the bed and swimming it through the nest. That usually produces a reactionary strike and accounts for 80 percent of the spawning bass he catches and *releases* during the year.

4

Larry Lazoen prefers a blackgrape with green glitter ribbon-style worm for the speed-worming technique.

There are exceptions to the method's year-round allure. As with all techniques, water temperature and bass activity levels are deciding factors. Once the water goes below the 50-degree mark, speed-worming isn't much of an option, Lazoen admits. During those colder-water periods, as well as cold-front conditions when the bass are inactive, Lazoen becomes a "dead-worm" fisherman along with most other avid bassers. And speed-worming is not very effective around scattered cover or structure in shallow water on bright, sunny days when the fish are likely to be holding tight to any object.

Speed-worming works in a wide range of water-clarity conditions. It draws strikes from impressive distances in crystal-clear water; produces consistently in the high visibility of Florida's tannic-colored water; and even scores in muddy water. "Fishing a tournament on (Alabama's) Lake Eufaula last year, the water we were concentrating on was all rolled up with mud from carp that were spawning," Lazoen adds. "Yet, speed-worming worked well. I caught a lot more fish than my partners, who were using spinnerbaits in those conditions."

This unorthodox worming technique is particularly productive in a variety of aquatic vegetation, but can also be effective around isolated wood cover (fallen logs, stumps and treetops) and vertical cover such as boat docks, standing timber and bridge pilings.

This is a particularly effective technique for fishing relatively shallow flats of vegetation. "By making long casts across large fields of grass or weeds where bass can be anywhere, your worm is in the strike zone much longer than it would be if you were to use the flipping or pitching technique," Lazoen explains. "The worm is in potential bass-producing water from the time it hits the water until it is in the boat."

Lazoen uses the speed-worming technique a little differently at three basic depths.

Surface fishing. When fishing thick fields of pads as well as heavy, matted vegetation that forms a blanket on the surface, Lazoen works the worm quickly across the top. His retrieve is so fast that it is similar to that of a buzzbait, rubber mouse or frog. The sight of a bass exploding through the jungle-like vegetation to inhale the worm is almost heart-stopping.

Subsurface exploring. With scattered vegetation like peppergrass, eelgrass, cabbage and milfoil just below the surface and boat trails and other cuts through heavier cover, Lazoen uses a steady retrieve to keep the worm just 2 to 4 inches under the water.

Deep vegetation. Lazoen has had outstanding success with this technique in deep vegetation. A prime example is Rayburn Reservoir where the hydrilla tops out at 6 to 10 feet below the surface. In this situation he works the worm much like a swimming plug, steadily moving it along the top of the weeds (using rod positioning to keep the lure skirting across the top of the vegetation).

In contrast to his methods for fishing vegetation, Lazoen's approach to working wood is to first move the worm slowly around isolated cover. Then he turns to the speed-worming technique. "You will be surprised how many times swimming the worm through the same area will trigger a strike," Lazoen claims. "That is especially true if the bass are not holding tight to the cover and are roaming around."

A major attribute of the speed-worming technique is its hook-up ratio. Lazoen believes that the additional speed increases your chances of successfully setting the hook.

"It's not like slow-worm fishing when you'll feel a bump, wonder if it is a fish and maybe not even set the hook," he explains. "Almost all of the bites you get while speed-worming are definite strikes. They'll hit it hard, often several times. And often you'll see the water boil behind the worm. You will sometimes see the strike, which allows you to react quickly.

"All you have to do is drop the rod tip to give the fish a little slack, let him swim with it momentarily, reel down until you catch up to him and then set the hook. If you have the presence of mind to do that, you'll catch virtually all of them."

Lazoen utilizes three types of plastic worms for his speed technique.

A ribbon-tail worm is used most often because of its built-in action. It is particularly effective when buzzed across surface vegetation, but it also works well over sunken weed beds. When fishing a few inches below the surface, Lazoen uses a slender worm with a sickle-shaped tail. For vegetation that has barely reached the surface, Lazoen prefers a paddle-tail version.

The worm weight varies with each situation. A 1/8-ounce, bullet-shaped sinker is well suited for speed-worming just below the surface, while a 3/16-ounce weight is better for working through pads or atop matted vegetation. And Lazoen prefers a 1/4-ounce sinker for fishing the deep hydrilla.

Unlike many anglers, Lazoen never pegs the bullet weight in place with a toothpick or rubber band. "With this technique you're steadily reeling it through the water, so the force of the water keeps the sinker up against the worm," he explains.

If you are starting to get the idea that, as a worm fisherman, Larry Lazoen is a little unconventional, consider that he limits himself to a single color — blackgrape with green glitter. Doesn't every fisherman from the weekend angler to the tournament pro own at least 50 different colors of plastic worms?

"That color has worked in every state I've ever fished, including Florida, Texas, New York, Kentucky, Tennessee and out West," Lazoen says. "People tend to make bass fishing too complicated, whether it be worm fishing, spinnerbait fishing or whatever. You don't need to complicate things by running up and down the blade sizes or in and out of the color charts. It is more important to concentrate on the mechanics involved with each technique rather than stocking your tackle box with every color available.

Line size is not a major consideration with speed-worming, according to Lazoen, because the bass often hit the worm out of a reactionary reflex. Lazoen uses 12 to 17-pound test Stren, but recommends that others use the lightest line they feel capable of fishing.

The choice of rod is important, though. For this technique Lazoen uses two versions of a 6-ft. 10-in. graphite rod. For fishing scattered and moderately heavy cover, he uses a rod with a slightly limber tip; for heavy cover he switches to a rod that has a little more backbone.

"The long rod is critical with this type of fishing," Lazoen adds. "It allows you to make longer casts, plus I hold my rod high — about 10 o'clock — which allows me to easily regulate the depth of the worm."

There are times when Lazoen's speed worming technique must take a back seat to the more conventional style of plastic-worm fishing. But by experimenting with different retrieves on each trip, you may find that more bass will find their way into your boat.

"Speed-worming isn't the total answer," Larry Lazoen reminds us. "It is just another technique for getting the most out of the most versatile bass lure there is."

Rattle Up Big Bass

Shaw Grigsby's partner on this tournament day apparently failed to detect the slight ticking noise that came from his worm as he finished his retrieve and prepared to cast again.

During the second day of the Bassmaster Florida Invitational on Lake Okeechobee, both Grigsby and his partner were using identically-rigged worms of the same color and size, the same line size and casting into the same pockets in the peppergrass. Yet, Grigsby was out-producing his partner in embarrassing fashion.

For every single bass the partner landed, Grigsby caught six. Finally, his frustrated partner begged for an answer. What could they possibly be doing differently?

The difference was a worm rattle.

While few bass fishermen nationwide may be aware of the practice of placing small rattle chambers in the body of plastic worms, Grigsby and other pros who travel the national circuit rarely miss a trick. And worm rattles are just another small piece of their vast array of weaponry and strategy.

And pros like Grigsby, Mickey Bruce, Paul Elias and Russ Bringger have discovered that rattling worms have a definite application in three situations: weedy lakes, fishing off-colored water and during spawning season.

"I think rattles are great because they add the dimension of sound to your plastic worm" says Grigsby, a former Red Man All American champion and BASS Masters Classic qualifier who lives in Gainesville, Fla. "It gives a worm a significant amount of sound, a surprising amount of sound. You can actually hear the ticking sound when lifting the worm out of the water."

Russ Bringger of Pompano Beach, Fla., won the 1986 Florida Bassmaster Invitational on Lake Okeechobee and is one of the state's most successful pros. Unlike other pros, Bringger uses a rattle in 100 percent of his worm fishing.

"I'm a big believer in rattles, particularly in heavy cover situations, which describes most of the tournaments I fish in Florida," he explains. "I think sound is important and I think the rattle triggers strikes.

"Even if you don't drop the worm right on the fish's head, rattles are effective. I've seen bass come from 4 or 5 yards away to get it while I was shaking it. I've seen them explode from 5 yards away and before you could realize it, he's already got the worm."

Bringger compares the value of the added attraction of sound inside of a plastic worm to that of the Rat-L-Trap, which is among the noisest crankbaits made. The Rat-L-Trap has long been known as a lure that would attract long-distance attention from bass.

It would seem that these tiny rattling sound chambers were designed with Florida fishing in mind. Every piece of vegetation that the worm comes into contact with sounds the rattle. "That's the key to the worm rattle's success in Florida," Grigsby says. "Instead of just dropping the worm along a ledge or open-water bar, you're actually bumping something continuously, so it's making noise almost all of the time it's in the water."

Former Super B.A.S.S. champion and Classic qualifier Mickey Bruce of Buford, Ga., believes the worm rattle can make a crucial difference when fishing for bedding bass. He caught almost 50 pounds of spawning fish with a rattle-pegged worm to finish second in the 1985 B.A.S.S. Lake Okeechobee stop.

"I had my partners in that tournament thinking it was the worm I was using that was making the difference between me catching a lot of fish and them catching a few," Bruce says. "But then I gave them the same worm and I still out- fished them.

"The difference was the rattle in my worm. Those bedding fish didn't seem interested in regular worms, but when I would shake that rattle two or three times, they would usually hit it."

Bruce is also a big-believer in using worm rattles for night fishing.

The pros have found that the noise emitted by the tiny beads in the rattle can often be the difference between striking out and limiting out in stained or off-colored water. The rattle enables bass to detect the worm from a greater distance in a situation where their vital vision is limited.

Both Grigsby and female bass pro Claudette Tircuit of Denham Springs, La., have discovered that current is a prime application for a rattling worm. "Current keeps the worm moving, so it's always making noise," Grigsby says.

There are three basic styles of insertion-type worm rattles on the market — glass, plastic and metal — although their availability is limited in some areas. Most of the pros seem to prefer the glass rattle.

The rattles are 1/2- to 3/4-inch in length and have a sharp pointed end so that they can be easily inserted into a plastic worm. While most anglers insert the rattle into the middle or tail section of the plastic worm, Grigsby prefers to position it in the head adjacent to the shaft of the Texas-rigged hook.

Bringger, owner of Gambler Worms in Fort Pierce, Fla., inserts a rattle in both the head and mid-sections of the worm. He often uses as many as three rattles in a single worm. "The thicker the cover, the more rattles I use," he says.

Rattles can be used with any type or style of worm. The Kangaroo Worm, made by Tom Mann's Fish World Lures, has a pouch that is perfect for holding one or two rattles.

Some anglers, including Grigsby, occasionally epoxy one or two rattles to the concave size of a large spinnerbait blade when fishing off-colored and even muddy water. Some Florida fishermen glue a rattle onto a Johnson-type weedless spoon, giving that lure a distinctive sound.

Chapter 2

Open-Water Worming

The legion of ardent bass anglers who are attracted to the waters of Lake Tohopekaliga and the rest of Florida's Kissimmee Chain of Lakes come prepared for war.

A 44,000-acre lake, Lake Toho is a body of water where big bass abound. And most can be found in the most impenetrable shelters available, notably thick mats of grass or reed-lined castles.

PROfile

To free these big fish from their protective homes, most Lake Toho regulars arm themselves with flipping sticks and 25-pound test line. That way, they can winch the resident monster bass from their homes.

Although he ranks among Florida's top flipping specialists, Wayne Yohn often takes an unusual approach to catching Toho's trophies. Yohn is a talented angler, who qualified for the prestigious BASS Masters Classic in 1983. But more impor-

Wayne Yohn is a worm-fishing specialist and for-mer BASS Masters Classic qualifier.

tantly, Yohn practically owns Lake Toho when there's money on the line.

Over the years, Yohn has won more than 50 tournaments and recorded over 100 other top 10 finishes. These tournaments range in size from club tournaments to national events, but all share an important common trait — all took place in the central Florida area and about half were held on the Kissimmee Chain of Lakes.

His success rate accelerated when Yohn discovered open-water worming.

"Back in the early '80s, the water level was real low," he says. "Most people had it in their mind that they had to fish the weeds to catch the fish.

"But the water level in the grass and cattails was so low that there was no place for the fish to live in there. These fish naturally moved to open water where there was more depth. That's when I started loving open-water fishing."

Yohn spent several days diagramming the lake with his chart recorder, particularly the open water areas where there was no visible cover or structure. But what he found were bottom irregularities, rock ledges, drop-offs and big holes.

And a great deal of fish.

It was then that Yohn taught himself the basics of open-water worming, techniques that have proven worthwhile in tournaments throughout the country.

"While everybody was pounding the weeds, I found places in the middle of the open lake that hold fish not only when the water is low, but throughout the year," Yohn says. "I've had just as much success when the water level was normal."

Yohn warns that anglers who master the technique of open-water worm fishing may die of loneliness. But not from a lack of action.

"Most people affiliate worm fishing with working the weeds or casting to the bank, particularly in Florida," he explains. "Most people think of worm fishing as shoreline fishing.

"With open-water fishing, you're casting at targets you cannot see, so it's a little difficult for some people to adjust to. But, believe me, it's worth the trouble to learn."

Since the targets aren't visible, this type of fishing requires two special tools: a depth flasher or chart recorder and a couple of weighted marker buoys.

"You need a flasher to locate these areas," Yohn says. "I ride around the lake with my depth finder on, looking for structure like sudden drop-offs or anything that might hold fish.

"In these lakes, some of the drop-offs are real fast drop-offs and some are subtle. The main thing I look for is drop-offs that have some structure in it. If it's not a real sudden drop-off, then I look for something there that might hold fish on a gradual drop-off. Like a old tree or rocks or something like that."

Most of the holes and drop-offs in Lake Toho range from 6 to 10 feet in depth, Yohn says.

To work such structure, Yohn uses a Texas-rigged plastic worm teamed with a 1/4-ounce sinker exclusively. He recommends a graphite casting rod of at least 6 feet in length. "I personally use a 6-foot rod," he explains. "I believe the longer rod gives me a lot more hook-setting power."

Worm color is dictated by the color and clarity of the water.

"For example, on Florida lakes, there is a lot of green water," Yohn explains. "On those lakes, I use a dark worm like a blackgrape or blue. In clear water, I use a solid black worm or a black with red glitter. I really like that combination. I've always heard that bass hate the color red and I get some savage strikes on that worm. In slightly off-colored water, I usually start with blackgrape and then go to a shad-colored worm as the day brightens."

Thad Lacinak admires an open-water beauty that fell victim to a worm.

Wayne Yohn prepares to boat an exhausted open-water trophy.

"For this kind of fishing, boat position is crucial," Yohn continues. "You need to take the wind direction into consideration, but the most important thing about boat positioning is to position yourself in shallow water and cast into deep water.

"A lot of people sit in deep water and cast into shallow water. But I think it's important to cast into deep water and work it real slow. This way, you're able to work the worm on the bottom more than you would if you're casting into shallow water and working it toward deeper water. By throwing deep and working it shallow, you're right on the bottom all the way."

Yohn is a stickler about an often overlooked facet of worm fishing.

"I don't throw anything but painted bullet weights," he says. "I use only black or purple. I know from past experience that fish can see that flash from the plain, unpainted lead. It's just another example of keeping the odds in your favor."

Another advantage of open-water worming is that it provides shelter for bass that seems to keep them comfortable throughout the day. Since the water is deeper than surrounding portions of the lake, the fish don't have to keep moving to seek shelter from the growing sun.

"This kind of fishing is not limited to early and late," Yohn says. "You can sit on these holes and continually pound it and you'll usually pick up fish throughout the day."

Chapter 3

Do-Nothing Trickery

For years, Jack Chancellor had been trying to get the bass fishermen of America to try his unusual lure, a bizarre-looking plastic worm he named the Do-Nothing Worm.

But his fellow tournament pros and the vast legions of bass anglers refused to conform to Chancellor's way of thinking and give the odd-shaped lure a try despite the two runs he made at the BASS Masters Classic — the most prestigious title in fishing — on the strength of the Do-Nothing Worm.

PROfile

But all of that has changed now.

Chancellor and his Jack Chancellor Lure Co. began to sense a change when the orders began to flood in on the heels of the Phenix City, Ala., angler's domination of the best bass pros in the country at the 1985 Classic on the Arkansas River. Chancellor used the Do-Nothing to take home $100,000 and the sport's biggest championship, a fact that didn't escape the country's fishing public.

Alabama pro Jack Chancellor created an incredible demand for his Do-nothing Worm by using it to win the 1985 Classic.

"It's been crazy around here since the Classic," Chancellor says. "All of a sudden, everybody is interested in the Do-Nothing. After all these years of me telling everybody how good this bait is, I guess it took this Classic (championship) to prove it."

Chancellor's Classic performance did indeed prove what he has said all along — that in certain situations, the Do-Nothing will catch a limit of bass as quickly as any lure on the market.

Although he is renowned as one of the country's top river fishermen, the personable Chancellor has developed several applications (including some unusual methods) for fishing the Do-Nothing.

But to understand his varied applications, you must understand the basics of what makes the Do-Nothing work and how Chancellor fishes it normally.

The Do-Nothing Worm ranks as one of the strangest-looking lures on the market, a 4- or 5-inch straight plastic worm with a pair of small (and extremely sharp) exposed hooks protruding from the bottom. The worm is tied to a 4-foot leader that is connected to the main line with a swivel. Above the swivel sits a plastic bead and a 1-ounce slip sinker.

Chancellor fishes the Do-Nothing on 14- to 17-pound test line, using 12-pound line for the leader. The lighter line is used for the leader so that the worm will break off when hung instead of the entire rig, which saves considerable re-rigging time.

"It's different. It's odd-looking. It's ugly," Chancellor admits. "It has absolutely no eye appeal at all.

"But it's the easiest thing in the world to fish. Women, children, anybody can catch fish on it. The guides in Alabama give it to their clients that have never fished before and get out on a sandbar or a little ledge and they catch fish. You don't have to set the hook with it. The fish just catch themselves. That's the good part about it."

The Do-Nothing Worm was so-named because you don't have to work it like most conventional plastic worms. There is no premium on agonizingly-slow movement and extraordinary sensitivity, like that required with traditional worm fishing. Chancellor fishes it the same way 90 percent of the time — raising his rod tip sharply to make the worm rise. With the 1-ounce sinker sitting 4 feet above the worm, that motion of the rod tip makes the Do-Nothing dart about frantically.

"I like to hop it around with my rod tip," Chancellor explains. "When you give it a pop, the weight hops up and causes the worm to dart behind it and that's what seems to attract the fish.

"I think it also helps that this big weight will drag across the bottom kicking up clouds of silt and mud. I think that gets the fish's attention. I think he probably thinks it's a crawfish or whatever and he's going to investigate it. Then here comes this little worm darting around behind it. If there's fish in the area, the Do-Nothing will usually find them."

Although Chancellor's greatest accomplishments with his pet lure have come on rivers, he says the Do-Nothing is very versatile and can be effective under a variety of conditions and cover.

"It's not just a river bait," he explains. "It's good in rivers and running water, but it's also productive in lakes and big reservoirs like Lake Eufaula.

"While I think current makes the Do-Nothing even more effective, it will also catch a lot of fish back in old creek channels and river ledges. In the spring, it's real good around sandy, shallow points or gravel points.

"But it's definitely a structure-type bait. It's not a bait that you would pick to go chunking along a bank. It's good in deep water, as deep as 35 or 40 feet, and it works in 2 feet of water."

Chancellor won the 1985 Classic by working a school of bass that were suspended around an underwater sandbar on the Arkansas River where the water rose from 30 to 7 feet. Positioning his boat in deep water and casting to the point of the sandbar, the smoke-colored Do-Nothing produced 45 pounds of bass in three days, enabling Chancellor to smoke his opponents.

The Do-Nothing Worm has proven productive in various types of waters throughout the country at the hands of Jack Chancellor. He has even found ways to fish it in lakes where the main structure is aquatic vegetation.

"Most people don't think of the Do-Nothing for fishing grass, but it can be a good bait in some cases where you're fishing around weeds," Chancellor explains. "At Lake Seminole (on the Florida-Georgia border), I've caught a lot of fish working the edge of the grass where it comes to a point.

"A couple of years ago, I even found a way to fish it on Lake Okeechobee. I took the weight off of it and went down to 10-pound line and put it on a spinning outfit. The line was tied directly to the worm, with no swivel, bead or weight on it. It's not real easy to cast and you have to cast it with the wind. When it hits the water, it starts sinking real slow. Our worms aren't made to float. But if you raise the rod tip — just pop it a little bit — the worm will pop back to the surface and start sinking again very slowly.

"That seems to really attract fish in that situation. Plus you can work it either along the edge of grass that comes all the way to the surface or keep it above the top of grass that doesn't quite come to the surface. But it's a weird feeling bait when it's worked that way. It feels like you've got a rod in your hand with nothing tied to the end of your line."

Chancellor has developed a couple of ways to make the Do-Nothing relatively weedless. One method involves taking a small length of stiff 40-pound line and sticking it through the eye of the hook embedded in the worm. You can then bend and mold the other end of the line to shield the exposed hook.

"The best way I've found to make this thing weedless is so simple I could shoot myself for not thinking of it sooner," Chancellor adds. "What you do is take two straight pins — the kind with the little flat head on it — and from the top side of the worm (not the side where the hooks are exposed) insert the pin through the eye of the hook all the way through it.

"You might have to adjust it a couple of times to get the angle just right to the hook. It's easy to do with our translucent colors, but you'll have to poke around some to find the eye of the hooks with some of the darker colors like black-grape. It makes a good little weedguard. The pins stay in it real good and it's possible to fish it in fairly heavy vegetation."

When fishing areas where the vegetation is light, you can often get away with bending the hooks inward slightly toward the worm. This will often allow

At top: the Do Nothing Worm unaltered; at bottom: Chancellor adds straight pins as weedguards to make the bait more weedless.

you to escape from the weeds, while not hampering your ability to set the hook.

While the Do-Nothing is renowned for putting quick limits in the livewell, Chancellor has developed a rather strange method of fishing it that can reduce the amount of time it now takes to catch a limit with his lure.

It often catches two bass at a time.

"I rig up two Do-Nothings using a three-way swivel," he explains. "I put one worm on a 5-foot leader and the other on a 3-foot leader.

"This has produced two bass at a time lots of times. But it feels weird fishing it this way. When you cast it out, you see all those lines crossing and tumbling through the air and you just know it's going to be a mess when you bring it in. But it's unbelievable how many times those lines don't get tangled with each other. What I usually do is thumb the spool right before the lure hits the water to help keep the lines straight.

"I've thought about adding more three-way swivels and more worms until you have so many you couldn't cast. It would be interesting to get into a school of fish, make one cast and wait until you thought all of the lines were hooked up with fish and catch a limit with one cast."

You can forgive Chancellor if he's gone slightly Do-Nothing crazy. But he insists that the tandem Do-Nothing rig is an excellent lure for catching schooling bass, particularly where there is current.

Chancellor has found that the Do-Nothing can also be productive in saltwater.

Some Gulf Coast fishermen have begun using chartreuse Do-Nothing Worms to catch speckled trout. They modify Chancellor's original rig somewhat, though, using a 1/4-ounce weight and a 2 1/2-foot leader.

"When you think about it, shrimp have a similar darting-type action," Chancellor says. "That little 4-incher really simulates a shrimp darting through the water."

Chancellor says the tandem Do-Nothing rig should be very effective for this type of fishing, since speckled trout usually travel and feed in schools.

To increase the versatility of the Do-Nothing, Chancellor developed a 5-inch model with a claw tail. The end of the worm resembles a split-tailed plastic eel and gives the Do-Nothing a little added action.

"There's probably dozens of ways to fish the Do-Nothing that I've never even thought about," Jack Chancellor says. "My best advice is to experiment with it. Once you fish it and catch fish on it, don't be afraid to experiment with it and try it in different areas and around different types of structure. I think you'll be surprised."

Guide Dan Thurmond releases a trophy catch back into the vegetation where it had been caught on a topwater frog minutes before.

Chapter 4

The Time-Honored Topwater Frog

From the time that early man first attempted to copy nature by carving wooden objects into forms that would fool gamefish, fishermen have always had a special affection for the top-water frog.

PROfile

Surface-fished frogs have evolved from their earliest and crudest forms (for which collectors now pay top dollar) to today's realistic amphibians, but all have shared a special place among fishermen, most notably bass fishermen. The allure of using this natural prey to fool largemouth bass has not wavered throughout the years.

This affair began as early as 1880, according to lure-collecting historian, R. Stephen Iwrin, M.D., who ranks topwater frogs third in terms of antiquity.

Illinois pro George Liddle is a past qualifier for the prestigious BASS Masters Classic.

The Kent Champion Floater was born in 1880, but was soon followed by the first rubber frog, made by Pfleuger (under the name of the Enterprise Manufacturing Company) in1885. James Heddon, father of artificial lure-making, began hand-carving surface frogs as early as 1890 and, at the encouragement of Dr. James Henshall (the first acknowledged expert and author of the first book about the black bass), introduced a line of frog-like baits, beginning with the Luny Frog in 1927.

The early frogs displayed marvelous ingenuity. In 1906, Shakespeare marketed the Rhodes Mechanical Swimming Frog, a patented surface lure that featured legs that seemed to kick as the bait was pulled through the water.

The day of the wooden frog is over, but not, apparently, the heyday of the surface frog. The allure of topwater frogs is evident in the role reserved for these lures by fishermen throughout the country, including the highly competitive professional tournament trails. Topwater frogs still catch fish, so even the pros rely on them.

All of the frog-like lures made today are constructed from rubber or plastic, in varying degrees of hardness. But a wide range of qualities exist and include both lures that resemble a frog only through its bulky form and some so lifelike that they could end up on the fork of a gig.

The most popular surface frogs used universally today are the soft rubber weedless floaters, like the Snagproof Frog, Bill Plummer Superfrog, Renosky Natural Frog and the Harrison-Hoge Super Frog. All are made of a very pliable rubber and feature limber, almost lifelike legs that shake and quiver when pulled through the water, slightly resembling the kicking action of a real frog. But, generally, these lures have very little built-in action; it has to be created by rhythmically moving the rod tip. These types of topwater frogs are largely weedless through the use of a wire weedguard or the positioning of the hooks pointing upward from the rear of the bait.

There are other types of soft rubber or plastic frogs like the Mister Twister Hawg Frawg, which come without hooks and are usually rigged Texas-style with a regular worm hook.

The most realistic topwater frogs on the market are designed for Burke Lures by famed big-bass expert and naturalist Doug Hannon.

Few men have spent as many hours studying and observing bass (both above and below the water) as Hannon, who worked with his wife Lynn to design the Frogbait, a semi-hard plastic frog that most resembles what a bass would eat. Hannon designed the lifelike line of surface frogs, but utilized the talents of his wife — a world-renowned wildlife sculptress — to bring it to life.

"I took the overall aspects of living frogs and exaggerated them somewhat," she says. "Living frogs display a pronounced back, which is absent in virtually every frog bass lure except Burke's. The bulging yellow eyes of my design give the bass an immediate suggestion of living prey, as well as a target for striking in dense grass, lily pads and surface weeds."

The Frogbait line includes five models with different intricate color patterns. All share the distinct advantage of appearing extremely lifelike when in the water, which Hannon says is crucial since bass are, by nature, sight-feeders. "A bass learns that certain forage is safe to eat by general cues the forage presents," explains Hannon, who has caught and released more than 500 bass that topped the 10-pound mark. "With a frog, the bass learns to spot powerful hind legs, large eyes and an arched ridge to the back, among other things. This lure captures the overall living profile and amplifies it somewhat."

Although it makes hard-plastic lures, Rebel has a pair of frog-like baits that have developed quite a following.

The Rebel Wee-Frog is a personal favorite, an ultralight crankbait that dives as deep as 3 feet, but can be fished effectively on the surface as well. When sitting still in the water, this floater/diver is submerged, except for its protruding eyes that peak out from the water much the way a real frog would position itself. The Wee-Frog line includes several realistic color patterns for each season.

The Rebel Buzz'n Frog is a larger bait with natural color patterns that assumes the same profile when sitting quietly in the water. But begin retrieving it and it suddenly takes the shape of a buzzbait. Its legs are molded into a diamond shape and spin, creating a buzzbait-like disturbance on the surface of the water. With its unique twin hooks (which point upward), the Buzz'n Frog is largely weedless and can be fished in the same places you would normally use a buzzbait.

Although frog-like surface lures have certainly passed the test of time by catching more than their share of bass, frogs are not a very prevalent food source for bass, according to Dr. Loren Hill, inventor of the Color-C-Lector and probably America's most renowned bass biologist. Disease and the continual draining of wetlands have significantly thinned out native frog populations and manmade reservoirs are practically void of them, Hill says.

Natural lakes, streams and farm ponds are the only waters where frogs have a presence, according to Hill, but even in those situations, the population is small. "In all of my studies looking at food habits of bass, frogs have been very rare," Hill claims. "But there is no question that bass are very efficient at catching them. That's one reason that the population of frogs in streams and farm ponds is going to be very low if you have a fairly dense population of bass."

If frogs are not a regular food source for bass, why have the topwater frog-like lures been so successful over the years?

"I think the appeal of these baits comes from their action and design," Hill responds. "Anything that is used to imitate a surface frog will definitely attract bass. These lures will always catch bass — even in lakes that don't have any frogs. The action of these lures is the key, because some of the places where these lures catch bass, the bass probably have never eaten a frog."

Frogs are an underrated food source for bass, claims Doug Hannon. In fact, when present, frogs are a preferred food item, a delicacy for largemouths.

"In my thousands of hours of documenting big-bass behavior, both on and under the water, I've observed bass eating frogs countless times," he says. "Bass, being the superior predators that they are, can take a wide variety of prey in their large mouths. And the biggest bass — the lunkers — get big by feeding on prey that is easily caught — like frogs."

That explains the allure of topwater frogs for both fish and fishermen.

"I find myself using rubber frogs more and more these days," Roland Martin says. "It's one of the standard baits now, just like a Johnson spoon. A Johnson spoon would have to be in everybody's tackle box. A guy is crazy not to keep one in his box. And a guy is crazy not to have a weedless frog in his box if he is serious about his fishing."

Frog-like lures were designed for fishing vegetation and little else. The most common applications for these weedless baits are lily pads, moss and exotic vegetation that has peaked out and matted on the surface. But Martin has also had good success fishing surface frogs in vertical vegetation like bulrushes and reeds — an unlikely application for these baits, it would seem.

Martin fishes the Bill Plummer Superfrog and Snagproof version in a variety of situations that stretch from spring through fall. It is a surprisingly effective lure for spawning bass, he claims.

"Any time you have spawning fish, many of them are going to be in almost inaccessible places," Martin explains. "On Lake Okeechobee, some fish will spawn in places so thick that you have to use totally weedless lures.

"A topwater plug is out of the question. Bedding bass love to hit a topwater bait, but you just can't fish it in that situation. But you can fish a weedless frog and, unlike a spoon, you can stop it and twitch it without it sinking to the bottom. These frogs are strictly a topwater lure and can even be fished in open pockets just like a Devil's Horse or Rapala. And it's the only completely weedless topwater there is."

Summer brings good surface fishing and Martin spends a considerable amount of time "frogging the pads," as he calls it. He concentrates on large lily pad fields, where bass seek the extra shade, added oxygen and cooler water that the pads provide.

Frogging the pads requires heavy tackle: a flipping stick and 25- to 30-pound test line for setting the hook and winching the fish out of the dense patches of pads. Martin fishes the surface frog slowly, allowing it to linger when pulled up on a pad or dropped into a small open-water pocket.

The rubber frog is a prime comeback lure for George Liddle in the early summer when the Mississippi River is at its highest and its banks become flooded. The Westmont, Ill., angler concentrates on that flooded shoreline and searches the vegetation for bass with a Johnson spoon. Once the spoon attracts a strike, Liddle immediately switches to a Snagproof Frog and thoroughly saturates the spot with the fake frog. "When I follow up with that frog, more times than not they will gobble it up," he says.

Prime-time for frogging, though, is September through November, when the vegetation is at its thickest and tends to create a horizontal mat on the surface of the water. As the vegetation dies and begins to break up, it is blown into weed patches that are still firmly rooted and the result is an almost impenetrable surface layer of grass. And a magnet for bass.

When the milfoil or hydrilla reaches the peak of density on lakes like Missouri's Lake of the Ozarks or Guntersville in Alabama, former BASS Masters Classic champion Guido Hibdon automatically sharpens the hooks on his rubber frog and begins randomly retrieving it along the top of the vegetation. The vegetation is so thick that it will support the weight of the frog and the bass are able to detect its vibration as it moves overhead.

In that situation, the bass usually take one of two tacts: blow up through the grass to inhale the fake frog or wait for it to fall into an open hole or pockets in the vegetation before grabbing it.

"From July through September on our lakes in the South, the moss gets so thick that we sometimes take the boat and run through it to try to tear it up and create some holes," says Hibdon, a longtime guide and tournament pro from Gravois Mills, Mo. "I can't tell you how many times I have done that and gone back the next day with that frog and caught bass from each of the holes we had made the day before."

For his frog fishing, Hibdon scores most effectively with the color pattern that most resembles the spring leopard frog. He fishes it on 17- to 25-pound line.

The most difficult aspect of frog fishing around heavy cover comes once the bass strikes. The thick vegetation makes it a challenge to set the hook effectively and then pull the bass — particularly a big bass — from its grasp. In fact, Hibdon doesn't usually even attempt to pull the fish free. Instead, he sets the hook as well as possible and, while keeping a taut line, goes to the fish, where a little gardening is in order. He actually pulls the grass off of the bass until he can get a firm grip on it.

The most common mistake with fishing topwater frogs — as with surface fishing in general — is setting the hook too soon. It takes a cool customer to be able to watch a bass blast though the vegetation and nail the frog while resisting the urge to set the hook. Nerves of steel.

"Frog fishing is an art in itself," Martin says. "To fish it right takes a lot of self-control. The secret is to pause the instant a bass takes the frog and give the fish time to get the lure completely in his mouth.

"The trick is to almost pretend you're fishing a plastic worm, because a frog is a soft plastic bait, too. When a bass grabs it, he'll likely try to eat it much the same as he would try to eat a plastic worm. When he strikes, he might have the frog only in his lips and you have to give him time to get it securely in his mouth.

"When the bass hits the frog, give him complete slack line and pause for two or three seconds. As he turns and dives into the pads or grass, he'll sort of gulp the bait again and that is the time to set the hook. When he's moving away from you, you have a far greater chance of setting the hook and that two or three seconds will usually give him time to get the frog completely inside of his mouth."

Experienced frog fishermen have developed a couple of tricks for altering the rubber creatures that have paid off handsomely. When the vegetation is at its thickest, Martin sometimes fills the Superfrog with BBs to create more noise. As it is being worked over topped-out milfoil or moss, this altered frog makes a surprising amount of noise.

Often, casting these light-weight fake frogs is almost impossible when the wind begins to build. Adding the BBs will give it the extra weight that increases

A selection of topwater frog imitations.

its castability. Dusty Pine, a two-time Classic qualifier from Birdseye, Ind., creates added weight by cutting a small slit in the rubber frog and inserting a Johnson-type metal spoon. In addition to making it heavier, the natural, built-in action of the Johnson spoon makes the fake frog come alive as it is pulled through the grass.

Although the standard rubber frog is weedless by design, you can make it even more weedless by carefully bending the hook-points in toward the body of the lure. Some frogs come with wire weedguards, but often it is necessary to substitute a heavier wire guard.

Bass fishermen have known since the days of James Heddon that surface frog imitations hold a special allure to their favorite gamefish. And a faithful legion of anglers — including some of the top tournament pros — still take advantage of that natural attraction whenever possible.

Chapter 5

The Pros'
Spinnerbait Secrets

If you asked the pros who travel the vagabond trails of the big-money tournament circuits to name the most versatile bass lure known to man, they would almost all be in agreement.

If you queried knowledgeable bass fishermen who cast for pleasure instead of cash throughout this country, the answer would likely be the same.

Spinnerbaits.

No lure produces fish under a greater variety of weather conditions, water clarity conditions, water depths, types of structure and cover.

A spinnerbait will produce in water ranging from a foot to 40 feet in the hands of an experienced angler. It will catch fish in muddy water as well as crystal-clear water. You can bump the stumps and entice bass. Or you can crank it through the thickest types of grass known to man.

You can even fish it productively in open water.

"I don't know of another bait that has the versatility of a spinnerbait," says Cliff Shelby, an executive with Ranger Boats and one of the country's most knowledgeable bass fishermen. "There are just so many ways to fish it."

Living in Flippin, Ark., there are very few lakes, rivers and streams in the South that have escaped Shelby's prowess over the years. He is a complete angler, capable of taking bass with a fly rod as well as a flipping stick.

PROfile

Bernie Schultz is a two-time Classic qualifier and winner of the 1990 Canadian Open and Golden Blend New York Invitational.

Shelby was asked to outline some of his most productive techniques for spinnerbait fishing.

"One technique that the people here in Arkansas use that is real effective and would work in plenty of reservoirs in other states is selecting the size of a spinnerbait by the time of the year," Shelby says. "The key is to match the hatch, so to speak.

"Match the size of the spinnerbait, particularly the blades, by the size of the baitfish at that time of year. As the new hatch of baitfish like shad takes place each year, you can approximate the size that they've attained right on through the year. Smart fishermen will follow it by changing the spinnerbait all year long.

"It's that simple. Different times of the year, the mass of the shad population are different sizes. You'll run into a school of shad and they'll all be an inch or 2 inches long. A successful fisherman knows he needs to look at the baitfish and before he can catch a lot of fish, he's going to have to mimic or imitate that size. Bass sometimes are very, very selective on size.

"Trout fishermen talk about matching the hatch. The closest a bass fisherman can come to matching the hatch is to approximate the size of the baitfish that the bass have congregated to prey on."

Estimating the size of the shad or minnows or whatever type of baitfish that are most prevalent is easier than it sounds.

"You select blade and spinnerbait size by visually inspecting the shad that are inside the belly of the fish you catch or seeing shad in the water," Shelby says. "You will often see the baitfish jumping and scattering around and you can tell what size they are. I'll even approximate that size with a crankbait throughout the year. Most people have never associated that with a crankbait, but that has always worked well with crankbait fishing, as well as spinnerbait fishing."

With size in mind, Shelby is a real believer in the productivity of the large willow-leaf spinnerbait that took the bass world by storm several years ago and became the hottest lure on the market and the B.A.S.S. tournament trail.

"It took a lot of people by surprise," he says. "But it's really not surprising to me because many times the size shad that are easier to catch and are abundant in certain areas and attract the bigger fish to the area are baitfish with about the body size of that No. 7 willow-leaf blade.

"We used to take advantage of this as much as possible, but a spinnerbait of that size hadn't been readily available before it was adapted from something else (Florida fisherman Chuck Faremouth invented the monstrous willow-leaf-bladed spinnerbait by teaming a salmon-type spinner with a bass spinnerbait). The biggest thing we used to use was something like a No. 5 Colorado blade. Spinnerbaits have traditionally been Colorado blades, although the willow-leaf blades are a lot easier to turn in the water.

Bill Dance is a big believer in the allure of spinnerbaits for big bass.

"The willow-leaf spinnerbaits are most effective because as the blade rotates, it creates a hologram almost of a baitfish's body."

Faremouth says there are some important considerations for selecting a willow-leaf spinnerbait that might appear minor on the surface.

One important factor is the arm length of the lure from the bend to where the willow-leaf blade is attached. It's important, he says, that this section of the spinnerbait arm be long enough that the willow-leaf blade extends past the hook "so that when a fish crushes down on the bait with this light wire, the willow-leaf will be behind the hook and won't hamper the hooking process."

Faremouth prefers lure designs that have the safety pin-type bends for all of his spinnerbait fishing — with and without the willow-leaf blade.

Texan Gary Klein obviously has more name recognition than Cliff Shelby or Chuck Faremouth. But he shares a common bond with those two weekend fishermen — he relies on a spinnerbait a great deal because of its versatility.

Klein, who in 1985 became the first pro fisherman to win $100,000 in a single year without winning a tournament, finished second in a Super B.A.S.S. Tournament held on the St. Johns River in Florida by using a spinnerbait technique that has consistently produced for him over the years.

It was early spring on the St. Johns and Klein was "bumping the stump" — ramming the spinnerbait against dead trees and submerged logs to increase the lure's vibration and alert nearby bass to its presence.

"I was catching some fish with a worm in the grass, but I noticed that all of my better fish were coming off dead wood, so I started working a spinnerbait," Klein explains. "By the third day of the tournament, I made a commitment to fish nothing but dead wood on the river where the better quality fish are.

"The fish were on stumps, logs and docks with laydowns (fallen timber). The fish were tight to the cover. You'd float a spinnerbait down to the tree and as soon as it would disappear, a mudfish or a bass would have it. I caught about 15 mudfish the last two days. I think the key was casting the spinnerbait about 10 feet beyond the fish and bringing it to where I thought the fish was at and I would just bump the spinnerbait against the wood and then float it up and over. I then let it flutter out of sight and started my retrieve. The fish almost always hit once the spinnerbait was out of sight."

Klein was using a 1/2-ounce double-bladed spinnerbait that sported a diamond-shaped head, chartreuse-and-white skirt and a chartreuse trailer. He used a combination of willow-leaf and Colorado blades — a small No. 3 willow-leaf blade with a silver No. 2 Colorado blade in front.

Fishing shallow water forced Klein to make long casts, which required a long rod. He was also casting sidearm to ensure that the spinnerbait made a relatively quiet entry into the water. By propelling the lure low across the water, Klein was able to get a softer presentation.

Veterans of the bassin' wars like Ken Cook, Roland Martin and Tommy Martin will tell you that to catch big bass as well, you have to penetrate the tranquility of the big fish as they take shelter. That means getting a lure through some incredibly thick cover and putting it right in front of the bass' nose.

Flipping a plastic worm is one way to penetrate these thick-cover hiding places. But flipping is a slow method, so you aren't able to cover much water.

A spinnerbait, though, covers water faster than any lure other than a crankbait. A crankbait can't penetrate grass and usually gets hung up too much in thick cover. But a spinnerbait can penetrate almost anything.

The most successful pros run their spinnerbaits through the roughest-looking cover and structure imaginable. Even vegetation as thick as hydrilla doesn't often stop the amazingly-weedless spinnerbait.

Another example of the versatility of the spinnerbait: because it's weedless, you can quickly work the spinnerbait through the thick portions of the grass and then stop your retrieve as it approaches an opening in the vegetation. The result is a lure that flutters to the bottom with a tantalizing action.

The same is true with a treetop, where knowledgeable anglers will bounce the spinnerbait off of the limbs and allow it to flutter downward for several seconds before starting the retrieve again.

Many fishermen put away their spinnerbait rod when a cold front passes through their area. It is a common thought that cold-front conditions mean finicky fish and require lures such as worms worked slowly in front of the bass to entice a strike. A fast-moving, reflex-action lure like a spinnerbait doesn't fit into that common theory.

But Tennessee's Charlie Ingram disproved that theory en route to winning the 1985 B.A.S.S. event on Truman Reservoir in Missouri. Ingram never hesitated when cold-front conditions dropped the water temperature by more than 10 degrees overnight.

Ingram decided to fish a flat area with about 4 feet of water and assorted standing and fallen timber. He was using a 1/2-ounce spinnerbait with just a single blade (a silver No. 5 Colorado) and a plastic trailer.

Realizing that the cold-front bass would not be as aggressive as normal, Ingram slowly rolled the spinnerbait through the cover. And at his best spot, where the flat area dropped off into a creek channel, Ingram worked the spinnerbait to the edge of the channel and then let it flutter over the edge. The fish all hit it on the fall. The result was almost 32 pounds of bass and $30,000.

One of the most interesting recent developments in spinnerbaits is the use of tin as a blade material. Top pro Bernie Schultz was looking for the ultimate clear-water spinnerbait when he designed the prototype for "The Blade" spinnerbait, which is made by the John. J. Hildebrandt Corp.

Schultz discovered that tin is only about 64 percent as heavy as lead, which makes the head of this spinnerbait significantly lighter than traditional bladed-baits. "That allows you to crawl the bait right along the surface," Schultz explains. "You can also keep the bait in the strike zone longer. I believe it will run at least 30 percent slower in the water than a lead spinnerbait."

Despite its weight, this spinnerbait casts surprisingly well and survives the impact of a rock or stump as well as any spinnerbait.

Schultz used the prototype to win the 1990 Canadian Open and Golden Blend New York Invitational. The same lure enabled him to finish second in the Golden Blend Championship in 1990. So the lure entered the market in the summer of 1991 with a track record.

Although this bait will prove to be effective in a wide variety of situations, Schultz says it is at its best in clear water — foreign territory for most spinnerbaits.

Spinnerbaits are among the most altered lures of all, which adds to their versatility.

The Blade comes in 1/4- and 1/2-ounce sizes and in three colors — silver shad, alewife combo and golden shiner. The blade combinations include tandem willowleaf, a tandem Colorado/Indiana and single willow-leaf blade. The look of The Blade is completed with a translucent silicone molded skirt.

If Schultz' success is any indication, spinnerbaits have now opened up a whole new area. Clear-water bass are no longer immune to the allure of the spinnerbait.

Chapter 6

Crash Course
On Crankbaits

It was in the swamps and bayous of southern Louisiana that Lee Sisson first discovered the potential of a wooden lure that ran deep and covered a great deal of water. It was a bait that he fashioned in his imagination and molded in his hands.

It was the first true deep-diving crankbait.

PROfile

"Back in those days, I fished a lot of tournaments and I was killing everybody," Sisson says today. "Just killing them because I had a bait that would go 8 to 10 feet deeper than anything on the market at the time.

"What really got me started was that I always wanted a bait that would dive deeper than a regular crankbait. When I first started doing this 25 years ago, there were a lot of crankbaits with a shallow lip in it. This was the time Fred Young came out with his Big O, so I knew this kind of lure would catch fish, but I wanted something that would go a lot deeper because I was catching fish in about 15 feet of water at the time.

In addition to being one of the foremost wooden lure designers in the country, Lee Sisson is an oustanding bass angler.

"The only things available at the time that would get that deep were worms, jigs and some kinds of heavy sinking lures. And I had fallen in love with crankbait fishing because you could expose a crankbait to a lot more fish. So, I started fooling around with lures and I came up with a bait that would run very deep and run true. And I started walking away with tournaments."

Sisson would soon meet noted luremaker Jim Bagley, who had seen and heard of his work. On the day they met, Sisson was hired. And, together, they proceeded to make refinements and innovations on crankbaits that enabled Bagley to command a significant share of the artificial lure market.

That home-made deep-diving crankbait became the Bagley Diving 'B', which was followed by the Kill'r 'B' series. And in the next 10 years, lure designer Lee Sisson would make a definite mark in the industry with innovations that found their way into the tackleboxes of most American fishermen.

After a decade with Bagley, Sisson decided it was time to fulfill a life-long dream. Today, he is president of Lee Sisson Lures, based in Auburndale, Fla. In addition to making creations for his own line, Sisson also designs wooden crankbaits for other companies.

Over the past 25 or so years of designing, testing and fishing crankbaits, Lee Sisson has accrued a knowledge that few anglers will ever obtain. But we can learn from his experience with diving baits and ideas on why bass strike lures.

"Over the last two decades, there has been a lot of research into strike stimuli, ranging from people like myself to university researchers," Sisson says. "While we obviously don't know everything, we all have some good ideas about why bass strike artificial lures.

"In my opinion, the number one strike stimuli is the vibration pattern that a bait produces. I believe that color and flash — sunlight reflecting off of a bait — are also strong factors, but the most important strike stimuli is that vibration pattern. A lot of people talk about sound and vibration. They are the same. All sound is, is vibration patterns. I think vibration patterns are really the key.

"Bass have lateral lines and also have an inner ear. So, the vibration pattern is what they pick up on long before they ever see the lure. It either turns them on or turns them off. Every so often, you'll catch a fish that's totally blind. Now, you know color didn't make a difference. That fish had to have zeroed in on the vibration pattern."

Sisson is asked to describe the action of a lure that gives off the ideal vibration pattern.

"First of all, bass, being a predator, will take advantage of a baitfish that's weak or injured," he replies. "What gets his attention is the vibration pattern of that injured baitfish, which is different from the vibration patterns he experiences normally in his environment.

"So you want a crankbait with an action that gives off a vibration pattern different from that of healthy baitfish and other bass. If it's different, this will alert the bass and get his attention that there's some easy prey around. The perfect action for this is a bait that has a real tight quiver rather than a wide wobble, which a lot of lures have. This quick, tight quiver sends a vibration pattern through the water that's unlike anything he normally he experiences. So the bass equates this unusual vibration pattern with the unusual vibration pattern he notices when a weakened baitfish is near."

Top female pro Penny Berryman of Arkansas cranks a boathouse on the Potomac River.

Understanding the action of a crankbait is a crucial first step in learning to fish it successfully, Sisson insists.

"That's an important rule for the guy who is just starting to fish crankbaits, as well as the guy who has been fishing them for a while," he says. "Either use a swimming pool or find a piece of water that is real clear and just cast and retrieve for a while before ever attempting to catch a fish with it.

"The idea is to see exactly what the lure does underwater. See how it runs and what kind of action it has. If you can find a treetop in clear water, run it through the limbs and see how it responds. Then you can have a visual picture of what that lure is doing down there while you're fishing it. That, alone, will make you a better fisherman."

Crankbaits are among the easiest lures to learn to fish, since the action of the lure will often attract a strike, regardless of the retrieve. This makes it an excellent bait to put into the hands of a beginning angler.

But even the most seasoned bass chaser tends to overlook some important facets of the mechanics of crankbait fishing, Sisson says.

"First of all, line size plays a very important role in the depth you attain with a crankbait," he explains. "I use as light of line as I possibly can get away with.

"You're simply going to get more depth with lighter line. The reason is that the lighter the line, the smaller the diameter and there's less friction coming through the water. The heavier the line, the more resistance there is. You'd be surprised in the difference between 10-pound test line and 20-pound. With the average crankbait, you can get a couple of extra feet with 10-pound test line. And, in some situations, an extra couple of feet can be crucial.

"But there's a point when you go below 10-pound test where you lose a little depth because of line stretch versus its diameter."

Another problem with using heavy line with crankbaits is the possibility of altering that all-important vibration pattern.

"You have to consider that anything that's coming through the water has a vibration," Sisson adds. "This is something that the people at Rebel have experimented with and found. They've determined that line diameter makes noise coming through the water.

"And heavy line can even change the vibration pattern of a crankbait. It's like tying a tail on a kite. The heavier line will deaden the vibration pattern and movement of a crankbait. The smaller the lure, the more critical that problem becomes, both in terms of depth and vibration patterns. A large lure can overcome the heavier line size much better than smaller lures."

Most bass anglers are interested in getting the maximum depth out of these deep-diving lures. But most aren't familar with the keys to attaining it.

"There are several things that help you reach the maximum depth," Sisson explains. "The longer cast you can make, the more depth you're going to get. That and line size are probably the most critical aspects.

"To get that long cast, a lot of people have gone to using big flipping sticks or long crankbait rods that can be cast with two hands. The distance of the cast is critical because you're working angles. Say you make a 50-foot cast, which is a long cast, and you're trying to get 20 feet deep. If you dropped the crankbait straight down, it would take almost half of your line to reach 20 feet. And you've also got to have some room for that bait to actually work its way down. So, you can just eliminate that 20 feet of your line. Now you've got 30 feet for that bait to work its way down to the structure and back up (as it nears the boat) in a single retrieve. And that's if you're able to make a 50-foot cast."

Two other problems can keep a crankbait from reaching the desired depth: overcranking and a poorly-tuned lure.

"Most people don't realize that you don't have to crank a crankbait real hard to get it deep," Sisson says. "With most crankbaits, just a moderate retrieve will allow the crankbait to find the depth that it will run at. That's probably the most common misconception there is about crankbaiting.

"Another way you lose depth is if the crankbait is not running dead-center true. If it's a foot off to the left, you lose some depth. If it's running 2 feet off to the left, you're losing even more depth. That's why it's important to run the crankbait in a swimming pool or some clear water to make sure it's running properly."

While all lure manufacturers design lures that are intended to run straight, veteran crankbait fishermen know there are times when a center-line diving bait isn't what the situation calls for.

By understanding the mechanics of the crankbait (how it's supposed to run and how to adjust its course), you can create a lure of unequaled versatility that has a wide range of applications.

"What you want to do with a crankbait is use that tool to do things that normally aren't done," Sisson says, explaining the practice of maltuning crankbaits. "The baits are really designed to do these things, but nobody ever does it. It's kind of like an adjustable wrench that's never adjusted or having a socket set with one socket.

"You need to be aware of other ways to use a bait when that particular application presents itself. What I'm talking about is tuning a bait to run off to the right or the left. This is a specialized type of fishing, but it often comes into play.

"Let's say you've got some type of vertical structure like boat docks or standing timber. A lot of times, there will be a sheer wall that comes straight down and the wave action has washed an undercut in it. The fish just sit in that undercut, which is common in the western lakes like Lake Powell. What works real well is making the bait run to the left or the right a little bit, so that it works its way into this undercut in the rocks.

"There's all sorts of applications for maltuning crankbaits. Say you're fishing around a pier or boat dock. By maltuning your lure, you can cast parallel to the pilings and the bait will actually run around each of the pilings and enter the shady areas where bass usually lay. You can do the same thing with standing timber. Tuning the bait the right way will make it hug that stick-up during the retrieve and actually get in behind that stick-up. This works real good on any kind of vertical structure."

Maltuning a crankbait to perform a specific task is simple to do.

"All you have to do is bend the wire at the nose of the bait just like you would to straighten it out," Sisson explains. "You just bend it the opposite way (you would to straighten its course) to make it run crooked — off to the right or left. It just takes a subtle adjustment.

"The easiest way to remember it is that, facing the lure, you take the nose wire or the split ring that you tie your line to and turn it the way you want the lure to run. If you want it to run to the left, bend it to the left. But with most baits, it takes a very minor adjustment."

The crankbait is a tool, Lee Sisson reminds us. It is one of the most versatile weapons a bass angler can own.

Rick Clunn has proven the allure of lipless crankbaits in tournament after tournament.

Chapter 7

Big-Deal No-Bill Crankbaits

Rick Clunn calls it his primary tool for locating bass, which is lofty status considering the credentials of the man.

The tool is the lipless crankbait, those vibrating, shad-shaped, flat-sided rattling lures that allow you to quickly cover water in search of active bass. In the case of the four-time BASS Masters Classic champion, the Rat-L-Trap is his best bird dog bait, the lure he ties on when there is ground to cover and time is short.

PROfile

Although he fishes it around a variety of structure and cover conditions, the Rat-L-Trap is Clunn's weapon of choice most often for a wide variety of aquatic vegetation, ranging from submerged milfoil to vertical bulrush strands. Vegetation is where a lipless crankbait can best strut its stuff, he says.

For Clunn, lipless crankbaits know no seasonal boundaries. As long as a lake or reservoir has some type of vegetation, he will automatically fish that lure.

Rick Clunn is a four-time Classic champion, former B.A.S.S. Angler of the Year and the first pro to top the million-dollar mark in winnings.

"The Rat-L-Trap and lures like it do several things for you," Clunn says. "You can control it over the top of the weeds with the position of your rod tip. With any submerged weed bed, the top of it will vary and this bait allows you to make quick, easy adjustments and still keep working just above the weeds.

"Weed fishing is notorious for having what I call non-positional fish — which means you cannot position the fish. Non-positional means you can't predict where they are going to come from. With vegetation, particularly submerged vegetation, you have to search for the fish unlike a stump row or stick-up. You know where those fish should be holding. The Rat-L-Trap is the best bait I know of for locating these non-positional fish. There is no doubt that the bait moves fish to it. The noise from the Rat-L-Trap will draw fish that are buried in the weeds out to see what's going on.

"It's the one bait that you don't have to present properly to the fish."

Clunn's victory in the Bassmaster Alabama Invitational in the spring of 1987 on Lake Guntersville is a classic example of the allure of lipless crankbaits to grass bass.

His pattern centered around isolated patches of submerged milfoil that were 1 to 4 feet below the surface in 5 to 13 feet of water. Although a few of the bass were still spawning, most of the fish were in a post-spawn mode and seemed to be holding around the edges of any bare spots on the underwater islands. Clunn conquered these spots with a 1/2-ounce gold Rat-L-Trap fished on 8-, 10- and 15-pound test line.

The Rat-L-Trap was the right tool for the situation, a bait that Clunn could use to skirt the top of the submerged vegetation and still attract the attention of bass hiding inside of it. The lipless crankbait has a bigger role in grass fishing than most anglers realize, Clunn says, but he warns that this type of fishing can be frustrating.

"If you're going to crank weeds, you have to put up with a certain amount of frustration," he explains. "You can't hardly make a cast without having to either slap the bait on the water or reach up and clean grass off of it. The average guy won't tolerate it. He'll either move out away from the weeds or find a place where there are no weeds. To be successful, you have to control yourself when fishing weeds and be willing to put up with fighting them all day long. There are many times when it would be easier to fish a worm or a spinnerbait, but they don't usually produce the strikes that the Rat-L-Trap does."

When working a submerged weed bed or the outskirts of a vertical wall of vegetation, Clunn emphasizes keeping the lure as close to the cover as possible. That will also increase your chance of getting hung up, but popping a bait free from the grasp of vegetation also triggers strikes from time to time.

Serious consideration should be given to the equipment involved in fishing lipless crankbaits.

Clunn uses an inexpensive 7-foot fiberglass rod. He has long been a proponent of using glass rods with fast-moving lures like crankbaits, believing that the graphite rods allow us to respond too quickly to a strike and often take the bait away from the fish.

"The best thing ever made for fishing lipless crankbaits is the 7 to 1 (gear ratio) high-speed reel," Clunn says, in reference to Daiwa's Procaster model PT33SH, the fastest baitcasting reel on the market. "It's value is not in the fact that it is so fast. The real key with this reel is that it is almost a variable speed control reel. I can really feel the bait with this reel. I can slow the bait down and speed it up without losing that feeling. With most reels, if you slow down, you lose the feel of the Rat-L-Trap momentarily, but not this reel. That kind of control is important when you are trying to run a crankbait just over the top of brushpiles or grass."

Clunn's choice of line size varies from situation to situation. Although he primarily uses 14- to 17-pound test, he adjusts the size of the line depending on the clarity of the water and the amount of fishing pressure in the area. In his Guntersville win, Clunn began the tournament with 15-pound line, but dropped to 10- and 8-pound line on successive days. Down-sizing his line was a major reason he was able to continue to catch fish off of the same spots, Clunn believes.

Although Clunn swears by the Rat-L-Trap for fishing vegetation, he insists it is a more versatile lure than most people realize.

"I've had good success with it in the fall of the year multiple-casting to boat docks," Clunn says. "It may take 25 casts to the same dock before you get a strike, but the good thing about it is that you can follow a lot of people throwing other baits like a spinnerbait or worm and catch fish off of the docks they just fished."

During a fall tournament on Lake Tawakoni (near Dallas), low-water conditions congregated the fishermen around the lake's boat docks, creating a situation where the anglers literally formed a line to fish each structure. Clunn watched as boat after boat struck out on dock after dock with more conventional lures. But when he followed the parade by making short pitch-casts under the dock, the Rat-L-Trap produced two or three strikes from beneath every pier.

"It's a reflex bait," Clunn says. "I think creatures in nature have to be entuned to subtleties to survive and sometimes you can change some little thing and give them a different look and that is enough to trigger a strike."

The noisy lipless crankbaits are also good tools for jump fishing schooling bass, as well as fishing muddy water.

For all of its benefits, a problem remains with the Rat-L-Trap and other similar lipless crankbaits that fishermen must recognize — its poor hooking ability. The basic design of the bait works in favor of a frantic bass. When a bass is struggling, the weight of the flat-sided bait provides enough leverage to work the treble hooks free on many occasions.

To remedy that situation, some of the tournament pros began modifying these lures by removing the rear hook (to avoid excessive fouling with the modified belly hook) and drilling a hole down through the body of the bait. They would then run the monofilament through the lure body and tie it directly to an oversized hook. That adaptation was the forerunner to Bill Lewis Lures' Pro Trap and the Cordell Slidin' Spot.

Lipless crankbaits have become one of Rick Clunn's best grass baits.

Clunn does not use the free-swinging version of the Rat-L-Trap, saying the problem of losing fish still exists despite the adaptation and he does not want to sacrifice the rear treble hook. Instead, he simply replaces the factory hooks with larger models and flares the barbs farther outward. "My hooks look like I've been pulling them out of stumps all day," Clunn says.

The biggest danger of a bass dislodging the lure is when it takes flight. In an effort to convince the fish not to jump, Clunn immediately buries 2 to 3 feet of his rod tip after setting the hook. Although that is often not enough to stop the initial jump, Clunn has enjoyed good success in keeping the bass from making subsequent leaps — the most dangerous part of the battle.

Despite its flaws, the lipless crankbait remains a viable tool for both locating and catching bass. "If a lake has vegetation in it, you had better be throwing one of these baits," Rick Clunn concludes.

Jim Bitter knows that 'kneeling and reeling' will add an important extra couple of feet to the depth of his crankbait.

Chapter 8

The Myth
Of Super-Deep Cranking

In the mid-1980s, several lure manufacturers introduced lures that go where no crankbait had ever gone before, breaking the 20-foot barrier. For a long time, that barrier seemed impenetrable, but that is no longer true.

PROfile

The earliest deep crankbaits were the Poe, made in California, Bomber's Water Dog and the Bagley DB-III, which hovered just around the 15-foot mark.

Today's super-deep diving crankbaits have opened up a whole new arena for cranking. But you still have to use a lot of tricks and advanced techniques to get even these new super-divers to reach the 20-foot mark. Reaching 20 feet is anything but easy.

Former Classic champion Stanley Mitchell admits that cranking is his favorite — and most productive — technique.

"There is a misconception that you can tie one of these new super-deep crankbaits on to 15-pound line, make a normal cast with a 5 1/2-foot rod and reach 20 feet," insists Roland Martin. "You couldn't get the newest of the new super-deep divers below 15 feet under those circumstances."

With super-deep cranking, you have to understand the laws of physics. There are three requirements for extra deep cranking: a long cast, light line and a long rod. If you use a long-enough rod, make a long-enough cast with light-enough line, you can reach 20 feet.

Then there is the kneel-and-reel technique that Paul Elias is famous for after winning the 1982 BASS Masters Classic. For years, a lot of anglers used long rods and stuck the tip down in the water, but never got down on their knees in the bottom of the boat. But that is a good way to get some precious extra depth.

That same year, Cliff Craft won a national tournament on Alabama's Lake Eufaula by making super long casts and cranking a DB-III on 8-pound line. He was getting his lure down about 16 feet, which is deep by any fisherman's estimation.

"The truth is that only a handful of today's crankbaits are capable of reaching the 15-foot mark — despite what advertisments claim— and should be classified as super-deep crankbaits," Martin claims.

The long rod accomplishes three tasks — it allows a long cast, enables you to crank with the tip in the water and helps better set the hook from a distance.

The size of line used dictates depth not in regards to the pound-test of it, but the actual diameter of the line. The larger the diameter of the line, the more depth-robbing friction that is created as the line is pulled through the water. For super-deep cranking, Martin advises disregarding the line manufacturers' line-strength claim and consider the actual diameter of the line. He uses Dupont's MagnaThin, which has the smallest diameter for each pound-test rating.

There are some inherent problems with cranking with light line in some of the places we fish, such as heavy brush and cover. Catching a big bass with 8-pound line in that situation is difficult. You often have to finesse them and play them a little lighter than normal. There is a problem, though, with trying to finesse a bass with a big 7 1/2-foot cranking rod that isn't very forgiving.

"After experimenting with these deep crankbaits, I have had good success with 8-foot rods made for steelhead," Martin says. "I cut the tip down to 7 1/2 feet and it makes a fantastic deep crankbait rod, because it is a little softer. These rods don't have the extra strong butt of a flipping stick, but it has the length and whip action necessary for making long casts and better fighting the bass. Long light rods bend more and maintain a steady pressure on the fish, while stiffer rods have less shock-absorbing ability."

Martin emphasizes that you cannot muscle fish in that situation. Also, be sure that your drag is set properly — really light. And the hooks on that crankbait have to be extremely sharp. These are the facets of light-line deep cranking that you can control.

The efficiency of the shallower crankbaits (10 to 13 feet deep) can be significantly improved by using the same techniques that allow the super-deeper crankers to reach maximum depth — using long rods and light line.

"Light line and crankbaits should not be strangers to each other," Martin adds. "The only time I use line as heavy as 20-pound test is when I am in tremendously heavy timber in places like Toledo Bend or Seminole. In that situation, you are just kidding yourself if you try to get by with 8- or 10-pound line. You're going to lose all of your fish.

"But I'm talking about shallower cranking in this situation, where depth isn't as important as the cover."

The super-deep crankbaits open up a whole new arena for summertime bass fishing. Before now, crankbaits have been traditional tools for spring and fall when the fish are suspended 5 to 15 feet deep. But the summertime bass in 20-foot depths are no longer immune to these ultra-deep divers. Before the advent of the new super-deep crankbaits, these fish had only been reached with trolling techniques like spoonplugging and long-line trolling.

"Now, summer structure situations like deep-water creek channels, underwater islands, rockpiles and brushpiles can be fished like never before," past Classic champion Stanley Mitchell says. "A big advantage of being able to work these types of deep-water structure in the summer is that you often find large schools of fish."

But the myth persists that with these new crankbaits, the average fisherman using average equipment can make an average cast with a 5 1/2-foot rod and use an average retrieve to reach that magical 20-foot mark. That just isn't so.

Joe Hughes, one of the most high-profiled anglers in the country, has spent considerable time explaining the fallacies associated with that belief for the past several years now. Forget for a moment that Hughes handles public relations duties for PRADCO, Inc., the parent company to Rebel, Heddon, Cordell, Bomber and other lure manufacturers (which was one of the companies that didn't dive head-first into the 20-foot-and-below craze). Instead, listen to the words of one of America's most talented crankbait fishermen as he discusses the subject of super-deep cranking.

When asked if 20-foot diving baits are a myth, Hughes replies "I'm not going to say that you can't get them that deep. But there are some inherent misconceptions in that. The person that reads the advertising is led to believe otherwise, but the truth is that you cannot use a 5 1/2-foot pistol-grip rod and expect to get one of these baits to the depths that are claimed. Personally, I'm not saying that they can't get that deep, but I can't get them that deep.

"The casts that are necessary and the line weights and lengths are very particular to whether or not you are able to get these baits down. I'm not casting stones, but people have come to me at my seminars all around the country, I think, because Rebel was conspicuous in their absence of getting into this mega-deep-running bait deal, and complained about these baits.

"The reason that we didn't (start manufacturing ultra-deep divers) was because of the efficiency involved. Fishing should be fun out there on the water and if you are going to fish in excess of 15 feet deep, you are going to beat yourself to death getting these baits to reach such depths. It is a very physical method of fishing.

"In summary, let me just say that to get 20 feet of depth out of a crankbait, you've got to be at the very top of your game."

Lee Sisson knows that tiny crankbaits will catch giant bass.

Chapter 9

The Art of Ultralight Cranking

Jimmy Rogers and Jimmy Nolan are versatile pros who are good enough to have qualified for the prestigious BASS Masters Classic. Lee Sisson is a nationally-renowned lure designer who has fished in every corner of the country and can work every type of lure effectively.

Jerry Simpson is a guide who spends most of his time flipping the submerged brush and timber of Missouri's Lake of the Ozarks.

PROfile

Each has his own style, his own successes.

But if you leave them alone and allow them to fish any way they prefer, each would chose the ultimate form of sport fishing   ultralight bassin.'

More specifically, each would choose ultralight crankbait fishing, a specialized art that produces consistently year-round and, at times, can out-produce any lure known to man.

Although they wouldn't have bothered to learn to master fishing the tiny diving plugs on thread-like line if the lures weren't productive, each admits he was originally attracted to it because of the sheer enjoyment involved. Ultralight crankbait fishing is

Past   BASS Masters Classic qualifier Jimmy Rogers is the host of the long-running Anglers in Action television series.

pleasure fishing in its purest form and isn't for the faint-hearted.

"I've caught a lot of fish every way you can catch fish, but when I get out on a lake or a little pond by myself, I just take my ultralight outfit and crankbaits smaller than most people have ever seen," says Sisson, who has an 8-pound bass on 2-pound test line to his credit. "As far as pure sportfishing, pure recreation, there is nothing that can rival hooking into a fish of any size on these little crankbaits, watching that rod bend and that fish take line."

Rogers agrees. "I find myself actually giggling and laughing when I'm ultralight fishing and I'm fighting a fish on that wimpy rod," adds the Lakeland, Fla., tournament pro and television show host. "I do it just for the enjoyment that fish of all sizes provide and then there's the challenge of maybe getting a big fish on light tackle."

"Whenever I can get my customers to take the time to learn to fish these little baits, they usually fall in love with this kind of fishing," Simpson says. "Not only do these little lures produce bass, but they'll catch so many other species like bream that it keeps my guide parties into action all of the time."

To understand the passion of these anglers toward ultralight crankbait fishing, it's important to realize just what the sport involves. The equipment usually consists of ultralight spinning gear (although a few companies, like Quantum with its 1510 reel, make baitcasting tackle that will suffice). That means a limber rod that allows you to apply some pressure to the fish without breaking the line and a small reel that does little more than store line. Ultralight crankbaiting involves line sizes ranging from 2- to 6-pound test, hardly the stuff of tournament champions.

And then there are the tiny crankbaits that, generally, run 3 to 10 feet. Most are less than 2 inches in length and weigh less than 1/4-ounce. They range from minuscule lures like Rebel's productive Wee Crawfish (1/10th-ounce) to heavier and deeper-running lures like Bagley's Honey B and Lee Sisson Lures' Diving Tiny Ticker.

While the sporting nature of such fishing is an attraction to many, these little crankbaits will also produce fish. Without that facet, there would be no self-respecting ultralight crankbait enthusiasts.

The light line is an important reason why these tiny lures produce consistently. The intelligent bass fisherman knows that line visibility plays a major role in a lure's ability to attract strikes. More importantly, with ultralight crankbaits, lure size is not an eliminating factor.

"The main reason these crankbaits catch more fish than larger lures is that you are not culling out the smaller fish on the basis of lure size," says Sisson, who developed the popular Honey B during the decade he served as the lure designer for the Jim Bagley Bait Company. "With large lures, you're going to catch some small fish, but there's a certain amount of small fish that you're automatically eliminating. The small lures don't eliminate anybody.

"And a lot of it has to with the feeding habits of bass and the fact that it's just easier for them to mouth or eat a smaller bait. I think there's some validity to the saying that big lures catch big bass, but you can catch big fish with little lures, too. It's like an elephant eating a peanut."

While ultralight diving baits produce throughout the year, they are particularly effective in the spring when bass seem to concentrate on the small panfish fry or newly-hatched shad, minnows and crawfish. This often creates a tough situation for anglers using more conventional-size lures.

"In the spring of the year when you have a lot of young fry hatched out, the natural forage of bass is actually smaller than it will be at any time of the year," explains Rogers, who qualified for the 1980 Classic. "During that time of year, they seem to zero in on a certain size of baitfish and often they won't take anything bigger. You can take a small crankbait during March, April and May throughout the country and catch as many numbers of bass as you can with anything. That's prime time for ultralight crankbaits."

"Another factor, especially in the spring, is the vibration pattern," Sisson adds. "Vibration patterns may be the number one strike stimuli, because predatory fish like bass are able to detect it from some amazing distances through their lateral lines and inner ear. A smaller baitfish has a completely different vibration pattern coming through the water than a larger baitfish or fish and bass will home in on that, especially in the spring when most of the baitfish are small. An ultralight crankbait gives off a different vibration pattern as it moves through the water than a larger crankbait, a vibration pattern that is close to the type of vibration pattern that the bass are concentrating on during that time of the year."

Although ultralight crankbait anglers aren't picky about when they fish these little lures, there are a couple of situations where the baits are the perfect solution to angling problems.

Jimmy Nolan, a talented bass pro who has qualified for two Classics, uses light line and ultralight diving plugs regularly in the clear waters of his home lake — Arkansas' Bull Shoals Reservoir. "In water that's super clear, it's to your advantage to automatically go to a small bait on light line," he says. "The reason behind that is with the super clear water, the fish have a better chance to examine the lure more closely and a smaller lure is easier to fool them with. And these little crankbaits like the Honey B, which I use a lot, are fast-moving lures, so that helps in that situation. Add to that 4- or 6 pound line that's not very visible and you can overcome a clear-water situation."

Sisson and others agree that in clear-water situations, a sound tactic is to use a smaller, fast-moving lure that presents a less-visible object than baits like a plastic worm or jig.

For years, tournament pros like Rogers have held to the common belief that you can combat the doldrums of passing cold fronts by altering your strategy in three ways: slow your retrieve down, work an area more thoroughly while remembering that the bass are likely to be tight to the cover and drop to a smaller lure. Rogers has found that ultralight crankbaits have been the answer to cold front-induced lockjaw on many occasions over the past few years.

"There is a definite cold-front application for these little crankbaits," Rogers says. "It's a small bait and you can work it slowly as well.

"When a cold front hits and I'm on a good crankbait pattern, I drop to a smaller lure and concentrate on working the area slowly and thoroughly. By experimenting in the Cypress Gardens pool near my home in Lakeland, I've discovered that you can really work these little crankbaits slowly and in a tantalizing fashion — a technique I've had good success with in cold-front conditions. I make as long a cast as I can and quickly get the lure down near its maximum depth. Once it reaches that depth, you can keep that lure down there while just barely turning the reel handle. A straight slow retrieve like that has produced well for me. Another tactic is using a balsa-lure like a Honey B or Bagley's Deeper-Diving Kill'r B-I. You can stop it and suspend it for a second or so. It will slowly begin to drift up and with a couple cranks of the reel handle, you can bring it back down and start the suspending tactic over again.

"You've got to remember that under cold-front conditions, a bass is not likely to dart out from the cover and grab a bait that's flying past him. If that bait is swimming toward him slowly, he'll often take it despite not being very active at the time."

There are some definite advantages to down-sizing your crankbait. But there are some disadvantages that should be addressed as well.

The foremost drawback with ultralight crankbaits is a significant loss of depth compared to its larger counterparts. With a smaller lip and diving plane (the top and back portions of the lure which help drive the bait deeper), the tiny crankbaits won't usually penetrate the 10-foot level, despite the fact that the small diameter of the light line presents very little resistance moving through the water.

But Sisson and Simpson have come up with a couple of ways of doctoring the small lures to attain more depth. Sisson often attaches a small bell-sinker to the O-ring of the belly hook of his crankbait, while Simpson has had good success with using a large slip sinker attached above a swivel a foot or more from his lure. "This is almost like a Carolina rig," says Simpson, whose favorite ultralight crankbait is Rebel's Wee Crawfish, a tiny, lifelike lure that has a legion of followers throughout the country. "It will run fine at a deeper depth and you can get great action by stopping it, letting it slowly float up and then start your retrieve again. This makes the lure suspend for a second and then dart toward the bottom."

Another disadvantage with ultralight crankbaits is that you won't be penetrating grassbeds or thick treetops with these lures, which are not weedless in any sense of the word. Instead, you are limited to open-water situations, as well as cranking the edges of weedlines, stick-ups, rocks and so on.

And this is one form of fishing that takes practice to perfect because of the ultralight gear and light line it requires. You aren't automatically born with the feel and sensitivity required for successfully fishing 4- and 6-pound line. But with enough practice, you will understand that even the lightest line — in the right hands — can handle the biggest bass.

"I think fishing 2-, 4- and 6-pound test line really hones your skills as a fisherman," Sisson says. "It really polishes your techniques because you have to actually play the fish.

"I think a major reason why fishermen lose fish today is that they don't play the fish. They're using 14- to 20-pound test line and they've got their drag tightened down. And when a fish hits the lure, unless the hook gets into a meaty part of the mouth, he pulls off. They physically pull the lure out of his mouth. Light line teaches you how to fight a fish on any size line."

"I think people are often scared to try this little line after fishing so long with bigger line that they're used to horsing fish with," Jimmy Nolan agrees. "With 4-pound test, I think a fisherman will start to respect the bass more. You can't simply horse him in. You've got to play him or he'll just break you off. I think you tend to get more of the bigger fish in on light line than you do with more conventional line sizes. With 12-pound line and up, you tend to not respect the fish as much and you either pull the bait out of its mouth or you break your line by trying to horse the fish out of cover."

Although there are some obvious disadvantages to using 4-and 6-pound line, today's rod, reel and line manufacturers have refined their products into real tools for the sporting angler. The rods are designed to be more forgiving of the fisherman's mistakes, while the drag systems of today are smoother and much more reliable than earlier models. And the drag is a very important part of fishing ultralight crankbaits.

Still, with ultralight fishing, it is critical that you concentrate on most minute details such as tying good knots, retying often, sharpening hooks, changing line regularly and keeping your tackle in good shape.

Ultralight crankbaits are not discriminating. These little diving plugs will attract fish — and fishermen — of all shapes and sizes.

Past Classic qualifier Neal Parker with a nice power-plant large-mouth that parted the grass to nail a Johnson spoon.

Chapter 10

Weedless Spoon Ways

Summer means plenty of sunshine and hot days, but, more importantly, signals the beginning of one of the country's most exhilarating types of bass fishing.

During the late spring and summer, there are few better artificial lures than the Johnson-type spoon. It produces more large bass than almost any type of lure because of one factor — you can run it through the middle of the thickest vegetation in the lake, which is where the big bass stay as the days grow hot.

"This time of year is excellent for spoon fishing," agrees Gene Lewis, a former guide on Florida's Kissimmee Chain of Lakes. "As we start to get into hot weather, these spoon fish start to come alive."

When summer rolls around, the Johnson spoons suddenly appear.

Johnson spoons are the ideal weapons for working pad fields. First of all, it is weedless, so you can

PROfile

The weedless spoon is largely responsible for Lake Okeechobee guide Richard Vance's Classic appearance.

cover a great deal of water without hanging up. And you can finesse the lure on demand and drop it into holes and pockets as it is being retrieved.

Kentucky's Ron Shearer will attest to the quality of spoon fishing.

It was during a 1982 B.A.S.S. tournament on Lake Okeechobee that Shearer came across a spoon pattern that gained him instant recognition, gave him his first national tournament victory and established his career as a fishing pro.

Shearer turned in a seven-fish stringer that weighed 36 pounds, 8 ounces — a B.A.S.S. record.

"Okeechobee is a phenomenal lake, particularly for spoon fishing," Shearer says. "Spoons were made for that lake."

During Shearer's amazing day, he was fishing a shallow, weedy bay with a 1/2-ounce Johnson Silver Minnow spoon, teamed with a white skirt.

"We got some good cloud cover that day," Shearer remembers. "I moved into some peppergrass and fished the little cuts in the grass. I was cranking it real slow, just wallowing it through the grass.

"I just sort of drifted from one cut to another when all of a sudden the action started. When the big fish hit it, they really swallowed it. I had to take needle-nosed pliers to get it out of their throats."

Shearer believes an important part of his success was the altering of the spoon's rubber skirt. After a couple of bass hit short and didn't contact the hook, Shearer trimmed the skirt to about 2 inches. It must have worked. He went on to boat bass weighing 8 pounds, 14 ounces, 8-1, 6-12, 6-1, 3-8 and a pair weighing 1-15 each.

Richard Vance is another spoon nut.

A former qualifier for the BASS Masters Classic, Vance has fished Johnson spoons throughout the country with great success. It was a Johnson spoon that enabled him to finish seventh in a B.A.S.S. tournament on Kissimmee and make the coveted Classic. And it is the silver or gold Johnson spoon that produces limit after limit for him during this time of year.

"The spoon is a very underrated lure in many parts of the country," Vance says. "But it has plenty of believers."

In his system, Vance juggles four colors of spoons and three colors of skirts depending on the water clarity and sunlight.

With bright sunshine and clear water, he uses a silver or gold spoon and white skirt combo. In off-colored water, he switches to a chartreuse spoon and skirt for high visibility. On overcast days, Vance relies on a black spoon with a yellow or chartreuse skirt.

Vance attributes a significant portion of his spoon success with the person-alized alteration he puts on each skirt. He always trims the longer lengths of rubber to match the shorter legs and then plucks much of the rubber completely off. He usually finishes with only a dozen or so rubber legs remaining intact.

"Trimming the skirt does three things," he explains. "First, you can cast the spoon better. Secondly, it will come through the grass and weeds better. And third, it gives the fish less to grab onto. He's more likely to grab on to the hook."

Vance usually retrieves the spoon as slow as possible without allowing it to get hung up constantly.

"I must start by saying that spoon fishing is very hard work," veteran angler Larry Douglas says. "There are many different ways to work a spoon from skipping it across the surface to bouncing it off the bottom.

"To work or control the spoon, I use a 7-foot heavy-action rod with 17- to 20-pound test line on a high-speed reel. This equipment is used because most

In 1982, a spoon produced the B.A.S.S. seven-bass record for Kentucky's Ron Shearer — 36 pounds, 8 ounces — that still stands.

spooning is done over grass or heavy vegetation and it gives the strength and power that's necessary in landing a large fish.

"I choose the size of the spoon by noticing the size of the bait that the bass are feeding on. When small bait is present, I use a 1/4-ounce spoon. With larger bait present, I use a 1/2-ounce model. Weather conditions and water clarity dictate the different colors of spoons. I will throw a silver spoon with a white or chartreuse grub as a trailer on cloudy days and a gold spoon with a yellow or chartreuse grub on clear days. Early in the morning, I'll use a black spoon with a yellow grub."

Douglas mixes his retrieves and the different types of spoons depending on the situation.

"I use three methods for retrieving a spoon," he explains. "Skipping the spoon fast across the surface, working the spoon slowly, just barely on top of the water and working the spoon to a pocket and then letting it fall briefly before resuming the retrieve.

"The Johnson spoon casts very easily by its design, but is difficult to keep on the surface. When I want to work a spoon very slow and still have good action, I switch to a Barney spoon or Captain Hogan-style spoon. These spoons have more buoyancy so they stay on top easier and fall very slow with good a fluttering action."

Douglas adds two important points about spoon fishing: keep the rod tip high during the retrieve and never set the hook until you feel the pressure of the fish.

Larry Wright, a Lake Okeechobee guide and former BASS Masters Classic qualifier, fishes spoons regularly and has developed a consistently successful plan of attack.

He uses a 1/2-ounce Johnson spoon, except for heavy winds, when he'll switch to a 3/4-ounce model. On sunny days, Wright uses a silver spoon teamed with a white grub, but switches to a gold spoon and chartreuse grub on cloudy days. Extremely heavy cloud cover calls for a black spoon and chartreuse grub combination.

"My number one method for working the spoons is to move the spoon rapidly over the surface," Wright says. "I use this method no matter what type of vegetation I'm fishing. If the fast-moving method doesn't produce, I slow my retrieve, but still try to keep the lure on top. If this fails, I slow the spoon even more, letting it fall into open pockets, and then after it drops, I pull it up and start my retrieve again.

"Always remember you can fish a spoon under most conditions. Try throwing a spoon in the bulrushes, let it sink to the bottom and then work it back like a plastic worm."

Few anglers understand the allure the weedless spoon as well as guide and tournament pro Steve Bushore.

"The equipment I use for spoon fishing is very important in working the spoon properly," Bushore says. "I use a 7-foot rod to help keep the spoon on top or near the surface. The rod must be a medium-heavy to heavy action with the backbone to haul a big fish out of heavy cover. The reel I use can handle 20- to 30-pound test line, which is so important in thick cover.

"The Johnson spoon comes in many different sizes, but I prefer the 1/4- and 1/2-ounce models. I use a 1/4-ounce spoon on days with a little wind or in cover that's not too thick or has a few inches of water over the grass. The 1/2-ounce spoon is my choice on windy days and in heavy cover so that I can control the spoon better and keep it in the water.

"I use three colors of spoons: silver for bright days, gold on bright days with cloud cover moving in and black on very cloudy days. I use only two colors of trailer, either chartreuse or chartruese/metalflake. And I use a 2- or 3-inch grub with a curly tail as a trailer.

"I prefer using a spoon in shallow water between 1 and 3 feet. Always look for Kissimmee grass, peppergrass or hydrilla. I work the spoon up on the surface so that it creates a little wake as it is reeled back to the boat."

Many anglers have discovered in recent years that one of the most productive spoons looks nothing like the age-old Johnson spoon.

Rebel's Talkin' Spoon doesn't resemble its more established counterpart, but the two spoons have something in common: both catch a great deal of fish in grass.

The foil-finished Talkin' Spoon in both silver and gold has proven particularly effective in most grassy lakes. Unlike a Johnson spoon, the Talkin' Spoon emits a rattling sound that many of its believers think helps attract bass.

It's an excellent lure for even the most dense types of vegetation like hydrilla.

Knowledgeable bass anglers use a variety of trailers on their spoons, including regular rubber skirts, short grubs and even plastic worms. Many of the top pros prefer the Burke Twin-Tail. Others switch to plastic worms for bass that seem to be hitting short or tentatively.

An excellent trailer for this time of year is one of the many plastic lizard- or crawfish imitations.

Regardless of the personal taste, summer marks the time when spoon fishing begins to heat up. And when it's hot, spoon fishing is among the finest angling sport available anywhere.

Texas pro David Fenton demonstrates the allure of the Pop-R.

Chapter 11

Last Secret Bait of the Pros

The year was 1979, not long after Rick Clunn had established himself as one of America's best bass anglers with back-to-back championship performances in the 1976 and '77 BASS Masters Classic.

On the heels of the most important victories of his career and the realization of a pair of life-long goals, Clunn was guiding a long-time customer when it dawned on him that he still had plenty to learn about the sport that many assumed he had mastered.

PROfile

It was on that day that his client, an average fisherman, taught Clunn a fishing technique that would ultimately help him — and others — win several national tournaments.

Almost by accident, Clunn discovered a tactic so good he would try to keep it as close to his breast as possible and a lure that became the secret bait of several pros on the B.A.S.S. and other tournament trails. It was a lure and technique so effective that a

Texan Zell Rowland is a two-time B.A.S.S. winner and five-time Classic qualifier.

handful of pros worked overtime to keep it to themselves by even going as far as buying up almost all of available lures in the southwestern United States.

The lure is the Pop-R, a small, 2-inch concave-mouth chugger made by Rebel that features a small white bucktail on the rear hook, a bait that has produced victories in several national tournaments for Clunn (U.S. Open), Zell Rowland (B.A.S.S. Super-Invitational), Mike Folkestad (U.S. Open) and others. But the Pop-R never received much acclaim from its tournament exploits because Clunn and others did such a good job of keeping it a secret.

But now, that has changed.

"We might as well talk about it," Clunn said recently when interviewed about the silent success of the Pop-R. "I guess the secret is out.

"I had never known anyone who had fished the bait before 1979 when I was introduced to it by one of my customers. I had used chugger-type lures for years, but this guy was fishing the Pop-R different from the way you were supposed to fish a chugger. He was using a real steady retrieve, instead of popping it. What really impressed me about the bait was he fished with me once a month all year-round and this bait and technique produced throughout the year. I fished with him six or seven months before it hit me what that bait was doing and how many good fish it was catching under all kinds of conditions.

"I started fishing it hard in 1980 in tournaments and it wasn't long before I began working hard at keeping the Pop-R a secret."

Although his success with the Pop-R in Texas tournaments didn't go unnoticed, Clunn and a handful of Long Star State anglers concentrated on keeping the deadly little lure their own confidential weapon. They spoke about it in whispers and only within their own circle. They never credited the Pop-R while on the victory stand (Rowland would not identify the "chugger-type bait" after winning the $72,000 first prize in the Super-Invitational).

And they helped create a shortage of a lure that was already hard to find. Because it hadn't sold well, Rebel officials had pulled it from the main catalog in 1979. A few were found scattered around the country in tackle stores, but were difficult to locate. When the Texans finished collecting the lures, the only way to get your hands on these chuggers in recent years was by ordering 300 or more of the same color from the manufacturer.

"When I finally figured out how neat this bait was, I bought all of them up," Clunn says. "Except for a stray box here or there in stores throughout the country that I hadn't found, there wasn't a Pop-R to be had. And right about the time I won the '83 U.S. Open and we had been catching a lot of fish on Sam Rayburn and Toledo Bend in regional tournaments, some of the guys in Texas got together and started making special orders of them."

Such clandestine efforts might seem silly on the surface. To understand their zeal, you must understand the power of the Pop-R in certain situations.

"It's one of the best reaction baits there is," claims Randy Fite, a seven-time Classic qualifier from Texas. "It's an extremely good, productive bait, especially for numbers of bass, but occasionally you'll catch a big fish on it."

"It is the only topwater bait I've ever seen that you could fish it all day long and get bit on it all day long," Rowland adds.

"It is different from other topwater baits in that it will actually cause fish to hit that are in that neutral mode and they're really not feeding," Clunn says. "That says a lot for an artificial lure."

All agree that the key to the Pop-R is the sound it makes when worked quickly across the top of the water. The pros describe it as a noise similar to that of a frantic shad skipping across the surface of the water to avoid a predator. It is a sound not usually associated with chugger-type topwater lures, which usually displace so much water when popped that it emits a "BLURP" noise.

Even as word of the Pop-R's charm over largemouth bass gradually emerged, the unusual method of fishing the lure kept others from copying the success of Clunn and the other privileged few. Most fishermen fished it slow and popped it hard — like they would work most chugger baits. And the Texans didn't tell them any differently.

The Texas pros found that the Pop-R is most productive when worked similar to the "walking the dog," a method of retrieving most commonly associated with a Heddon Zara Spook. It involves rhythmically twitching the rod tip, while retrieving the lure. The result is a quick, side-to-side action of the Zara Spook that has proven productive for years.

"Most people think a chugger should be fished slow and go 'KAPLUNK, KAPLUNK,' " explains Clunn, the only four-time Classic winner. "The Pop-R can be fished that way, but you won't catch many fish that way. And if you do, you could have caught those fish with any type of chugger.

"But with this bait, you want to work it fast. The Pop-R will actually dart, go under, hop out of the water and dart back and forth like a Zara Spook. Every once in a while I'll chug it, but most of the time I fish it with that fast, darting motion. And it makes a sound that's hard to describe. The best way I can describe it is it sounds like a shad flitting across the water. And that's one reason why the Pop-R is such a great bait. I'll tell you what, I've seen whole schools of bass when they're not even schooling come up and chase this little bait. They literally go bananas over this little bait at times when I cannot get them to hit anything else."

"Most people think that they have to work any type of topwater lure real slow to entice the fish into striking," adds John Torian of Hemphill, Texas, a guide on Toledo Bond and a former Classic qualifier, who has long been privvy to the Pop-R's magic. "But a bass is capable of catching a fast-moving bait. The Pop-R has proven that."

Although the Texans say the Pop-R will produce throughout the year, there are certain conditions and times of the year that it is most effective. Clunn says late spring through late summer is prime time for the Pop-R.

The most critical condition for Pop-R success, all agree, is water clarity.

"You need some clarity to the water for the Pop-R to be most effective, which is why it has done so well in the U.S. Open, which is held on Lake Mead (a clear, mountain lake)," Clunn explains. "The key is that water clarity. It will bring them as far as the clarity of the water will allow. You can catch them on it in muddy water, but it's not nearly as effective. You have to slow it down and when you slow it down, it loses its special little talent."

"Out on Lake Mead where the water is super clear, I've had fish come up from off of the bottom 30 feet deep to hit that bait," Rowland adds. "They look like a little torpedo coming up. It's really exciting."

Fite agrees with Clunn and Rowland, but emphasizes that a Zara Spook will also draw vicious strikes from deep-water bass. A major difference between those lures, though, is that the fish often strike just short of the Spook and are hard to hook, while the bass seem to almost inhale the Pop-R. That translates into more celebration and less frustration.

Surprisingly, Clunn and his fellow Texans use heavy line with the Pop-R, even in clear-water situations. But Fite contends that line visibility is not much of a factor with surface strikes, while Clunn maintains that the heavy line (he recommends 17-pound-test) is necessary to produce the proper action from the tiny chugger.

"It works so much better with heavy line," Clunn says. "When I fish the Pop-R with light line, the bait will try to go under. I don't mind that a little, but with light line it will often go under and try to stay under on you. The heavier line keeps it on the surface better where it can work."

Clunn also alters the Pop-R by sanding off a little of its lower lip and putting lighter hooks on it. Rowland constantly experiments with the lure by sanding it mouth to create different sounds. "For example," he says, "you can sand the whole lower lip off to the point where it is sort of tucked back underneath the bait and it will give you that desirable sound 10 times louder than what it normally does."

There seems to be applications for several types of structure and cover for the Pop-R.

Rowland won the Super-Invitational on Tennessee's Lake Chickamauga by paralleling the edges of the milfoil patches. Another effective pattern was working the Pop-R across the top of milfoil that was submerged slightly below the surface. In clear-water lakes like Mead, the pros work the Pop-R on the surface above submerged boulders and rock piles. And some have good success working it around standing timber in typical southern reservoirs.

When he won the U.S. Open, Clunn concentrated on deep-water points and brush.

Unlike recent years, the average fisherman now has no trouble getting his hands on a supply of Pop-Rs. Although Rebel officials had decided to remove it from their catalog when sales fell below 1,500 in 1979, they began to recognize a sudden interest in the little chugger as word of its heroics leaked out. When the number of 300-plus special orders began to increase significantly, Rebel officials decided to begin actively promoting the Pop-R again. Since its resurrgence in 1987, PRADCO officials have sold more than a million Pop-Rs.

The secret of the Pop-R is out — much to the displeasure of the pros who had been dominating with it and the pleasure of the average bass angler who can add still another tool to his arsenal.

Chapter 12

Tauber's Tips for Topwater

The towering cypress tree has stood guard here for 100 years or more in this corner of the lake. It stands far out in front of the rest of the tree line, its presence an obvious, textbook example of where a bass should be.

Rich Tauber approaches the lone tree, but pauses to rumble through his tackle box. He quickly wipes away the perspiration accumulating from the mid-day sun and ties a King's Sling knot to secure a green-and-yellow Zara Spook in place.

Careful about his boat positioning, the California pro makes a long cast that settles about 5 feet past the tree. Then, with the touch of a surgeon and the rhythm of jazz pianist, he begins to bring the Spook alive. As the lure approaches the tree, Tauber shifts into a more subtle gear and seemingly makes the cigar-shaped lure walk completely around its half-submerged knees.

As the frog-patterned Spook enters the shaded part of the water, the base of the tree seems to explode with activity. A longtime inhabitant has objected to the intrusion of the Spook and does its best to inhale one of James Heddon's greatest creations. Within a matter of seconds, Tauber subdues the 5-pound-plus largemouth, works the hooks loose and returns it to the same shady pocket of the lonesome cypress.

PROfile

Californian Rich Tauber is one of the top pros in the country with both a U.S. Open title and a Classic appearance to his credit.

Rich Tauber lands a nice bass that couldn't resist the noise of the Pop-R worked quickly across the surface of the water.

"Now that's what topwater fishing is all about," Tauber exclaims. "The weekend fisherman considers topwater baits to be something you fish early and late. But some of the bigger topwater fish are caught in the middle of the day.

"Topwater baits, as a group, are overlooked. The reason I fish topwaters so much is that they're probably one of the lesser-fished baits, especially in tournament fishing. Jigs, worms and spinnerbaits dominate the tournament trail, but a few guys like Charlie Campbell have shown how effective topwater baits can be. My greatest successes as a tournament fisherman have come on topwater baits.

"Plus, I really enjoy fishing them. I can see my bait working the entire time. Seeing the fish strike is no big deal. It's always fun, but it's more important to be able to watch your bait work to be able to see what it takes to trigger a strike. I get a lot of enjoyment in seeing what movements make the fish react. And then putting those movements into a topwater bait and seeing it produce again. Also, you are keeping the bait in and around visible cover so you're keeping it around the fish more often. I love it because it's target-shooting."

Tauber has made a career out of disproving the myths of surface fishing. Although many fishermen consider topwater lures to be limited in the times and situations when they will produce, Tauber's career as a tournament pro has shown just how untrue such thinking tends to be. In fact, it was a Zara Spook that gave him the biggest moment of his career (winning the U.S. Open) and surface lures have paved the way to an appearance in the prestigious BASS Masters Classic.

In the process, Tauber has developed a system of topwater fishing that has proven productive on lakes, reservoirs and rivers throughout the country.

Tauber is asked to describe the ideal conditions for surface fishing.

"My ideal situation would be a water temperature in the 70-degree range. The clearer the water, the better. I like real, real clear water for topwater fishing. Add to that submerged cover like vegetation, rocks or wood in 4 to 7 feet of water. Throw a topwater plug over the shadows, cracks where you can see a little dark spot in the clear water, and you will enjoy some of the greatest action you can have fishing."

Obviously, the prime conditions for topwater action are limited, but Tauber has proven that these lures can be effective in a variety of situations. As a rule of thumb, he fishes surface baits in water of at least 60 degrees in temperature.

"For me, topwater baits aren't limited to early and late," Tauber emphasizes. "They're all-day baits for me. You shouldn't always follow the so-called rules for topwater fishing. Bass are obviously most vulnerable in a low-light situation, but I won the U.S. Open (on Lake Mead) fishing a topwater bait in the middle of the day. It was 110 degrees with 90-degree water temperature when I caught all of those fish. And I caught them all from 10 in the morning until two in the afternoon. And there hadn't been a cloud for a month."

Although Tauber has an extensive surface system, ranging from tiny chuggers to plastic rats, his unabashed favorite topwater lure is the Zara Spook.

"To catch quality fish — 2 pounds and up — I consider the Spook to be the best surface bait of all," he explains. "The Spook is a great draw bait. And the clearer the water, the more effective the Spook is. I think you get better quality fish on a Spook than any other surface bait, particularly the Spook that is white and has a green back and silver glitter.

"I work a Spook much like you would a buzzbait — pretty consistent in speed. I give it a little pause every third time. I always keep in one rod position. The bait will walk on its own because it's tail-weighted and the nose slides back and forth. You don't want to do too many wild things with a Spook because it's a hard bait for the fish to track in the first place. The more consistent you move it, the easier it is for the fish to find and the more success you will have. You'll get more hook-ups on the strikes."

The Spook performs best on 14-pound test line for Tauber. That line size has good castability, yet it is strong enough to control a big bass. And to ensure its action, he advises using a split ring on the nose of the bait or tying a King's Sling knot for freer movement.

Perhaps the best overall surface lure for catching sheer numbers is the Rebel Pop-R, according to Tauber. The Pop-R is a small, subtle chugger with a concave mouth. Years ago, some of the Texas pros discovered its uncanny allure for catching bass when fished in an unconventional fashion — quickly across the top of the water instead of being slowly popped and paused.

"I usually work it fast and try to imitate a feeding fish on top of the water," Tauber says. "It's kind of an impulse or reaction-type strike where the fish is down in the cover and not even thinking about feeding, but that quick chugging sound stimulates the fish enough to get it to look up. I think the curiosity brings them up and then their mood changes when they see the bait and they hit it."

The Pop-R is well-suited for working isolated targets like brushpiles and willow trees. But Tauber avoids using it on long weed lines because it cannot be fished quickly enough to be efficient in that situation.

"I don't fish it as fast as the guys in Texas do," he adds. "I fish it more deliberately and pause it a lot. I give the fish a chance to get it. I catch 90 percent of them when the bait is sitting still in the water, so I fish it more like a chugger."

Two of Tauber's topwater tools are often not classified as surface lures in the minds of some anglers — the buzzbait and plastic rat.

Tauber's topwater system includes other types of surface baits like propellor lures (like a Bomber Rip Shad), which are most valuable when the bass are feeding heavily on shad, and smaller stickbaits like the Zara Puppy, a small, subtle version of the Spook which shines on super-shallow fish.

In the early spring when the bass are shallow, but inactive, Tauber utilizes a minnow-style lure like the Rebel Minnow or Rapala, which he considers small, finesse baits. The idea is to use a lure that will trigger these still sluggish bass into striking.

Two of Tauber's topwater tools are often not classified as surface baits in the minds of some anglers.

His belief in buzzbaits was reinforced in 1984 when Tauber won a Western Bass event on a Cordell Squeaky Pete. The bass were suspended on the ends of points about 10 feet below the surface and in 20 to 30 feet of water. The noisy bladed bait proved to be the best lure for bringing the bass up.

"I try to fish a buzzbait as slowly as possible and still keep it on top of the water and basically try to develop a sound or commotion that is productive," Tauber says. "If I get it where it's churning just right and I get a few strikes, I try to tune into the sound of that speed."

Although the country has seen a resurgence in interest in the hollow-bodied, plastic rat, Tauber has long been a believer in its ability to attract vicious strikes in situations where the vegetation has matted on the surface of the water. "This can be a real exciting bait when fished around topped-out grass, isolated holes with good depth and clear, open-water pockets," he adds. "I don't do a lot with the bait. Throw it out past the cover, reel it quickly across the grass and stop it in the pockets.

The Heddon Zara Spook, one of Tauber's favorites, is perhaps the most time-honored surface lure of all.

"The key with the rat is setting the hook. Once I get a bite, I usually drop the rod and count to 10. I really try to count to 10. If you jerk early, you'll lose the fish. And don't expect to bring the fish out. Instead, keep a tight line and go in after it."

Selecting a rod is a crucial part of topwater fishing, according to Tauber, who recommends a 6-foot medium-action graphite model. He prefers graphite over fiberglass because of its strength and quick reaction, factors that often come into play when setting the hook from a distance.

To follow Rich Tauber's career is to understand the multi-faceted allure of the topwater bait. He has certainly proven that "topwater baits are big-bass baits."

Roland Martin's first topwater strike came on a Zara Spook and weighed about 5 pounds — but it was a striper.

Chapter 13

Roland Martin's
Surface System

If you surveyed the bass fishermen in America who have experienced different types of the sport and asked them what is the most exciting form of bass fishing, the vast majority wouldn't hesitate to answer "topwater fishing."

The "tap-tap-tap" of the plastic worm will never be the same once you've been an audience to the visual excitement of a vicious topwater strike played out on the surface of a shallow-water flat.

Roland Martin, one of the most successful tournament fishermen of all-time and host of a highly successful nationally syndicated television show, admits he was hopelessly hooked on topwater fishing at the age of 12.

PROfile

Tournament pioneer Roland Martin holds B.A.S.S. record for victories (17), Angler of the Year titles (nine) and Classic appearances (19).

"I still vividly remember my first topwater strike," he says, smiling. "I was only 12 at the time, but I remember working a topwater plug along the shore of Lanier Lake in central Maryland, where I grew up.

"A little bass, about 1 1/2 pounds, boiled at the plug. The fish didn't really get it the first time and I jerked it clean out of the water and up into a tree behind me. The boil looked so big, I just knew there was a 5- or 6-pounder out there. When I cast a second time, the bass sucked it in and this time I managed to catch him. That was really exciting to a 12-year-old boy and it still is today."

Roland Martin has lived the dreams of every fisherman, travelling to exotic places in pursuit of a variety of gamefish, yet he actually gets excited when he talks about surface lure fishing.

"In my opinion, there's nothing more exciting than topwater fishing for bass," he continues. "I've fished for bass all over the world, using every conceivable method and technique, but I've yet to find anything to top the thrill of seeing a big swirl behind the plug and a big bass come out of the water to engulf the lure.

"It still gets my adrenaline flowing. As a fisherman, if you don't get excited over topwater fishing, you're probably dead."

Through the years, Martin has refined the art of topwater fishing into a systematic approach that can work for anglers of all skills in all parts of the country.

Martin breaks his topwater attack into three categories of bass and four types of lures.

"With topwater fishing, you're dealing with three kinds of fish," Martin explains. "Spawning fish in the spring of the year, schooling fish in the summer and individual feeding fish from spring until the fall. The trout fishermen talk about 'matching the hatch' and that's what I do with topwater fishing.

"I use four types of plugs. I depend on swimming minnow-types like the little Rapalas, chugger-type lures like the Sam Griffin lures made here in Clewiston (Fla.), propeller lures like the Diamond Rattler or Devil's Horse and buzzbaits like the Floyd's Buzzer, which is made by Blue Fox."

To further "match the hatch," Martin uses the conditions around him to help dictate the type of topwater lure he'll use. He says the basic criteria for successful topwater fishing is clear water, warm water, little or no wind and low-light conditions.

"When you get those conditions together, you can really be in for some exciting fishing," Martin says. "That's a topwater fisherman's heaven."

The most exciting fishing of all takes place during the spring, when nature sends the large female bass to shallow-water bedding areas to spawn.

"When the water warms up to 62 degrees, the fish will usually be spawning," Martin explains. "So, then you've got a situation where the fish aren't hitting out of hunger. They're hitting out of a protective instinct to protect their nest.

"So, you prey on that little bit of predictability of the bass. The bass is anything but a predictable creature, but spawning season allows you to take advantage of the fact that you know they will be protecting those beds.

"Consequently, you want to intimidate these fish with the right lure worked slowly along the beds."

Martin believes the best intimidation lures for spawning fish are swimming minnow-type lures. His favorite is a small No. 11 Rapala in gold or silver. "It's a universal spawning lure from Connecticut to California, for largemouths in Florida and smallmouths in Canada. It will work anytime the fish are on the beds, except when the water is extremely muddy."

That small plug, which measures just 4 3/8-inches in length, has produced two 10-pound trophy bass during spawning situations in Florida for Martin.

The idea behind this particular attack is to intimidate the bass into striking by allowing the lure to lay over top of the bed, where it will aggravate the protective bass. To do that, you'll need a little cooperation from Mother Nature. Too much wind and rough water will not allow the plug to stay in one place very long. You also need water that isn't too muddy or cold.

"I cast that little Rapala past the bed and retrieve it slowly until it's right over the bed," Martin says. "Then I twitch it a couple of times and let it sit. That's usually all it takes."

Water depth is an important factor. Martin contends that a topwater lure will be more effective in shallow-water bedding areas than deeper spawning situations. "The fish are more likely to hit a lure in 2 feet of water than in 5 or 6 feet."

Locating bedding areas and spawning fish is usually a simple matter. Martin uses his airboat for a high perch and looks for the white rings the bass create by fanning the beds. Smallmouth seem to prefer bedding around rocks and boulders, while largemouths will bed around grass, stumps or logs. Polarized glasses are helpful for locating bedding areas.

Martin is asked what the ideal conditions would be for this type of swimming minnow for spawning bass.

"Give me a 2-foot weedy flat with little pockets and holes where the fish are spawning," he replied. "The water temperature would be 62 degrees with little or no breeze and you would have low-light conditions, like an overcast day. I would consider that a limit situation."

Martin would like the same conditions for the other types of topwater fishing in his system, when he is stalking individual fish located on points and around isolated cover. "For me, the topwater season begins with the full moon in the spring around Easter in the South (a little later in the North) and runs through September," he says.

During this period, topwater success usually comes during the traditional fishing periods of early morning and late afternoon, according to Martin. For this type of fishing, Martin likes a chugger-type lure. His favorites are a Sam Griffin Nippin' Sam or Jerkin' Sam lure, Heddon Chugger or Zara Spook.

"These lures are most effective when they're fished around brushy, weedy cover and stumpy points," he says. "Although you, again, want fairly shallow water, I've seen these chugger-type baits bring big fish up from deep places because they make a lot of noise when they're popped on the surface.

"Sunshine is not the best topwater condition, but I've seen the propeller-type baits work on bright and sunny days. With a prop bait like a Devil's Horse, the sun's rays reflect off the lure, giving it a flash that attract bass, plus the propeller makes a little noise."

When fishing during the warmest months of the year, Martin recommends looking for bass under heavy cover like large lily pads, hydrilla patches and boat docks. A noisy surface lure can often get these fish to come out from hiding and strike.

One of the best ways for catching single, isolated bass in open water, Martin says, is making long casts and working a Zara Spook very slowly.

Perhaps the most thrilling form of topwater fishing is when the bass are schooling in the summer and chasing shad, a common occurrence on southern reservoirs and lakes.

"In lakes that don't have shad, the bass stay around the shoreline searching for bluegills," Martin explains. "In those big southern reservoirs where there are schools of shad, the bass will often follow them out into open water and suspend beneath them."

Schooling season usually runs from June to late October, while August, September and October are the prime months. During this time, you'll often see the bass, which normally inhabit points, bars, timber and weedlines, on the surface breaking shad. Armed with a pair of binoculars, it's usually just a matter of chasing the schooling fish.

For casting into these schools, Martin recommends a topwater minnow like an Original Rapala or Countdown Rapala. "Again, match the hatch," he says. "Rapala makes a couple of Countdown models (Nos. 5 and 7) that are just about the same size as the threadfin shad in the fall. Silver is usually the best color."

Another good lure, according to Martin, is a heavy, sinking plug like the Near-Nothing, which can be worked very fast and has a concave mouth that pops loudly.

While it's common to catch plenty of small fish from these schools, Martin targets the bigger bass from time to time. The smaller fish are usually on top and the larger bass are ambushing the baitfish from below. A heavier surface plug can often be deadly on big bass.

For the hottest times of the summer, Martin likes to concentrate on buzzbait fishing, an exciting surface form of fishing that is often overlooked by the average angler.

"With a buzzbait like a Floyd's Buzzer, I can cover a lot of water and locate fish," he says. "When it's the hottest part of the summer and the fish don't seem to be hitting anything, more often than not, they'll hit a buzzbait.

"In the summer when the water temperatures soar to over 80 degrees, I buzz shallow coves, pockets and flats, especially around isolated cover like stumps, weedlines or any half-submergent cover. Chances are the noise from the big blades will aggravate the fish into striking. And buzzbaits usually produce bigger fish."

While many anglers return home to wait out the scorching summer temperatures of mid-day, Martin can usually be found casting a buzzbait. "The biggest bass I've ever caught on a buzzbait have come that way and consistently. The secret is to work it around heavy, heavy cover like a weedline or boat dock."

Mickey Bruce scored with a small topwater plug worked on the edge of a grass line.

Buzzbaits can also be effective in off-colored water, since bass rely more on sound than vision to ambush the noisy bait. And it's the one topwater lure that doesn't require low-light conditions to be effective.

In summary, Martin says "topwater fishing is not only is exciting, it's not that difficult to learn and perfect. You'll be glad you took the time to add this type of fishing to your arsenal."

Michael Dyess believes there is no better trophy lure than a jig.

Chapter 14

Kings of the Jig

Ask former MegaBucks champion and BASS Masters Classic contender Lonnie Stanley to name the absolute best big-bass bait and, not surprisingly, the Texan's answer would be the rubber-skirted jig. "It's the best year-round big-bass bait throughout the country," he claims.

PROfile

That is Stanley, as in Stanley Jigs, perhaps the best-selling of all of the lead-headed lures. But there is plenty of evidence to support Stanley's contention that, when it comes to catching quality fish, you cannot beat a jig.

"We did a survey about two years ago of several of the major tournament trails and went through their books as far as three years back to document which bait was used to win the most tournaments," says Stanley, one of the top pros in the country. "We found that 68 percent of all of the tournaments held in every month of the year were won on a rubber-skirted jig. I think that's impressive."

Personable Lonnie Stanley is a pioneer in jig design as well as a past MegaBucks champion and Classic qualifier.

It shouldn't surprise many to know that Stanley has become an expert at fishing the bait, particularly the jig-and-pig (a jig teamed with a pork chunk trailer) and jig-and-plastic crawfish combinations. He has developed the sensitivity of a rare gem-cutter when it comes to working the jig in heavy cover ranging from vegetation to brush. But he is quick to give the lure a lot of the credit.

"I think a jig can imitate three members of the bass' food chain, which is why it is so effective," Stanley explains. "By changing the size, color and type of trailer, it can imitate a crawfish, perch or a lizard. Not many baits are that versatile."

Stanley never fishes a jig without a trailer.

"With plastic trailers, you can do a lot of different things with jigs," Stanley says. "With our Craw Worm, you can get a loping motion. Frogs and crawfish lope up and down as they come through the water. Then there are screw-tail worms and snake types that wiggle. You can change the whole complexion of what a jig looks like by changing trailers. You can put a pork lizard on it and it will lope and wiggle at the same time.

"And a lot of people screw up their jig fishing with what they put on the back of it. I've seen them put a whole 6-inch worm on the back of a jig. But I've always had better luck by not using a trailer any longer than about 3 1/2 inches below the hook. Anything longer than that hampers the motion of the bait."

Over the years, the techniques of flipping and pitching have been tailored for fishing lures like the jig-and-pig. These close-quarters techniques enable the angler to accurately present a bait in seemingly impenetrable cover almost without disturbing the water. But when it comes to flipping and pitching, Stanley believes that most fishermen make a major mistake by overlooking the importance of boat positioning and the influence of their trolling motor. Stanley says he chose a MotorGuide 765 because its quiet operation allows him to sneak up on his targets.

Lonnie Stanley has one final bit of his advice for his fishing disciples.

"If you're not catching fish on a jig, usually you're fishing too fast," says Stanley, who could rightly be called the Lord of the Jig. "Speed is the most important consideration, followed by the three Cs of jig-fishing — concentration, contact with the bait and confidence. Once you get all of those things together, it's unbelievable what you can do with a jig."

Texan Michael Dyess has spent much of his professional career exploding the myths involved in jig fishing.

You know the ones — jigs are not productive summer baits; and jigs are not suited for fishing weedy cover.

"I think one of the biggest mistakes people make is not fishing a jig in the summer, which is probably one of the best kept-secrets in fishing," claims Dyess, a former BASS Masters Classic qualifier and a true expert on the rubber-skirted lure. "That's especially true with grass.

"We fish a jig year-round in moss. One of the things we've found is that the fish are never going to leave that moss. There will always be some fish in that moss that can be caught on a jig. And in the summertime, you're going to catch the larger fish on a jig because it has a larger silhouette than other lures."

Kentucky's Corbin Dyer proved the jig's allure in both situations when a summertime catch in 1985 proved to be the fourth-largest seven fish stringer in B.A.S.S. history. He used a jig-and-pig to coax a 31-pound-plus stringer from the weedy waters of Lake Okeechobee.

Gary Klein has learned to fish rubber-skirted jigs in grassy lakes.

But that message still escapes most bass anglers.

"People are reluctant to fish a jig in grass and get hung up," explains Dyess, who is an executive with Stanley Jigs, Inc. "But you can always pull that grass off. The truth is, whether you're fishing the break of the grass or holes in the grass, a jig is certainly one of the most effective baits for working those types of things."

Winter has long been consider by knowledgeable anglers to be prime time for jig fishing.

"The coldest time of the year can be the best jig fishing of the year," Dyess, says. "While everybody is out deer hunting, a few determined fishermen are catching some of the biggest bass of the year.

"It is the greatest jig time there is because during the coldest times, the bass are staged on cover, whether it be grass or wood. Instead of being suspended, you will find them related to structure that is obvious. You can then work that piece of structure completely and if you are slow and precise enough, you can catch some big fish without a lot of finesse."

To illustrate his point, Dyess recalls a recent late January day when a tournament on Lake Conroe produced some of its finest fishing of the year. The weather was so miserably cold that the guides on their rods were accumulating ice, but the tournament *average* was almost 4 pounds. The secret, Dyess, says, was loading the jig with a pair of large No. 11 Uncle Josh pork chunks to slow its descent as much as possible.

That is an important tactic because an agonizingly slow fall is the secret to scoring with a jig-and-pig in the cold times. Dyess also fans out the bristles on his weedguard to get more resistance and slow the fall even more.

Dyess' main winter weapon is a 3/8-ounce black Stanley jig with a large black pork chunk, fished on 14- to 20-pound test line with a heavy-action flipping rod.

"I look for cold-water fish in the textbook areas — sloughs where they can move up as the water warms, creek channels and along the edges of deeper points," Dyess adds. "They aren't hard to locate."

Dyess cautions that the nonaggressive strike of these sluggish bass is often undetectable and recommends watching your line at all times. Most of the strikes come on the fall of the jig.

Although the color combinations of jigs almost rivals that of the plastic worm, Dyess utilizes three primary combinations — black/blue/brown, black/blue/purple and black/chartreuse/lime green — for most fishing situations. Water clarity is the primary factor that dictates jig and trailer color, according to Dyess. In clear water, he uses black/blue/purple with a black trailer. Off-colored water calls for black/blue/brown with a brown or black trailer. Especially muddy water demands brighter color combinations like black and orange or black and red with a dark trailer.

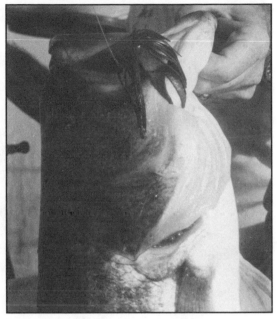

TROPHY TAMER: The jig-and-pig is unparalleled by any other lure when it comes to attracting bragging-sized bass.

Dyess is a pork fan when it comes to jig trailers. A No. 1 Uncle Josh pork chunk is his choice of trailer about 99 percent of the time.

A third Texan, Gary Klein, is one of the country's top heavy-cover fishermen and innovator who developed his own line of Tournament Lures jigs several years ago. From his boyhood days in California, Klein has developed a jig-fishing system that spans the spectrum of fishing situations — from light-weight jigs in deep, clear water to shallow brush in southern reservoirs.

"The common mistakes that I see frequently is a lot of anglers have a tendency to be very slow on the hookset or they do not handle their fish strong enough," Klein says. "Most anglers don't set the hook hard enough. I don't know if they are timid or what. You really need to get that hook point in the fish and once it's hooked then you're going to land the fish.

"Another problem I see with anglers when it comes to jig fishing is that they don't fish it enough. We always have the tendency to put it down too quickly."

Stanley, Dyess and Klein — the kings of the jig — are living proof that the rubber-skirted jig is not only among the best trophy-bass lures known to man, but it is also one of the most versatile.

Veteran North Carolina pro Jerry Rhyne was instrumental in the enormous popularity of Creepy Crawler-type jigs.

Chapter 15

A Different Kind of Jig

It has been one of the latest trends on the Bassmaster Tournament Trail in recent years, as well as the hottest bait and a semi-secret.

It produced every bass weighed in during the entire 1987-88 tournament season for veteran North Carolina pro Jerry Rhyne, paving the way to his ninth appearance in the prestigious BASS Masters Classic and securing a third-place finish in the Texas Invitational on Sam Rayburn. In addition, it produced both a second-place finish for Texan Jon Hall and a third-place showing for Alabama's David Yarbrough in the 1989 Arkansas Invitational. And the number of top 25 finishes it quietly ensured are too numerous to mention.

PROfile

Shaw Grigsby is a two-time B.A.S.S. winner, four-time qualifier for the BASS Masters Classic and former Red Man All-American champion.

It is the Creepy Crawler, an eastern version of still another western innovation. And although you have not read a great deal about its eastern exploits, the Creepy Crawler has had an impressive presence on the tournament trail in recent years.

Rhyne is the man responsible for bringing the lure to eastern waters. In the late 1970s, Rhyne discovered the allure of Bobby Garland's Spider Jig while fishing a tournament on enormous Lake Powell in Utah. Soon after returning to North Carolina, the productivity of the bait impressed Frank Jennings, one of Rhyne's bass club partners, enough that he began making the bait by hand.

Jennings and son Jeff, under the banner of the Lakeside Bait Co., began massproducing the Creepy Crawler. And thanks to the largely unpublicized successes of Rhyne and others, they have had to work hard to meet the grassroots demand for the lures.

The Creepy Crawler is almost identical to the Spider Jig, a longtime standard weapon for the deep, clear and rocky reservoirs of the West. But its resemblance to a regular jig ends with its lead head. The bait sports a smaller hook than conventional jigs, along with a light, breathable plastic skirt (much like a tubejig) and a twintailed trailer similar to that used on spinnerbaits. The bait is assembled both with and without a monofilament weedguard.

Rhyne believes its attraction lies in its resemblance to a crawfish, which are a universal food source for bass. But the pros say its beauty lies in its versatility, which greatly outdistances a regular jig.

"It has the appeal of a Gitzit, but it's more versatile than either a Gitzit or a jig," claims Yarbrough. "It combines the qualities of a jig and a Gitzit, along with the action of the twintail trailer. That gives it more of a three-dimensional look as it moves through the water and it comes alive even when it just sits on the bottom."

Florida's Shaw Grigsby says both the Creepy Crawler and Spider Jig have a tantalizing descent not found with conventional jigs. The plastic tubejig-type skirt gives it added buoyancy by flaring out as it falls, while a typical rubber-skirted jig tends to be more streamlined and compact as it descends.

"The biggest advantage with the Creepy Crawler over regular jigs is that the skirt on it can be made in the same colors and combinations of colors that you can get with the Gitzit," Grigsby says. "The plastic skirts can be made with some clarity in them, so that you can have clear glitters and smoke glitters and a lot of other colors you can't get with normal jigs.

"It's always an advantage to be able to present something to the fish that they've never seen before, particularly on the most heavily pressured lakes and reservoirs. One of the few baits that fish don't get accustomed to is the plastic worm and I believe that is because it is so lifelike and comes in such a variety of colors. The Creepy Crawler has those qualities."

The plastic trailer adds another enticing quality not usually found on conventional jigs, making it an excellent drop bait. Grigsby believes the successful hookup ratio of the Creepy Crawler is superior to that of standard jigs because of the small diameter hook and lack of a wirebrush weedguard.

The combination of alluring features on the Creepy Crawler make it a good tool for fishing a wide variety of cover, structure and clarity situations. Although the lure is most effective in clear water, it will produce in almost any clarity (other than water that is significantly stained).

For Grigsby, the Creepy Crawler is at its best in open water, particularly around deep structure. "With a deep drop off, most people either fish with a Carolina-rigged plastic worm, jigging spoon or crank it," he explains. "But the Creepy Crawler gives you a more subtle approach, which can really pay off."

No cover or structure is immune to the Creepy Crawler, according to Yarbrough, who fishes it in some heavy-cover situations where Rhyne and Grigsby prefer conventional jigs. Its plastic skirt doesn't seem to penetrate thick vegetation as well as a rubberskirt on a jig, although oiling it down with a fish attractant helps.

Rhyne fishes the Creepy Crawler differently than a rubber-skirted jig. "I keep the Creepy Crawler moving all of the time," he says. "I constantly swim it, although I speed it up and slow it down a lot. Most of the strikes come as I accelerate it."

Generally, the strikes on the Creepy Crawler are subtle, so Rhyne constantly watches his line and relies on a supersensitive feel honed by years of experience.

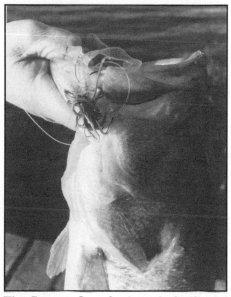

The Creepy Crawler is an imitation of the Garland Spider Jig, which has long been a popular lure out West.

Some versions of the Creepy Crawler featuring a foam head have recently been introduced. "The floating head model makes the Creepy Crawler an even better all-around bait," Grigsby says. "That will allow you to put it on a Carolina rig and float the jig just above vegetation or a dropoff. That should be especially good here in Florida, where we'll be able to use a jig without the weight of it dropping it into the weeds."

Few lure designers have had the impact of Bobby Garland with his Fat Gitzit tubejig.

Chapter 16

The Tiny Lure
That Changed Bass Fishing

The enthusiasm in Roland Martin's voice is still vivid in my memory bank. The year was 1982 and Martin had recently returned from an extended fishing trip on the western desert lakes of Mead and Powell. He had made an exciting discovery and was anxious to share its news.

PROfile

"I just saw the most amazing jig," Martin began. "It's made by a friend of mine, Bobby Garland out in Utah. It's made out of plastic and the body of the jig has 30 or 40 little tentacles, so it looks like a little octupus as it falls through the water. They are throwing it in the cracks in the canyon walls and for bass they can see. It's a tremendous bait."

Years later, Martin would refer to the lure as the "finest sight-fishing bait ever made."

The lure was the Fat Gitzit, the forerunner of the tubejig that is today an integral part of any serious bass enthusiast's arsenal. It was the Gitzit that started the tubejig craze and today, despite dozens of soft-plastic copies on the market, this entire genre' of fishing is referred generically as "Gitzit fishing."

Guido Hibdon, who is credited with bringing the Gitzit eastward, is one of only two men to win consecutive B.A.S.S. Angler of the Year titles.

The Gitzit was born in the mind of Bobby Garland back in 1964. It wasn't until the mid-1970s that it captured the imagination of his fellow western anglers who discovered its unparalleled allure in the deep, clear reservoirs where they plied their trade. But it was in the mid-1980s that the Gitzit migrated into eastern waters where it created an entire legion of believers in waters considerably different in biological nature.

The Fat Gitzit became the Lure That Changed the Face of Bass Fishing in the 1980s as light line and finesse fishing began to dominate tournament circuits from Georgia to California. Although the Gitzit was the leader of a pack of down-sized finesse lures jokingly referred to as "sissy baits," it suddenly became the answer to several fishing situations, ranging from pressured bass to clear-water sight fishing.

It was its acceptance in the East that made the Gitzit such a major-league player. And its popularity among eastern fishermen can be directly attributable to one man.

Guido Hibdon discovered the Gitzit by drawing Garland as a partner in a tournament on Lake Mead. Garland gave him a day-long education in tubejig trickery and Hibdon came away extremely impressed and determined to apply this magical little bait to the clear waters of his home Ozark Mountains lakes — Table Rock, Bull Shoals and Lake of the Ozarks.

After proving the bait's potency to his own satisfaction, the Missouri pro demonstrated its allure to the rest of the fishing world. Most of us took notice in back-to-back tournaments in which Hibdon's tubejig produced 48 and 50 pounds (and fourth and first places, respectively, in national tournaments). From that point on, the Gitzit soared in popularity.

Garland was not surprised that the lure would score consistently in eastern waters. "I had fished a Gitzit in the Ozarks and even won a national tournament at Table Rock with it," says Garland, who now makes his home in Arkansas. "I knew that the bait catches big fish and it is a consistent bait in winter, summer, spring and fall. And I knew that it would catch fish in dirty water as well as clear water.

"And it didn't surprise me that it would catch bass in grass lakes, which is a big reason why it caught on so well in the East. The first time I fished the prototype of this bait in a tournament, I caught my limit off of a grassbed in Lake Havasu on my first five casts. Then I went into the river and began fishing some tules (lily pads to you easterners) in fairly clear water with a little color to it. I use it on a 1/16-ounce lead head on 25-pound test line and used my flipping stick. I had five bass that weighed 20 pounds and then proceeded to cull every bass I had in the livewell. So I knew it could be quite effective around vegetation."

Finesse fishing actually scared some pros away. Contrary to some belief, however, the Gitzit is not a difficult lure to fish.

"It is a real easy bait to fish because the Gitzit shines with fish that are actively feeding," Garland explains. "It has a built-in action that works automatically while it's sinking. As a matter of fact, I've fished it with a lot of people who had rarely fished and they've beat me out of the back of the boat. That's a characteristic of this bait.

"But there is an art to fishing it and if a person knows which way to work it under the right conditions, it can be deadly all of the time."

The Gitzit created some high-profile disciples and ignited several careers to great heights. Among those are Shaw Grigsby, who has won two B.A.S.S. tournaments on tubejigs en route to becoming perhaps the finest sight fisherman in America, and Hibdon, who went on to develop the highly successful "G" series of tubejigs for the Lucky Strike Manufacturing Co.

But few understand the intricacies of tubejig fishing as well as its original inventor.

Through the years, Garland developed three sizes of Gitzits for different situations. Garland utilizes the 2 1/2-, 3 3/4- or 5 1/2-inch version depending on the prevailing size of the forage fish or the species of bass he is targeting. The smallest Gitzit is best suited for catching smallmouth and Kentucky spotted bass, while largemouth will assault even the Jumbo Gitzit.

Garland most often uses the smallest Gitzit on jig heads ranging from 1/16- to 1/2-ounce in size. As a rule of thumb, he never goes heavier than 1/4-ounce in the winter, but as heavy as 1/2-ounce in the summer. Depth, obviously, plays a role in jig size. Garland uses the 1/16-ounce head in shallow water, 1/8-ounce in water 8 to 12 feet deep and 1/4- or 1/2-ounce in depths of 13 feet or more.

"There are exceptions," he interjects. "Sometimes in the summertime when the fish are real full from a lot of feeding, I'll use a 1/4-ounce head and use it in shallow water to trigger a strike that I couldn't get with a slow fall. But other times, the fish want that slow fall, especially with suspended bass that are, say, up under a boat dock.

"I will occasionally take a 1/16-ounce lead head and cut it down real light for the times when I find fish up real shallow in moss beds or tules or suspended under boat docks. That super-slow fall has worked quite well for me at times. But I probably fish the 1/4-ounce head on 6- to 14-pound test line most of the time."

Although Hibdon, Grigsby and others have proven the versatility of the tubejig in diverse water and cover conditions, the Gitzit is at its best in clear water. "Not because I'm its inventor, I really believe the Gitzit is the best sight bait available," Garland claims. "The reason the bait works best in clear water is that the action of it often triggers a strike on the fall. When the water is a little dingy, the fish have trouble homing in on it."

And although the roots of the Gitzit are firmly planted in open-water structure in depths that most eastern anglers never knew existed, tubejigs are outstanding baits for shallow-water applications. That is especially true around aquatic vegetation. Innovative weedguards and an impressive new hook (Shaw Grigsby's High Performance Hooks enable tubejigs to be rigged Texas style) have converted the traditional exposed-hook bait into a weedless offering.

In a tournament on Nevada's Lake Mead, Bobby Garland shared his Gitzit tips with Guido Hibdon, who obviously learned well.

"There are always going to be some straggler fish up shallow if you go to the right part of the lake and these are the fish I would rather target," Garland explains. "I'll throw the bait to the edge of a bush on the shady side several feet beyond it. Keeping my rod tip high, I bring it back to the bush and then lower the rod tip to let it fall down into the shadow of the bush or rock or moss bed. That's when it will get nailed.

"If the action is slow, sometimes you need to get it down on the bottom and sort of bulldoze it along the bottom real slow."

Although the tubejig is most often taken during its initial descent, Garland has developed a pair of slightly unorthodox techniques for this type of finesse fishing.

"I've caught a lot of fish in the summer just by dead-sticking it," he says. "Just allowing the bait to lay beneath a bush and not move it at all. The fish will pick it up and start moving away with it. The reason being that the tails of the bait will stick up off of the bottom and wiggle. I've observed them in clear water and a lot of times a bass will get close to the bait and watch it.

"The tails are moving and he's watching it. Then when you move it a little, the bass will follow it. All of a sudden, that jig head will

Tubejigs Tricks

√ Fill the hollow body of the bait with attractant or even pieces of Alka-Seltzer.

√ Create a floating tubejig by inserting Styrafoam and fish it on a Carolina rig.

√ Add a crawfish imitation as a trailer for added attaction.

√ For sluggish, deep-water bass, thread a tubejig over a lead jigging spoon.

√ Use a drop of Super Glue to keep a tubejig or trailer in place.

√ Glue a rattle chamber on the shaft of the hook.

dig into the bottom and it will take a funny flip and the bass will inhale it.

"Another technique that has worked well for me in a tournament situation involves fishing a good ledge or point that drops off of the main channel — a place that holds a lot of fish, but these fish get pounded so much that they have wised up. In this situation, I've learned to stay back a ways and throw the Gitzit up shallow on the point and then start shaking it real hard as it comes down off of the point. That action seems to ignite a strike on fish that are heavily pressured."

Good advice. After all, who could doubt the creator of the Lure That Changed the Face of Bass Fishing.

A plastic trailer gives a weedless spoon a little added buoyancy.

Chapter 17

Dress for Success

For Jerry Rhyne, the feeling of deja vu was undeniable.

As he positioned the trolling motor and prepared to fire another cast at a large peppergrass bed on Lake Okeechobee, the North Carolina veteran pro couldn't help thinking about the tournament there the year before and a scene from that event that was to be replayed right before his eyes.

PROfile

The situation was exactly the same.

On this day, Rhyne was hot, catching keeper after keeper by running a spinnerbait through the shallow aquatic grass. But his partner on this day couldn't buy a strike. A year before on the same lake, he witnessed the same type of frustration coming from the back of his boat.

"I've been fishing tournaments a long time and I can tell you it's never a real pleasant situation when you're catching a bunch of fish and your partner can't even get a strike," says Rhyne, a perennial

Perennial Classic qualifier Guy Eaker of North Carolina is one of the most innovative pros in the country.

qualifier for the prestigious BASS Masters Classic. "You would like to help them out if you can.

"The same thing had happened on Okeechobee the year before, which flashed into my mind. And the only difference I could see between what my partner and I were doing was the fact that he didn't have any kind of trailer on his spinnerbait and I did. The year before, I gave my partner a trailer and he immediately started catching fish. My partner in this particular tournament wasn't as open to my suggestions. I kept suggesting he try a trailer, but he kept attributing my success to my ability to fish a spinnerbait.

"I finally talked him into trying it. And on the first cast, he caught a 8 1/2-pounder. I can't tell you how many times I've had that kind of thing happen with trailers."

Manufactured in a mind-boggling array of colors, sizes, shapes and textures, trailers have a definite role in bass fishing, which the nation's pros prove tournament after tournament. Today, it's rare to find an experienced angler who doesn't dress up his spinnerbait, buzzbait, spoon and jig when the situation calls for it.

Call it fishing's version of Dress for Success.

The situation certainly demanded a trailer in the scenario that Rhyne described on Lake Okeechobee.

"The difference between my catching fish and my partner striking out was the buoyancy that my trailer was providing," explains Rhyne, who is recognized as one of the country's top spinnerbait fishermen. "Those fish were lying on top of the peppergrass near the surface. As you brought the spinnerbait by a little opening in the grass, the fish would nail it. Without a trailer, his bait was staying down and pulling and tearing the peppergrass. The trailer allowed you to not only to keep the spinnerbait near the surface, but also to slow it down. That gave the fish a little more time to look at it."

Bouyancy is the most important reason for adding a plastic or pork trailer to a spinnerbait, according to those surveyed.

"Almost any type of trailer adds some degree of buoyancy to your spinnerbait," Rhyne adds. "Buoyancy is critical for guiding a spinnerbait in the exact path you need to and for keeping the bait in what I call the strike zone longer."

Rhyne uses a trailer for 99-percent of his spinnerbait fishing. Most of his fishing is done with a trailer of his own design, the Dancin' Eel (manufactured by L.C. Lures), which is a straight piece of plastic with a split-tail. The only time he doesn't add a Dancin' Eel to his spinnerbait is when he is fishing deep, clear water. In that situation, he prefers a Mr. Twister grub as a trailer, which is better suited for working the spinnerbait quickly across the surface of the water.

The one-percent of his spinnerbait fishing that doesn't include a trailer is limited to burning a willow-leaf spinnerbait through the top of shallow-water vegetation.

Former Classic champion Jack Haines, a guide on famed Toledo Bend, is another spinnerbait trailer fanatic. You will never find him fishing a spinnerbait without a piece of plastic or pork trailing behind it.

Besides giving a spinnerbait "a little added attraction," Hains uses, primarily, a curl-tail type of trailer, short plastic worm or grub to both make the lure

Various types of trailers that can be used to dress up a rubber-skirted jig.

float a little higher in the water on a steady retrieve and fall more slowly through the water when used as a drop-bait.

A trailer is particularly important when the water temperature falls below 65 degrees and the fish become somewhat inactive. It is during that time when the slowest lure presentation possible usually pays big dividends. Hains says trailers are not nearly as crucial during the hottest months of the year when bass are most active.

The balance it provides to the lure can be critical, according to Gary Wade, a two-time Classic qualifier from Greensboro, N.C. Wade insists that the added balance created by a floating trailer helps keep the head and hook of the bait running in the proper (downward) position as it is pulled through the water.

And when the head and hook are pointed downward, a spinnerbait is less likely to get hung up in vegetation or submerged tree limbs, he says.

Veteran West Point (Georgia) Lake guide Tommy Mike believes that bass will actually mouth a spinnerbait longer when it feels the soft-textured trailer, which translates into more successful hook-ups.

"In my opinion, any type of trailer is better than none," says Mike, a guide for stripers and largemouth bass on West Point since 1975, who has a masters degree in fisheries biology from Auburn University. "Not only does the more bulky appearance created by a trailer attract big fish, I've seen plenty of evidence that they are likely to hold onto a spinnerbait with a trailer considerably longer than they will a bait without one."

It is for that reason that Mike uses a small piece of a plastic worm to cover the hook of his buzzbaits. Many knowledgeable buzzbait anglers use an entire plastic worm or pork strip to get added buoyancy, which is critical with this type of surface fishing.

Shaw Grigsby uses a plastic Burke Split-tail Eel and a double curl-tail trailer for most of his spinnerbait fishing, but he emphasizes that there are times when a trailer can actually be a hinderance. He recalls tournaments on Arkansas' Bull Shoals Reservoir and Lake Havasu in Arizona in which he was fishing bank structure surrounded by current. The added buoyancy of a trailer floated the spinnerbait past the structure much too quickly for the fish to react.

But there is no occasion when he does not use a trailer while jig fishing.

"It doesn't matter what time of year it is or what the situation, the first thing I do when I fish a jig is put on a pork chunk," Grigsby says. "I love pork chunks, but there are just so many things that work well with jigs — plastic worms, Craw (crawfish-like) Worms, fireclaw worms and so on."

Like with spinnerbaits, pork and plastic trailers add both action and buoyancy to the rubber-skirted jig. Since jigs are primarily a drop-bait, buoyancy can be especially critical when cold temperatures require the slowest descent possible.

"I'm partial to pork because I think the fish may hold onto it a little longer," Grigsby says. "There are times when you can't take it away from them. I've seen times in practice when you can't pull it out of their mouths."

Apparently, thousands of American bass anglers share Grigsby's sentiment toward the lowly piece of pork. The Uncle Josh Bait Company of Fort Atkinson, Wisc., has made sure that pork-lovers have a wide variety of pig products to choose from. Fishermen can now dress their spinnerbaits, jigs and spoons with pieces of pork in the shape of a split-tail eel, straight-tail eel, twin-tail, leech, spring lizard and frogs of various shapes, sizes and colors.

A popular Uncle Josh product is a pork worm that can be used as a trailer or fished like a plastic worm (an artificial, artificial worm, so to speak).

The biggest problem with using pork trailers comes during the hottest months of the year when the pork chunks have a tendency to dry out quickly. Keeping a pork trailer fresh can be a real hassle, so Grigsby often uses a plastic crawfish-type trailer instead, both during the summer as well as tournament practice days.

While a wide variety of plastic jig trailers exist, there are a couple of plastic products designed for especially for pork enthusiasts.

Bass Pro Shops of Springfield, Mo., markets the Hot Chunk, a small, thick-textured piece of plastic that resembles a frog-shaped pork chunk, and the Lit'l Whiff Foam Chunk, which sports crawfish-like legs and a foam scent pad for holding fish attractant (for die-hard pork users, Pro Bass Shops markets a Sav-A-Pig, a foam enclosure designed to keep a jig-and-pig from drying out while it is still tied on, but not being used).

A unique trailer product is the Dri Rind, made by the Fred Arbogast Co. of Akron, Ohio. The Dri-Rind feels like soft leather but takes on a different appearance and feel when it absorbs water. Because it needs no special care, its makers say the Dri-Rind is the answer to the mess and bother of pork.

While Uncle Josh's No. 1 Jumbo Frog and No. 11 Pork Frog are standards for jig fishing, veteran smallmouth anglers emphasize the need for down-sizing the pork trailer. Florida pro Steve Daniel, qualifier for the 1985 Classic, is an excellent jig fisherman who drops to the smaller No. 101 pork chunk for luring smallmouths.

Gary Klein of Montgomery, Texas, one of the pioneers of jig fishing in the West, is a fan of Uncle Josh's Big Daddy, the larg-

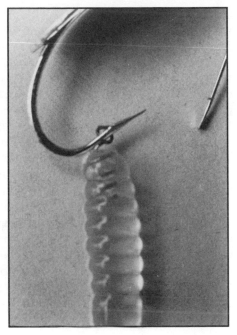

A tiny corkscrew device helps keep a plastic trailer securely in place.

est (4 inches in length) and heaviest of the pork chunk family. But he says there are a few times when jigs are more productive without a trailer of any sort. "For years, I never threw a jig with a trailer on it," Klein says. "You can catch more fish without a trailer in the springtime when the bass are on the bed and other times when they aren't very aggressive and are short-striking the lure."

Just as it is rare to see a jig without some sort of trailer, few fishermen would ever consider fishing a weedless spoon without a piece of plastic or pork behind it. Veteran spoon enthusiasts say a trailer is more critical with a Johnson-type spoon than other types of lures because it not only seems to make the lure more attractive, but also enables the lure to run better through the vegetation.

"Balance is very important with a weedless spoon," claims Gary Wade. "The balance that a trailer gives a spoon can make all of the difference between catching fish and missing fish.

"A spoon that has no trailer has a tendency to slide through the water and it doesn't create very much resistance, so you tend to get a big bow in your line. That slack line often leads to missed strikes. If you put a piece of plastic on a spoon or turn the skirt around backwards, it creates more drag, which enables you to keep a tighter line and miss fewer strikes."

In addition to better balance, a trailer adds action to a spoon, slows its sinking rate (which is important for surface and sub-surface fishing) and helps keep it from spinning as it comes through the water.

A plastic worm trailer can make a weedless spoon even more weedless. It is a simple trick: push the head of a 6-inch worm onto the weedguard. Then bend the the hook slightly outward so that it will penetrate the worm and then the put hook point through the worm (similar to the Texas-rig).

Although it received little attention, Burke Lures of Traverse City, Mich., has introduced an ingenious little device for keeping trailers in place. Burke's Corkscrew is a half-inch piece of metal wire fashioned into the shape of a corkscrew. The upper end is rounded for fitting over the hook of a spinnerbait, spoon or jig. The corkscrew shape begins at the other end and enables you to screw this tiny wire into the head of the plastic trailer.

The result is a small harness that keeps the trailer riding in the proper position as it is pulled through vegetation and other types of cover. The Corkscrew, which is also excellent for anchoring a plastic worm to the hook for normal worm fishing, keeps an amazing grip on plastic trailers.

Regardless of the type of trailer used for spoons, spinnerbaits and jigs, it is obvious that dressing a lure with some type of trailer is a time-tested technique that produces more fish than lures that are fished naked. Dressing for success works.

Chapter 18

Bass Fishing's Top 10 All-Time Lures

Taking a retrospective look at any facet of life can be challenging at best and frustrating at worst. That is particularly true when attempting to compile a list of the "all-time best" of anything.

In compiling bass fishing's Top 10 Lures, an attempt to identify and recognize the best bass-catchers of all time, there were dozens of worthy candidates in every shape, form and fashion. Since the Indians first sharpened and polished bone to make the first fishing lure, the innovative nature of man has produced a mind-boggling array of underwater decoys for fooling largemouth and smallmouth bass. They have ranged from the mundane, such as a piece of polished steel (jigging spoon) to the sublime like the early surface plugs that sported the actual skin of frogs and snakes.

PROfile

Missouri pro Charlie Campbell has built a career around his prowess with a Heddon Zara Spook.

And although there is plenty of room for dispute, some artificial lures stood out from the crowd, making their selection to our first-ever "best list" a must.

But there are a few others that were squeezed out for various reasons by baits that were deemed slightly superior by our panelist of experts that included top longtime tournament pros, renowned guides, lure-makers, tackle industry representatives, respected fishing writers and some legendary members of the bass-fishing fraternity.

In selecting Bass Fishing's Top 10 Lures, more than 50 baits were considered, using simple criteria. The lure has to be a proven fish-catcher that has passed the test of time and still remains a viable weapon. Some legendary baits like the Arbogast Jitterburg and Hula Popper have long been best-sellers, but are not overly productive lures by today's standards. In contrast, the Fat Gitzit tubejig has been one of the most popular lures of the 1980s, but it doesn't have the longevity — the track record — to earn a spot on our illustrious list. Lures that are both good fish-locators and catchers scored extra points, along with baits that are easy to fish.

With that said, here then is Bass Fishing's Top 10 Lures:

THE UNDISPUTED CHAMPION

Longtime *Sports Afield* Angling Editor Homer Circle summarizes the opinion of our star-studded panel: "The plastic worm has to be the No. 1 bass-catcher of all time. There is so little that you can do to fish it wrong. It is weedless and can be fished anywhere that bass live. It revolutionized bass fishing as we knew it."

The venerable Circle, as well as anyone, understands that the advent of the soft plastic worm completely changed the face of bass fishing. Noted luremaker Nick Creme is considered by many to be the father of the plastic worm, but the first crude versions were shaped out of a new synthetic material called polyvinyl chloride resin in 1949. Although the modern-day advancements in texture and the coloring process make the early plastic worms seem especially primitive, our fathers found them to be far superior to the rubber worms they were accustomed to fishing (the first rubber worm was patented in 1860).

Finally, here was a bait that closely resembled the body shape and move-ment of the food sources of bass such as snakes, live worms and eels. And the softer, more pliable texture created a bait that responded in a more lifelike manner with each twitch of the rod tip and was far more sensitive to the touch than the rubber versions.

In addition, its soft texture was more realistic than the hard baits, which caused bass to hold onto it longer (even digesting it) before rejecting it. That has led to the development of a plethora of other soft plastic forage fakes such as lizards, crawfish, frogs, grubs and jigs.

As a result of the developments in plastics, these lifelike worms forced bass anglers to slow down; to learn the art of finesse fishing; to develop a "feel" for the bass and its habitat. Before the introduction of the plastic worm, bass fishing consisted of two basic approaches — quickly covering water with fast-moving lures or slowly working a topwater plug on the surface of the water. It did not take long for the fishermen of the 1950s and '60s to discover that there was a better way and a superior bait for catching both largemouth and smallmouth bass.

And when the so-called Texas rig was developed — the method of embedding the hook point into the body of the worm to make it weedless — the popularity of the plastic worm surged even more. Finally, there was a bait that could be fished where the biggest bass lived — in dense aquatic vegetation and brush.

On lakes, reservoirs and rivers across the country, the plastic worm remains the most popular artificial lure and is easily the best-selling bait of all. Although it is now made in every color scheme and style imaginable, the plastic worm still retains the basic lifelike characteristics that enabled its forerunners to significantly alter the sport of bass fishing.

THE SPINNERBAIT SOLUTION

History notes that the spinnerbait was first advertised in lure catalogs as early as 1925. Although they don't much resemble what we consider spinnerbaits today, the Lou J. Eppinger Company's early offerings included the Shannon Single Spin and Hula Hula, which had a large rotating blade.

It was the development of the safety-pin style of spinnerbait that launched the lure to its present status as one of the best bass baits of all time. The Houser Hell Diver and Dragnetter of the early 1950s were among the original baits that featured the so-called safety-pin shape that made them run smoother and more weedless beneath the surface of the water.

The beauty of the spinnerbait is in both its simplicity and versatility.

With a basic built-in action, the spinnerbait will produce fish for anglers of all skill levels just by simply retrieving it at almost any speed. The flash of the blades and the vibration they emit are well-documented attractants, which eliminates the need for the fisherman to actually finesse a nearby bass into becoming interested.

The versatility of the bait scores big points as well. Not only can a spinnerbait work over a school of bass, it is an excellent tool for locating scattered fish, which are drawn to its vibration and flash. Although most American anglers fish the bait relatively slowly in shallow water, the spinnerbait is by no means limited to that application. There are times when it is most effective when buzzed just inches below the surface of the water, making a considerable wake. And veteran Georgia pro Cliff Craft has enjoyed good success over the years by bouncing a spinnerbait along the bottom in deep water (20 feet and below).

When Florida fisherman and Michigan transplant Chuck Faremouth combined a large salmon trolling blade with a large spinnerbait back in 1984, he created the giant-bladed willow-leaf spinnerbait, which started a big-bass craze throughout the country. The No. 5 to 8 willow-leaf shaped blades proved to be superior to any other blade type in terms of attracting trophy bass. The basic premise of the safety-pin spinnerbait had gained new life through the continuing innovation of the modern-day fisherman.

FAT-BODIED CRANKBAITS CHANGE CRANKING

In the mid-1960s, 65-year-old fisherman and tinkerer Fred Young began toying with a new idea for a lipped diving plug. Crankbaits had been around for years, even some that sported metal and wooden lips, but Young was determined to unleash a creation that was unlike anything available to fishermen.

Little did he know that he was about to change the art of cranking forever.

In 1967, Young surveyed the diving plugs on the market and found that all had slender shapes — similar to either a minnow or a shad. How much appeal would a larger, fat-bodied crankbait have, he wondered. With his talented hands, Young fashioned the first of the famed Big O crankbaits from a piece of balsa wood and crankbait fishing has never been the same.

With its angled plastic lip and squat, bulky shape, the Big O became the pattern that today's lure makers still follow when building a medium- to deep-diving bait. And for obvious reasons. "The reason the Big O started the trend toward the fat-bodied crankbait is because of the vibration pattern that it puts out," explains renowned crankbait designer Lee Sisson. "Compared to smaller, more streamlined crankbait shapes, the Big O style of bait has a vibration pattern that is much wider and covers more area, so bass can detect it from greater distances. And the fast, tight wobble of these types of crankbaits make them attractive to bass that detect them visually."

The most successful crankbaits of our time, like Bagley's B series, Rebel's R series, Rapala's Fat Rap and others, still feature the basic characteristics of the original Big O. But some impressive refinements have been made to make cranking even more productive. Innovations in lip design have created plugs that can break the 20-foot mark and, in the hands of a knowledgeable angler, can be fished in places that Fred Young would have simply avoided.

To earn a spot on our Top 10 list, fat-bodied crankbaits are obviously top sellers and good fish-catchers. But these diving baits are also excellent tools for quickly covering large areas of water to locate bass. And, another point in its favor, is that its built-in action can catch fish for even the novice angler.

We owe it all to Fred Young.

A REVIVAL OF SORTS

The rubber-skirted jig and pork chunk combination has been around for 60 years or so, but it was in the mid-1970s that the bait experienced a rebirth — thanks to the burgeoning national tournament scene.

It was during that time that bass pros like Roland Martin reminded us what our fathers had known for years — the bait combination is irresistible to both largemouth and smallmouth bass. In fact, Martin used the jig-and-pig to win an unprecedented three consecutive Bass Anglers Sportsman society tournaments in 1979-80. As a result, the jig-and-pig has become a mainstay for top competitive anglers.

Martin, the all-time tournament king and a tackle innovator in his own right, believes (and has proven) that the jig-and-pig is the best big-bass bait of all. Its appeal, primarily, is in its bulky appearance, which resembles the body shape of a crawfish, a delicacy to bass. Unlike many fishermen, Martin believes that the jig-and-pig is the top trophy lure throughout the year. Although some fishermen switch to a plastic worm in the warm months, Martin spent an entire summer documenting that while the worm caught more fish, the jig produced an impressive 4-pound average.

The only disadvantage to this heavy-cover bait is that it takes some skill to fish it successfully. For the experienced fisherman, the jig-and-pig is an all-time great fish-catcher. But it requires some adjustment time for the less experienced angler.

THE TOPS IN TOPWATER BAITS

If there is one surface lure that has passed the test of time it is the Heddon Zara Spook, which has been drawing vicious strikes for more than three decades.

"The Zara Spook is a timeless lure," says Missouri's Charlie Campbell, considered the dean of the topwater fishermen in America. "It has remained a favorite bait for topwater fishermen because of its ability to find fish and its ability to finesse them into biting. No other topwater bait does that combination of things as well."

The fat, cigar-shaped stickbait was born of a simple design. There is nothing fancy about it. And it is the one bait that has not seen significant refinement over the years. The original Zara Spook will produce just as well as those scheduled to come off of the assembly line tomorrow.

The Zara Spook is the opposite of a spinnerbait or crankbait in that it has no built-in action. It takes some skill to work the bait properly. For most knowledgeable fishermen, that means "walking the dog," a rhythmic method of using the rod tip and reel handle to make the bait dart from side to side at a rather quick pace. This surface darting action draws bass from impressive distances. After quickly working the bait across open-water areas, the Spook is then paused and finessed around individual pieces of structure.

That ability to find and finesse fish deserves a ranking among the best bass-catchers of all time.

THE RAPALA REMEDY

No list of the top bass lures of all time would be complete without the original floating Rapala, the most successful minnow bait of all time. Several million Rapala buyers can't be wrong.

For many of us, our first surface strikes came on the slender minnow-style lure with a small angled plastic lip. Whether twitched along the surface or darting below the water line, the Rapala has the natural action of a wounded baitfish and has long been one of the best "sight baits" known to fish and fisherman.

The floating Rapala and subsequent sinking and diving versions are also among the most popular trolling baits. And the Magnum Rapala, which sports a larger lip, has quietly become one of the most productive of the so-called subsurface "jerkbaits" on the national tournament scene. Enough said.

THE WEEDLESS SOLUTION

The Johnson Silver Minnow spoon may not have the history of some of our Top 10 member baits, but it deserves such lofty status based on its longtime following in the South and a growing legion of believers in northern states. Its growing popularity can be attributed to the continuing spread of aquatic vegetation throughout the country.

It is in hydrilla, milfoil, peppergrass and a myriad of other grasses that the Silver Minnow and similar weedless spoons can strut their stuff. With its built-in wobble and flash, the Johnson spoon gives off a vibration that bass can detect through even jungle-like vegetation. And with its metal weedguard, the spoon can penetrate almost any type of growth.

Spoon fishing is most exciting when the vegetation has topped out on the surface. Most of us can recall heart-stopping moments when a bass explodes through a thick surface mat to attack a spoon it had been trailing for several yards.

Almost every tacklebox in America houses a weedless spoon.

THE RAT-L-TRAP REACTION

The Heddon Sonic, circa 1957, is believed to be the originator of the sinking, vibrating shad-shaped crankbaits that are so popular today. But in what may be the surest sign of its popularity, those types of lures now referred to generically as "Rat-L-Trap fishing."

The Rat-L-Trap was designed by Bill Lewis, a longtime lure manufacturer from Alexandria, La. The 1/2-ounce Rat-L-Trap ranks among the best selling crankbaits and is a standard tool for fishing above and around vegetation because of its ability to attract bass to its vibration.

"I think the Rat-L-Trap definitely deserves to be on the best all-time list," says Rick Clunn, "because so many people are able to catch fish on it without a high level of skill. I think what makes a lure an all-time great lure is not that the guys in the know can catch fish on it. It's that the average fisherman can score with it."

BUZZING BASS

The Fred Arbogast Co.'s Sputterfuss and Sputterbug are considered the first churning prop baits that we have come to refer to as buzzbaits. But it was the original Lunker Lure with a large aluminum propellor that has remained among the best bass-locators of all time.

Like the Rat-L-Trap, these noisy surface lures draw fish from considerable distance. And anglers of all skill levels can quickly become proficient with it.

In recent years, knowledgeable fishermen have learned that the buzzbait is much more versatile than it was once considered. It is no longer a bait used only when bass are most active. We have come to learn that the buzzbait can be an excellent tool for pinpointing bass during all but the coldest times of the year.

A CURE FOR FINICKY BASS

The 10th and final member of our all-time list of lure greatness may surprise some. That position belongs to the humble jigging spoon, a slab-sided piece of polished steel that was first popularized by saltwater fishermen.

But bass enthusiasts have learned that lures like the Hopkin's Spoon are among the most effective for catching bass when they are the most difficult to entice, notably during cold fronts as well as the hottest and coldest times of the year.

There is no better tool when the water temperature drops below 45 degrees and the bass stack up along deep, open-water structure. Using a depthfinder to target the finicky bass, a jigging spoon can be presented vertically, which is often the only method for convincing the sluggish fish to bite.

It may not be glamorous, but the jigging spoon deserves a small share of the glory on our list of Bass Fishing's Top 10 Lures.

SECTION TWO
TECHNIQUES & TIPS

Shaw Grigsby is a strong believer in tubejigs for clear water.

Chapter 19

De-Mystifying Finesse Fishing

The lake will remain nameless. The names of the participants have been changed to protect the guilty.

It is Saturday morning on a large southern reservoir and, predictably, the launch ramp is packed with a line of boats and boaters. After a short ride, we arrive at our destination to find that lines and waiting aren't limited to the launch site.

PROfile

This is a spot commonly called the "Hawg Alley." Every public lake seems to have one — an area of the lake that gains an outlandish reputation for out-producing every other portion of the reservoir.

In this case, Hawg Alley is a line of deep-water hydrilla located along a sharp drop-off in which the water begins at 5 feet and bottoms out at almost 20. The result is a combination of structure and cover that has made Hawg Alley the place to be during this time of year.

We watch as a line forms at one end of the grass and the anglers begin to electric motor along the weedline, casting every few yards. In an orderly line and friendly fashion that would have made our elementary teachers proud, each boat gets a chance to work the vegetation. And once they complete the 100-yard long grassline, each fisherman runs back to the end of the line to begin again.

This is a typical Saturday morning occurrence, we are told.

Transplanted Texan Gary Klein is one of the country's most accomplished pros. His impressive resume includes five B.A.S.S. victories, a B.A.S.S. Angler of the Year title and 10 Classic appearances.

But atypical of Hawg Alley is that on this morning, few fish are being caught. By noon, we have seen two fish boated, two others lost during the fight. Still, the parade continues.

The monotony ends when one angler boats a bass on two consecutive casts. And then a 4-pounder comes three casts later. He has quickly attracted everyone's attention, but the guys who are fishless all around him are too embarrassed to ask how he was scoring while they were being skunked.

But I don't embarrass easily.

After a few minutes of idle chatter, he unveils his secret — light line and a small, 4-inch worm. He had been scoring with a technique that America's bass pros have come to call "finesse fishing."

Former Angler of the Year Gary Klein understands well the value and productivity of finesse fishing. It is a technique that he learned out West and has adapted to natural lakes and manmade reservoirs throughout the country.

"As a tournament fisherman, I have a lot of the same problems that face the average weekend angler," says Klein, who now lives in Texas. "In the major tournaments, I'm faced with sharing my most productive water with a large number of other tournament fishermen. The same goes for the weekend guy who has to spend his precious day off fishing a public lake that gets a lot of pressure.

"Both are examples of having to combat heavy fishing pressure. One of the best ways I've found to overcome it is learning finesse fishing — light line and small lures. And I really feel like we're going to have to fish light line a lot more in the future just due to the fact that the fishing pressure continues to build each year. And finesse baits will catch fish behind a lot of boat traffic and a lot of fishing pressure.

"A finesse bait fished slow and subtle is often the answer to fishing in a crowd."

Finesse fishing isn't the easiest type of bass fishing to learn. It requires some skill with light line, which Klein learned while growing up in California and fishing the deep, clear reservoirs of the West.

His favorite finesse lures are the small Gitzit, a hollow-body skirted jig that is impaled on a 1/16-ounce jig head, and the Little Bit Worm, a 3 1/2-inch curl-tailed worm that is manufactured in California (several eastern companies market similar small worms).

The Gitzit is a simple-looking lure that has enjoyed remarkable success throughout the country. Designed by Bobby Garland for fishing the sheer rock bluffs and cracks in canyon walls in the West, the Gitzit has become standard equipment on the Bassmaster Tournament Trail.

The man who should be credited to bringing the Gitzit East is Guido Hibdon, a veteran Missouri pro and five-time B.A.S.S. winner. After fishing a tournament on Lake Mead with Garland, Hibdon headed East with the ugly little bait and left a string of impressive tournament performances in his wake. Two examples illustrate that point: In Super B.A.S.S.-IV on Florida's St. Johns River, the tubejig produced almost 49 pounds of bass and a fourth-place finish. At a national tournament on Georgia's Lake Lanier, Guido and the Gitzit caught 50 pounds and 4 ounces to win. And that was for just two days of fishing.

In the 1986 Classic on Lake Chickamauga, North Carolina's Jerry Rhyne caught more than 120 non-keeper bass in two days by fishing the Gitzit along a concrete retaining wall that separated the Sequoyah Nuclear Plant from the main lake.

"The Gitzit craze across the country goes to show that a lot of anglers are under the impression that there is that magic lure out there and the Gitzit is it," Klein says. "The Gitzit is not a magical lure, but it produces fish under a variety of conditions.

"On a 1/16th-ounce head, the Gitzit is one of the best finesse lures. The lure is very, very effective due to the fact that it is small. It's the size of the average baitfish — about an inch-and-a-half in length. It's especially good in clear water, but it's also productive in off-colored water, too. The only disadvantage to the bait is that you have to fish it on light line; 6-pound test is the best. But to the good, all-around anglers, that isn't a big disadvantage."

While most of the Gitzit's eastern success has come in shallow-water situations, Klein and other westerners have learned to fish it around deep-water structure. "First of all, the Gitzit is at its very best when it's fished vertically," he explains. "The key to the bait is its spiral fall that produces little air bubbles that really seem to attract fish.

"The most effective way to catch fish on a Gitzit is on the initial drop, especially in shallow water. In shallow-water cover, the Gitzit usually doesn't fall more than about 3 feet before a fish hits it. I fish the Gitzit deep and have a lot of success, too. It takes a long time for that little bait to reach 30- and 40-foot depths, but once I get it down there, I drag it or let it drift with the trolling motor. That's a real effective method."

It was with another finesse lure that Klein won the 1985 Bassmaster Georgia Invitational on Lake Lanier. During three days of fishing, Klein put together three limits of small fish, but his 23 pound, 13 ounces, was enough to secure his second B.A.S.S. victory.

Klein's climb to the top came on the strength of a small 4-inch straight-tailed worm, which he fished around deep-water boat docks in the clear water of Lanier. The western-born technique is called "doodling" or "shaking."

Doodling is another form of finesse fishing that Klein refers to as deep-flipping. He uses the 4-inch worm on a 1/0 hook and a 3/16-ounce slip sinker on 6-pound line. Using a flexible-tip 5 1/2-foot spinning rod, Klein would quietly approach a boathouse and make a short pitch to its vertical pilings. While the worm was falling, he shook the rod tip slightly to give the lure extra action. Once it reached the bottom, Klein would raise the worm a few inches off of the bottom and shake it several times.

The technique proved irresistible for Lanier's plentiful spotted bass population.

Another finesse worming technique that Klein consistently scores with involves using the Little Bit Worm on a 1/8-ounce jighead. Because of the exposed hook, this worm rig is limited to open-water situations, but Klein has good success by jigging and shaking it around deep-water structure. "With that 1/8-ounce jighead and 6-pound test line, you get a good fall from the worm," he says, "so you can cover a lot of water during a day looking for bass."

Finesse fishing requires light line, but that does not mean avoiding the places where bass hide.

On the contrary, with enough practice and concentration, you can learn to fish light line in some heavy cover conditions successfully. Not only will you have the luxury of the added strikes that light line attracts, but you can take advantage of it by successfully boating a large percentage of those strikes.

"People have the wrong idea about light line," says Kentucky pro Ron Shearer. "It enhances your ability to catch fish more than it hampers you.

"Of all of the trophy animals that I've harvested over the years both hunting and fishing, my best personal trophy is a 6-pound, 5-ounce smallmouth that I caught in Dale Hollow on 4-pound line. I've caught a bunch of 5- and 6-pounders on it. And you'd be surprised at some of the rough places I've gotten those big smallmouths out of on light line."

Gary Klein is one of the few pros to master the highly specialized art of light-line flipping. While flipping usually involves heavy tackle like a stout 7-foot rod and 20- to 30-pound test line, years of experience have enabled Klein to learn to flip 8-pound line in thick vegetation with great sucess — a technique that requires extraordinary concentration and considerable skill.

For light-line flipping, Klein uses a 4- or 5-inch worm instead of the worm size most commonly associated with this heavy-cover technique — 7 or 8 inches. "I use a small-diameter worm because I will be using a smaller hook to go with the lighter line diameter," he explains. "With this worm, you don't have to worry about setting the hook hard. With a sharp hook, you can just pull the hook into the fish. The smaller diameter worm just means there's less plastic for me to have to drive that hook through."

Klein also switches to a 7 1/2-foot rod that features a slow (flexible) tip and a stiff butt section. Klein prefers a fiberglass rod for all flipping, claiming that the touch-sensitive graphite rod causes most fishermen to react too quickly before the bass can inhale the lure.

By down-scaling the tackle used for catching well-hidden, bigger bass, every aspect becomes crucial, even down to the most minute matters like re-tying regularly and keeping the hook-point extremely sharp.

"With light-line flipping, you're fishing where the big bass live just like you would with regular flipping," he says. "And hooking good fish on light line in heavy cover is a dramatic experience."

111

"Perhaps the most crucial part of light-line flipping is the mental and physical conditioning of the fisherman. A fisherman can break 8-pound test line real easy, especially if he is not concentrating on exactly what he's doing. You have to concentrate and condition your reflexes to react to the strike without over-reacting and breaking the fish off on the hook-set."

With light-line flipping, the angler is faced with a seemingly impossible task once a big bass strikes. With only a second or two to react and decide a strategy, there is little room for error once the battle begins. "Once you have the fish hooked, he basically has you hooked for a while," Klein says. "You have to try to lead the fish out of bad places, but you have to be easy with him. If he's headed toward heavy cover, you basically have to let him go ahead, unless the fish will turn easily.

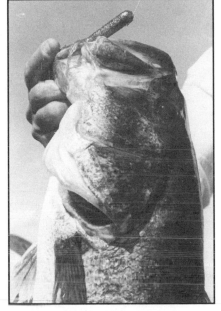

"There are two basic strategies: If you can get him into some open water, fight him for a longer period of time while he's in the water and then try to ease him into the boat (or net the fish). If you're fishing around heavy vegetation and you can't easily turn him, let him bury himself up in the grass and go get him."

More than ever, boat positioning becomes a critical factor in light-line finesse flipping.

The allure of the tubejig is one reason why macho men now admit to fishing sissy baits.

"If I know there's some fish sitting in real heavy cover, with 25-pound line I will just go right in, flip the worm on top of him and haul him out," Klein explains. "With light-line flipping, you have to approach it with a different attitude.

"Instead of trying to bully him out like you would with normal flipping, you're going to have to play with him more. First, I will flip the perimeter of whatever cover I believe he's holding in and try to draw the fish out of that cover. If that doesn't work, I'm going to go in after him and worry about what I'll do once I have the fish on.

"You have to think more about boat positioning. You have be in the best position to make an accurate flip, while at the same time positioning the boat so that you can lead the fish out of trouble once you hook him."

While finesse fishing requires a patience and skill that will not interest all bass anglers, it is another weapon, another tool for the times when fishing is tough or the water is crowded.

Chapter 20

Long-Range Flipping

When the technique of flipping was introduced to bass fishermen back in the mid-1970s, it practically revolutionized the sport, particularly among tournament anglers.

Here was a method of getting to the hard-to-reach places where the big bass thrive and a way to get them out of their well protected homes. Not only did flipping put you where the bigger fish dwell, it also allowed a softer lure presentation and better accuracy to place a worm or jig into a tiny hole or pocket in the heavy brush.

And flipping quickly captured the imagination of a nation of bass fishermen. Today, it is impossible to be competitive in tournaments or attain consistent success as a weekend angler without relying on the flipping technique from time to time.

Flipping is a fairly simple art, so fishermen of all skill levels have been able to master it to some degree. The result has been bigger bass and more bass for most anglers.

PROfile

Tennessee's Charlie Ingram is a four-time B.A.S.S. winner and a Classic regular.

But there are a few intelligent and innovative fishermen who have taken the art of flipping to a few advanced stages. And these anglers have set themselves apart from others with their consistent success on the tournament scene.

Roland Martin is probably the world's best known bass fisherman and certainly the most successful professional angler of all-time with more than 20 major tournament titles and Angler of the Year awards to his credit.

Charlie Ingram of Columbia, Tenn., established a name for himself on the Bass Anglers Sportsman Society trail by winning three national tournaments in four consecutive events.

Although he doesn't have the name or fame of a Roland Martin or Charlie Ingram, Chuck Faremouth is a highly successful tournament angler and a thinking man's fisherman. The Lake Worth, Fla., angler has finished in the top 20 percent of almost every tournament he's ever competed in and, although most of his tournaments have been on a local or state-wide scale, he has finished in the money in four national events.

An innovative angler who is constantly looking for a new angle, Faremouth is the creator of the so-called Okeechobee Spinnerbait, the large willow leaf bladed spinnerbait that became the fishing industry's hottest lure in 1985.

What these three knowledgeable fishermen have in common is a technique that could be called long-range flipping.

Although each has his own method, all of these men share the same objective — to reach fish that are easily spooked from farther away with the same delicate lure presentation that traditional flipping provides.

Each of these fishermen offer the aspiring tournament fisherman and weekend angler alike an insight into a technique that will mean improved success rates and more enjoyable times on the water.

Roland Martin has been practicing a form of long-range flipping for several years, but it wasn't until recently that his competitors have begun to pick up on it.

"I've been doing the long distance flip cast for years," he says. "In 1980, I won a tournament on Toledo Bend with the all-time record for 21 bass— over 80 pounds. And I caught most of those fish with the long flip cast.

"The reason I was so successful was that Toledo Bend is a great place to flip, but the water that spring was so clear — clearer than normal — and with a regular flip, you would scare the fish if you got close to the timber and brush. I recognized the problem right away —on clear lakes, it's just hard to flip.

"The whole reason I started the flip cast was to cast a jig into heavy cover in clear water. In the next tournament on Eufaula, which I also won, the water wasn't so clear, but I started using the flip cast more and more because it was just an easier way to flip. I could flip to a log that my partner couldn't. I could reach stuff that they couldn't. Consequently, I was catching more fish. I do a lot more long-distance flip casting instead of traditional flipping."

With Martin's technique for long-range flipping, he can expand the normal range of conventional flipping (from 10 to 20 feet) into a comfortable range of 25 to 30 feet. "That extra 10 or 15 feet farther than the normal flip is extremely important," Martin contends. "That extra distance is a big edge when you're in tournament competition. And it's a super big edge when the water's clear. With the long-distance flip cast, I can get to those 35- and 40-foot targets that you normally just can't flip to."

Roland Martin's long-range flipping technique was born of necessity.

Martin describes his long-range flip cast: "You push the button and swing the lure back to your hand. Now, I'm holding the lure with my left hand. The line is going straight to the rod tip and straight down to the reel. I'm holding the button in on the reel, so it's in free spool and now I'm thumbing the line.

"By swinging the rod and pulling the lure way back, I swing the rod tip out with an underhand flip. I'm flipping about like you would be putting if you were a golfer. My hand goes up and my rod starts at the water level and then goes up to a 45-degree angle. My left hand goes back and then it goes forward. I release the jig or the worm and the whole thing is just a few inches off the water as it travels. Even with a 30-foot cast, the lure might not get more than 3 feet high. So, consequently, it has a very quiet presentation.

"It takes practice to get good at it. It's not quite as accurate as regular traditional flipping because you're dealing with larger distances. But the flip cast is very accurate, because you're using a pendulum motion. You're swinging the lure on a 7- or 8-foot swing coming off that rod tip. And I'm using my hand to guide the lure instead of just letting it swing free. There's less room for error. By starting the lure off with my hand, I can kind of aim it. You can actually line it up like you're shooting a rifle or a bow and arrow."

"The fact that I can flip long distances separates me from a lot of guys," says Ingram. "Not many people have picked up on it much yet, but they will. It's just a matter of time before other people start taking advantage of it."

Ingram's sole criteria for deciding between long-range flipping and the traditional method is water clarity. "If the water's not too clear, the regular short flipping method works fine," he says. "But this is much more effective in clear water."

It was during the middle of a long Tennessee winter that Ingram developed his long-distance flipping technique and that practice has paid off handsomely.

"I have 16-foot ceilings in my house, so I flipped inside the house one whole winter," Ingram recalls. "That's when I really started experimenting with it and learned how to do it. I used a little plastic donut for a target and I just kept moving it out farther until I got to where I could flip as far as I wanted to accurately. It takes a lot of practice to sharpen your hand and eye coordination."

To achieve a greater distance, Ingram has developed a flipping version to fly fishing's false cast. First, he lets out enough line for a normal flip. While that line is being flipped out (as a false cast), Ingram pulls more line off of the reel and places it in his mouth.

When the lure completes its second pendulum swing, he simply allows the weight of the bait to string out the entire amount of line he has freed from the reel.

Because the lure travels just above the surface of the water as it heads for the target, "the lure presentation is soft and quiet like the regular flipping. It's got to be. If you don't, that destroys the whole effect of it.

"You can't let the lure get too high or it will splash. You just skip it right across the water. You get to where you can actually skip that thing back under bushes and stuff. It will hit and skip another 3 or 4 feet way back under the cover. It also works real well around docks."

The combination of Ingram's long range flipping expertise and clear line was instrumental in his victory on Lake Okeechobee in 1984, a surprise to most observers, who predicted that a local hotshot (does the name Roland Martin ring a bell?) would walk away with the top honors.

On Okeechobee, Ingram was flipping into pockets and holes in shallow-water grass from 20 to 30 feet away. Other anglers were attempting, unsuccessfully, to move in close enough to the cover to catch fish by conventional flipping.

During his hot streak on the B.A.S.S. tournament trail, Ingram used the cast to catch spooky clear water bass in the grass and stumps of the Mississippi River in Wisconsin, as well as fallen timber in Missouri. A spinnerbait was used for both victories.

No type of cover or structure is immune from Charlie Ingram's long-distance flipping attack.

"This cast adds another dimension to flipping," he says. "With this cast, not only are you able to avoid spooking fish with quiet, accurate casts, but you can hit so many more spots in a day's time, because the cast is one continuous motion. You're not wasting time reeling it back in and casting again."

Chuck Faremouth has never enjoyed flipping as much as casting. He freely admits that, but he is smart enough to know that flipping is often the key (and sometimes the only route) to consistent big bass catches.

Understanding the benefits of traditional flipping (particularly the quiet lure presentation and accuracy), Faremouth was introduced to an underhand cast by an avid bridge fisherman in south Florida. The saltwater angler used the cast because he didn't have the space to cast, since there was a constant flow of traffic behind him on the bridge.

Faremouth took the basic priniciples of the bridge fisherman's underhand cast and developed what he calls "the swing cast," an impressive and effective way to present a bait. The swing cast is perfect for regular casting, but one of its most important attributes is its ability to transform flipping from close-up work to a long range affair.

"I would never debate the importance of flipping to a bass fisherman," Faremouth says. "So I was looking for some sort of cast that would give me the same kind of accuracy and lure presentation that flipping provides from 1 to 15 feet.

"I can now flip with the same accuracy and soft presentation from 15 to 30 feet and I don't have to worry about spooking nearly as many fish. I think that's one reason I've had more success with the long-range flipping compared to the traditional form of flipping."

Another advantage of Faremouth's swing cast over the conventional flipping technique is apparent once a fish strikes the lure.

"A big difference and advantage my cast has is that there is no slack line," he explains. "As long as I don't have any slack line, I'm in a better position to feel and handle a fish.

"With this cast, I'm always on point."

Faremouth details the basics of his swing cast: "With this cast, the first thing you need to do is feel the bait. On a standard 6 1/2-foot rod, let out half of the length of the rod — about 3 and 3 1/2-feet of line. Use the rod to make the lure do a complete 360-degree turn (so that the lure swings past your ear) a couple of times until you get a feel for the lure.

"Once you complete the 360-degree rotation, you've got the inertia of the bait moving towards the target. All that has to be done at that time is just point the rod toward the target and release it at the proper point (about the time the lure passes your shoulder). It will travel about a foot above the water and you have complete control over the lure during its flight. If you see you're throwing past your target, you can stop it, simply by thumbing the spool.

"The swing cast is much simplier than it sounds. Every fisherman I've ever shown the cast to has picked it up in about a half-hour of practice."

Since the cast keeps the lure traveling low across the water, the chances of spooking bass are greatly reduced and it is much easier to get the bait into some hard-to-penetrate places.

"With this cast, I have the ability of throwing over limbs, through limbs and farther back in the weeds and up under boat docks," Faremouth contends. "And it's not as tiring as traditional flipping since the lure does all the work."

Although all three of these talented anglers have their own versions of long-range flipping, they all have something in common — they realize that distance flipping is another important weapon in a bass fisherman's arsenal.

They share the ability to "reach out and touch someone."

Chapter 21

Heavy-Handed Techniques For Bass

It had the makings of a bass fisherman's nightmare.

A cold front had passed through overnight, dropping the temperature by 18 degrees. On this particular morning, all semblance of wind had disappeared and a bright, cloudless bluebird sky greeted anglers.

PROfile

Apparent signals that a tough day was ahead.

While other tournament fishermen fretted about the conditions, Russ Bringger calmly began rigging up his flipping stick. But he wasn't preparing for just any flipping technique. He was readying his heavy cover special, a tactic designed to produce results during the toughest times — cold front and hot summer days when the fish bury themselves deep into heavy cover for shelter and protection.

Florida's Russ Bringger is winner of the 1986 B.A.S.S. tournament on Lake Okeechobee.

When the day was over, Bringger had collected another good limit and cashed another top 10 paycheck. Another day at the office.

Once again, a technique he calls "poking" didn't fail him.

"These types of days can be the most frustrating days of all for fishermen," explains Bringger, a talented Pompano Beach, Fla., pro and champion of the 1986 Florida Bassmasters Invitational. "You can be on the fish hot and heavy to the point where they're chasing your bait and go in there the next day after a cold front has come through and you'd think somebody had come through there and seined the place. You'd think there's not a bass in the whole lake."

"But we know from experience, what biologists tell us and everything that has been written about bass that the fish have a tendency to get as far up under heavy cover as possible, where there is shade, warmth and protection from the elements (during cold-front conditions). It's the same in the hot summertime when they will hold under thick cover to get shade and comfort. I've found that big bass really have a tendency to do this. But in Florida, where I live, the problem is that the fish will often get under grass so thick that you can't get a lure to them. At least not with conventional methods. That's when poking becomes a real tool for fishermen."

Although most of Bringger's success with the poking technique has come in his native Florida lakes, the fundamentals of this tactic should give bass anglers another weapon for grass fishing everywhere, including the thick milfoil beds of Tennessee's Nickajack Lake, the jungle-like hydrilla found in Texas lakes and the coontail moss of Lake Seminole.

Bringger's poking technique was devised as a way to penetrate thick mats of hydrilla and water hyacinths that blanket the surface and grow so dense that the bottom vegetation (and even the roots of the hydrilla stalks) die. That creates a huge open-water cavern beneath this blanket of greenery, the ideal habitat for bass, particularly big bass that recognize it as a protected comfort zone.

But penetrating this sphere of safety isn't easy. Weedless lures like plastic worms and jigs are required, but conventional flipping is often useless. Enter Bringger's poking technique

The technique involves using a long rod (a flipping stick is ideal) with plenty of backbone, heavy line (20- to 30-pound test), a pegged 1-ounce bullet weight and a large plastic worm (8 or 9 inches in length). He also uses a fish attractant to lubricate the worm and help it better penetrate the aquatic jungle.

The technique begins with the worm and weight reeled up tight to the top guide. Then with the reel on free-spool and a thumb holding the spool securely, Bringger begins literally poking the rod through the vegetation, wrestling with the surface cover until he finally penetrates the thick mat. Once the rod tip manages to puncture through the vegetation, he then releases the spool, allowing the worm to sink to the bottom. After jigging the worm a few times, he repeats the process in another spot along the vegetation. He works an area thoroughly, sometimes poking just 6 inches from his previous point of penetration.

"You have to literally shove the rod tip down anywhere from a foot to 3 feet deep to get through the stuff," Bringger says. "These are times when flipping is absolutely no good, yet there are fish in these places. Poking is the only way to get a lure in front of these fish."

When selecting likely cover for poking, Bringger concentrates on the thickest vegetation that has the deepest water beneath it. It stands to reason that the deeper the water, the larger these open-water caverns will be. He works the edge of the vegetation first, but then runs his boat up into the vegetation and

Russ Bringger winches an Okeechobee bass from heavy cover.

begins poking around the boat. If the water is deep enough (more than 5 feet), Bringger believes this activity will not usually spook fish in the vicinity.

"I've found this to be a good big-bass technique," Bringger says. "You could poke all day long and get only three strikes, but, usually, you'll have three good fish. And it's exciting. Think about it: you have an 8- or 9-pound fish with only 8 or 9 feet of line out. You can really have a battle on your hands."

Landing big bass under these conditions would seem almost impossible, but Bringger has had good success using a very simple method. "I set the hook hard, quickly pull the bass up to the underneath side of the vegetation and start gardening," he says. "I've found that when you pull a big bass up into that heavy cover, they have a tendency to quit fighting. Then it's a matter of actually gardening. You have to reach down and start pulling grass off of the fish until you can get enough of a hold to put the fish in the boat."

Russ Bringger's poking technique is a viable weapon for the times when bass fishing is the toughest, another tool for grass fishermen.

At times, both fish and fishermen are attracted to it.

Bass seek it for shelter, shade and protection. Bass fishermen are drawn to it because their prey are. Sounds simple enough, right?

But fishing heavy cover isn't all that simple. It is a specialized form of fishing that can mean attempting to penetrate huge mats of water hyacinths in Florida, thick hydrilla in Texas or nightmarish entanglements of milfoil in one of the Tennessee Valley Authority reservoirs throughout the South.

Once the vegetation reaches a certain degree of density, an angler's weapons are limited. Weedless lures like worms and some jigs are obvious choices, but the difficult part often comes in attempting to penetrate the cover. Matted hydrilla, milfoil and hyacinths can often eliminate conventional flipping, forcing some fishermen to simply find another area to fish.

But Barry Cummins has developed a flipping technique that can solve that problem, whether it be milfoil on Alabama's Lake Guntersville or the hydrilla fields of Lake Lochloosa in north Florida. He calls it his "hammer flipping" technique.

"I can't tell you how many times this technique has produced for me when a cold front had forced the fish to get tight to heavy cover or in the summertime when nothing else is working," says Cummins, a Fort Pierce, Fla., angler who owns the Gambler Worms Co. "Everybody knows that fish like to find heavy cover in those conditions, but the problem lies in getting your lure to the fish. Conventional techniques sometimes just can't break through thick grass."

Hammer flipping involves the use of a flipping stick, heavy line, 1-ounce pegged bullet weight and a small plastic worm (4 to 6 inches in length). The smaller worm can work through the grass better than a larger piece of plastic.

Its concept, basically, involves taking out a length of line (as you would with conventional flipping), pitching it upward (similar to normal flipping fashion) and once the lure reaches its apex, driving it sharply downward through the cover. This is a technique where a combination of the big rod and good timing translates into grass-penetrating brute force.

If the worm breaks through the top layer of vegetation, you then simply release the spool and allow the lure to sink. If the worm only dents the cover, Cummins jiggles the worm a couple of times in an attempt to help it slide through. Failing that, he repeats the unusual flipping technique.

"What you're dealing with often is a mat of vegetation that is thick on the surface, but sparse a couple of feet below the water," Cummins says. "The hammer flipping technique gives you a way to penetrate that thick mat and reach bass that are using that surface mat as shade and protection.

"The surprising thing about this technique is that it doesn't seem to spook many fish, which is the opposite to what most people would think. Although you're crashing it through this thick surface grass, I've found that bass seem to be more attracted to the noise than scared by it. Once I've broken through the grass, I'll usually jig up five, 10, 15 times and I've had bass come from considerable distances to eat it on the 15th time I jigged it. Because you're fishing in the type of cover where big bass hide, there's a great feeling of anticipation with this technique."

Cummins cautions that it takes practice to become proficient at hammer flipping, which relies on timing to create enough downward momentum to penetrate those hard-to-reach places. Once you master this basic slam-dunk approach to fishing, you can then teach yourself to gain extra distance of flipping upward and outward before hammering the surface of the vegetation.

The Florida pro made a believer out of former Super B.A.S.S. champion Mickey Bruce during a national tournament on Lake Okeechobee.

"Some of the places we were fishing was so thick that we would try this flip 15 or 20 times before we could force it through the grass," Bruce recalls. "We were fishing floating mats of hydrilla that were so thick on the top that they had choked out everything underneath it. There was about a 2-foot thick mat on top, but once you got it through, the worm would free-fall to the bottom."

All it took to impress Bruce was an 8-pound, 9-ounce bass that inhaled his worm while sharing the boat with Cummins.

Considering the thick jungle of grass involved with this technique, you would think that successfully landing a big bass in wall-to-wall vegetation would be difficult. But Cummins has had good success with a simple technique that involves setting the hook hard, winching the bass to the bottom side of the surface grass "and then doing a little farming. I just keep a tight line on him with one hand and carefully pull the grass away from him with my other hand. Finally, you'll find him and be able to pull him into the boat."

Crude, but effective. An apt description of hammer flipping as well.

Woo Daves and partner work a dock on Virginia's Lake Gaston.

Chapter 22

The Doc's Tips
For Boat Docks

When Greg South arrived in Pine Bluff, Ark., for the 1984 BASS Masters Classic, the Arkansas River was an unknown entity to him, unchartered waters, so to speak.

To make up for a lack of practice time, South attacked the Arkansas in a logical fashion. He simply sought out structure that was familar to him from the days he had spent on his home waters of Lake Gaston in Virginia.

Being a stranger to the Arkansas, South sought such structure as logs, stumps, pilings and boat docks, the very structure he felt comfortable fishing. He found plenty of those, but it wasn't until he discovered numerous boat docks in the Pine Bluff harbor area that the Richmond, Va., angler began to feel at home.

"Boat docks are one of my favorite structures back home and probably my most productive pattern," South said. "And it's one of the most overlooked structures by the average angler."

Virginia's Greg South is a two-time Classic qualifier and runner-up in the 1984 Classic on the Arkansas River.

South is obviously a boat dock veteran. In fact, he turned Al Linder on to a Lake Gaston boat dock pattern in 1977 and Linder went on to win the Virginia Invitational. South finished fifth.

And the 41-year-old doctor of radiology rode the strength of his boat dock pattern to 50 pounds of bass and second place in the prestigious Classic. He took advantage of one of the simplest patterns available to the 41 Classic anglers and in the end, only four-time Classic champion Rick Clunn could out-distance him.

Fishing with his father in pre-practice, South spotted a series of docks and scored immediately. During one practice day, the two men caught 22 bass off the docks, including three that weighed about 5 pounds.

The personable South left Pine Bluff with confidence that he would have a productive pattern when he returned three weeks later for the Classic.

"The reason I thought the pattern would hold on the docks was because these docks had plenty of water, as much as 12 feet," South said. "In a lot of the lakes we fish at home, the docks might have only 2 or 3 feet of water and if the water level drops just 6 inches, it can kill your dock pattern."

The pattern did, indeed, hold up for South. But there were others who fished the docks, but had little success.

"Some of the guys, like Roland Martin and Ricky Clunn told me they had practiced on the docks, but they didn't have much luck," South said. "I fish the docks a little differently than most people and think that made a big difference."

First of all, South uses spinning tackle, instead of the more traditional baitcasting equipment that dominates the pro circuit.

"I fish spinning tackle a lot and I'm very comfortable with it, which is very important," he explained. "With spinning tackle, I'm better able to skip a worm well back under the docks into the shady areas.

"I think most people come by and fish the front edge of the docks, but they never get back into the parts of the docks where most of the fish are. That's probably the most important part of dock fishing."

To accomplish that, South had a specially built graphite rod that was made by inserting a 6-foot casting rod blank into a cork spinning rod handle. The result is a 5-foot-2 rod ideal for skipping a worm beneath the narrow openings between the dock and water, but yet has enough backbone for setting the hook, then fighting the fish.

"Most people think of spinning tackle in terms of light- or medium-action type equipment," South said, who spends much of his dock time fishing on his knees to get a better angle. "I wanted a spinning rod to be just as strong as a casting rod because I don't hesitate to use 12-, 14-, 17- pound test line on spinning reels."

During the Classic, South kept three rods rigged with 10-, 12- and 17-pound line and would go to the lightest line in the clearest water.

"For the most part, I used 12-pound test line around the docks," he explains. "It's a little easier to use on spinning tackle than 17 and I didn't break off a single fish during the Classic."

South believes another factor that separated him from other Classic contenders who tried the dock approach is the size of the slip sinker he used. "I use a 1/8-ounce slip sinker for 90 percent of my dock fishing," he said. "That weight

Boat docks are a universal structure for bass.

allows the worm to sink much more slowly than the weights that most of the guys use.

"In fact, Roland said that was probably the reason he didn't do well on the docks. I'm very comfortable with that weight. That size weight makes a better entry into the water and a smaller splash than the bigger sinker that makes the worm sink much, much faster. I had a lot of my strikes when the worm was falling."

Although he picked up an occasional fish along the edge of the docks with a buzz bait early, South's most productive weapon was a 6-inch purple firetail Mister Twister Phenom worm. "To me, that's absolutely the finest worm," he said. "If I had to pick one worm to use anywhere in the country, that would be it."

When fishing the worm beneath the docks, South uses several variations of the retrieve depending on the type of structure around the wooden pilings. Most of the time, South says he "sort of leads the fish in the right direction for a second before setting the hook. That can keep you from getting tangled up and out of trouble."

Boat docks are a great hot-weather structure, South insists.

"One factor that helped my pattern was the days of clear skies and high, bright sunshine, which tends to move the fish to the docks. Those are usually the best days for this type of fishing."

And boat docks are usually productive areas throughout the year, except for the coldest periods of winter. "It's been my experience that boat docks are very good except in the dead of winter," he said. "Using my experience in Virginia, once the water warms up to about 50 degrees, the docks begin to be effective again. Summer is without a doubt the best time, though."

Through experience, South has learned to eliminate some docks from consideration. On the Arkansas River, he ignored the floating docks and concentrated on the traditional wooden docks that have pilings, which hold fish. His most productive piers had plenty of cover, brush that had been planted by some hard-working local crappie fishermen.

Obviously, the doc prescribes a little dock fishing to cure what ails you.

Chapter 23

Doug Hannon's
Schooling Bait

The schooling bass action of mid-summer/early fall may be the most exhilarating of all times for anglers. As the bass gang up to chase massive schools of shad, bass fishermen gang up to chase them as they explode along the surface of the water in a feeding frenzy not seen during other times of the year.

It is not called "jump fishing" for nothing. Once you "jump" a school of bass terrorizing a shad pod, you usually only have a few minutes to skip a heavy spoon or rip a vibrating crankbait through the whitewater action before the bass disappear. Temporarily, hopefully.

It can be the most exciting — and sometimes the most frustrating — moments in bass fishing.

While crankbaits, spoons and some topwater lures are the traditional weapons for taking schooling bass, Doug Hannon has developed a unique rig for this particular type of fishing. It is a rig that seems to produce bigger bass and allow him to continue to catch fish in the school longer than with other bait choices.

Naturalist, innovator and educator Doug Hannon has more than 500 10-pound-plus bass to his credit.

Although he has been fishing the rig for just a years and insists that more exploration is needed, Hannon, Florida's famed big-bass expert, has had some impressive success with his schooling special.

The basic rig consists of combining a topwater lure with a small plastic grub.

Although Hannon prefers a Heddon Zara Spook or Bagley's big Stick-Up, any large stickbait (with a weighted tail) will work in this rig. The stickbait is tied to the end of 14-pound test line. The grub is fashioned to a 14-inch leader that is connected to the main line with a blood knot 15- inches from the nose of the stickbait (a swivel can be substituted for the blood knot).

The result is a small grub that swims about an inch in front of the large surface lure, giving it an appearance of a small predator fish (a bass) pursuing a small baitfish (a shad).

It is an illusion that seems to fool schooling bass with great consistency.

"The key to this rig is the presence of the baitfish added to the lure that creates a chase scene," explains Hannon, who has more than 500 10-pound-plus bass to his credit and is well respected for his study and observation of the species. "That's why it is so productive during the whole schooling scenario when the bass are actively chasing shad.

"With other schooling baits like a jigging spoon and crankbait, you are simply duplicating a shad. But with this rig, you're duplicating the whole schooling scenario. What triggers bass to feed in a school is other bass chasing and breaking apart the school. If you only give the fish one stray shad to chase, a bass might chase it down, but he may also hesitate because he might miss the opportunity when the pack breaks into the big school and there's plenty of easy meals around. But if you give that bass the sight of a fish chasing a shad, he will usually commit and come look at it. He may interpret that as the initial stages of the school explosion."

Because he is simulating the complete chase scene, Hannon's rig allows him to stay in the school longer than traditional lures. Hannon says he has been able to catch bass from a single school for almost two hours with this lure combination.

Although schooling bass are typically small fish, Hannon's rig seems to produce an inordinate number of large bass. A prime example was a late-summer fishing trip on Florida's Lake Okeechobee, in which an 8-pound bass fell victim to Hannon and his rig.

"There is a common misconception that the schooling activity involves only small bass," Hannon says. "It used to be with school bass that a big bass was rare. You would catch 100 bass of the same size 12 to 15 inches, but a big bass was the exception.

"But with this rig, you'll catch a lot of 4- and 5- pounders — fish you wouldn't have believed were part of that feeding school. This rig seems to draw some very big fish from out on the edge of the school because these big fish will also exploit the smaller school bass in a cannibalistic fashion. Once a bass chooses an individual baitfish far enough away to be isolated from the protection that the turmoil and distraction that the mass of activity provides, he becomes a vulnerable target. When a small bass chases a shad 30 or 40 feet from the center of the schooling activity, he is liable to get eaten by a very large bass."

Doug Hannon's innovative schooling bait scores consistently.

Hannon casts the rig both directly ahead of the feeding frenzy, as well as in the middle of it and off to the side of the school (attempting to lure a big bass). His retrieve varies, but a productive way to fish the rig is to start and stop it (using the the rod tip). This makes both the predator and its prey perform the dart-and-stop chase ritual that can be a strike-triggering mechanism.

Another effective retrieve is the "walk the dog" technique best known for fishing a Zara Spook. Walking the dog involves rhythmically using both the reel and the rod tip to make the lure dart back and forth across the surface of the water as it is retrieved.

The Zara Spook, one of the oldest of topwater lures, is the ideal surface bait for this rig, according to Hannon, because of what it represents when fished alone.

"The secret to this schooling rig is the aspect of attracting a predator fish with another small predator fish, rather than with strictly a prey-type lure running away from the bass, which is what almost all lures represent," Hannon explains. "I think the reason the Zara Spook is such an effective lure and always will be is that it could never be interpreted as a baitfish. It is too big and has a pursuit, high-energy action that imitates a predator trying to catch something."

Although it was designed to take advantage of schooling bass, Hannon says this unique rig will produce bass that are less active and during other times of the year. He fishes it around vertical structure such as standing timber and boat docks, as well as along weed edges.

The predator-chasing-prey scenario will often ignite the feeding instinct in less active bass when they are not schooling, he says.

When selecting lure color, Hannon prefers using a stickbait in a brown or other dark-colored pattern to represent a small bass. The grub is white to imitate a shad.

Because the grub runs about an inch in front of the surface lure, it very seldom tangles. And a well-tied blood knot will easily slide through the tip guide, so the rig is remarkably easy to cast.

Another schooling-bass rig that Hannon is experimenting with uses a white popping bug (most commonly used by fly fishermen) instead of the grub. Worked quickly across the top of the water, this rig has proved productive in some schooling situations.

That rig works for the same reason that the stickbait-and-grub produces impressive catches of schooling bass — it creates the classic predator-prey chase scene with a sense of realism that active bass can't seem to ignore.

Chapter 24

Don Caggiano's Big-Bass Primer

Don Caggiano fashioned the reputation of a lifetime during two hot and windy days on Florida's Lake Okeechobee.

It might sound a little strange to say that a New Yorker took advantage of the South's largest and perhaps best bass factory. But by the time Caggiano had returned to his Tarrytown, N.Y., home, he had taught the good ole boys, masters of southern plastic worm fishing, some mighty impressive lessons.

On two consecutive days, Caggiano returned from the massive shallow-water lake with a monster swimming in the livewell of his Ranger. For the first time in Bass Anglers Sportsman Society history, Don Caggiano became the first man to win the largest bass award for the two biggest fish of a tournament.

Caggiano made even Okeechobee's hardened big-bass experts take notice when he brought in a 9-pound, 5-ounce largemouth on the second day of the tournament and followed that with a 9-pound, 13-ounce specimen the final day, both on a plastic worm.

PROfile

New York pro Don Caggiano, a past Classic qualifier, has the distinction of winning two daily big-bass awards in a single B.A.S.S. tournament.

But he took home something worth much more than that. He had created a legend of sorts.

Today, Caggiano downplays his experience of an angler's lifetime, saying much of his success must be attributed to luck. But Caggiano's big bass techniques used during his visit to the Big O provide fishermen on every skill level with an important lesson on catching big bass on a plastic worm.

Caggiano's success story centers around a 50-yard stretch of reeds in Lake Okeechobee's Monkey Box area, one of the most famous fishing holes in the country. This one reed patch would provide Caggiano with a little over 40 pounds of fish, which was good enough for 10th place, but more importantly, it provided him with some legendary big bass action.

"I had fished there in practice and had caught a couple of fish that would have weighed almost 4 pounds each," Caggiano says. "I drew a partner on the first day of the tournament who said he had some good fish located in the rim canal, so we fished there all day and I caught four or five little fish.

"I went right back to my spot in the Monkey Box the second day and I caught a 3-pounder right off the bat. I caught another little one, a 13-incher, soon after that and things slowed down a little. It was about 11 o'clock when the first big one (9 pounds, 5 ounces) hit. At that point, I said to myself, 'I'm just going to stay here.' I just continued to go back and forth along this 50-yard stretch of reeds and pretty soon I had another small one, which gave me about 14 pounds at that point.

"On the third and final day, there was no doubt where I was going to go. I caught a fish the first thing that morning, just like the day before. At 10:30, I caught one that weighed over 7 pounds. At 11 o'clock, I caught the 9-13. By 1 o'clock, I had six fish that weighed over 20. At about 2 o'clock, I lost one that was bigger than both of the 9- pounders.

"I know you hear fish stories about the big one that got away, but I had just caught a 7 and two 9s, so I had something to compare him against. He was huge. I couldn't be too disappointed about missing him though. But it would have been nice to bring in one over 10, along with the 9s and a 7. It probably would have come close to breaking Ron Shearer's record."

In the 1982 Florida Invitational, Lake Okeechobee yielded a B.A.S.S.-record to Shearer for a seven-fish limit weighing 36 pounds, 8 ounces.

On the strength of his outstanding final day stringer, Caggiano jumped from 42nd to 10th and staked claim to his first BASS Masters Classic appearance.

Caggiano's ticket to Pine Bluff, Ark., and Classic XIV was a 5 1/2-inch blackgrape Ditto Baby Gator Tail worm, which he teamed with a 3/0 Tru-Turn hook, a 1/4-ounce sinker and 20-pound Trilene line. He was pitch-casting it around the scattered clumps of maidencane that were surrounded by some of the thickest cover on Okeechobee.

"I think the reason this area was holding so many good fish was that it was about a foot deeper than everything else around it," Caggiano says. "It was about 4 1/2 or 5 feet deep and everything around it was about 3 1/2. Out of that same area, I saw six fish over 8 pounds caught during the tournament.

"I couldn't get close enough to flip to these fish. They were real spooky because they weren't on the bottom, they were suspended. They were real tight against the thin clumps of maidencane that was surrounded on three sides by solid cover. There was no way you could present a bait to any fish in that real

Don Caggiano with one of his two Okeechobee 9-pounders.

heavy cover, unless you could swim a live shiner under there. But these fish were coming out of the thick cover to feed and that's why I was able to catch them around the thin stuff."

The 9-pound, 5-ounce fish was the biggest bass Caggiano had ever seen (his previous best was an 8-pounder caught on the St. John's River during Super B.A.S.S. I), so he decided to have it mounted after the second-day weigh in. "I was going to release the big one that first day," he says. "I had never lost (killed) a fish in a bass tournament and I've only killed four since 1963 and those were mounted. I was ready to let that first big fish go, but I thought I might never do that again.

"And it was a real surprise to do it all over again and even better the next day."

Although Caggiano has some definite big-bass techniques that we can all learn from, he emphasizes the luck factor.

"You have to be lucky to catch big fish and I was," Caggiano explains. "When you hook big fish like these, it's not just impressive, it's downright scary. If they don't jump, you don't know exactly how big they are, but when they jump and you see how big they are, you start thinking about all the things that can go wrong and usually do.

"With these big fish I caught, I had my boat positioned on the only open side of the vegetation. There was solid cover on all three sides and I only had about 10 feet to play those big fish. That's where luck comes in. You can have the knowledge and the skill to make the bait presentation perfectly, to feel the bite and to set the hook, but then it's mostly luck. Because you really can't control those big fish. They're just too powerful in shallow water and there's too much cover around.

"Those big fish jumped at least three times each in that little 10-square-foot area. I had good partners who did a good job with the net and I got a little lucky with the fish. The first 9-pounder bent that Tru-Turn hook at a 90-degree angle, because he was heading for the dense cover and I had to put my thumb on the spool to stop him because if he ever got in there, I'd never get him out. He bent the hook, but luckily the line didn't break or the reel didn't come off the seat or the rod didn't break or the hook didn't pull out.

"There's about a 30-second period when you hook a big fish and try to get him in that seems like an eternity. They're such powerful creatures. That big fish I lost was a prime example. I'm 6-foot-5 and I got my arms up in the air, but that fish pulled me down to my knees and I had my wrists in the water with the rod under the boat."

Although he is a plastic worm fanatic, Caggiano's tackle box isn't nearly as colorful as most bass anglers' treasure chests.

"I don't believe in owning 50 colors of worms," he says. "I fish just five colors that I have great confidence in — blackgrape, purple, motoroil, black with a blue tail and a purple with a fire tail. All are Ditto Gator Tails, which is

Flipping heavy cover is Don Cagginano's top big-bass technique.

a curly tail that goes through thick cover real well and has the greatest vibration with just the slightest twitch of your rod.

"I've found that these worm colors will catch fish in almost any lake in the country. In the years that I've been fishing national tournaments, I have never failed to catch fish on a Gator Tail of these colors. I'm talking about from New York to Wisconsin to Okeechobee to Texas."

Caggiano refuses to get "scientific" about worm color.

"I switch pretty often if I'm not getting any action, but there's no scientific reason for it," he explains. "I'll usually start off with the blackgrape, which is an excellent color in Okeechobee or New York. I won a tournament in Connecticut (1981 Connecticut State B.A.S.S. Federation championship) on that color.

"I don't believe color is all that important. It's overrated. Most of the colors are made for the fisherman, not the fish. It's more important to have confidence in a bait. Confidence is one of the key factors of bass fishing. You can use the dumbest-looking lure in the world and if you have confidence in it, you'll stay sharp and fish it hard. That makes a difference."

Asked the most common mistakes he sees among plastic worm fishermen, Caggiano listed two: mismatching the hook and sinker and setting the hook improperly.

"Matching the right size hook and sinker is important," Caggiano explains. "I used a 1/4-ounce sinker at Okeechobee, which is pretty heavy for the kind of depth (4-5 feet) I was fishing. But it wasn't too heavy when you consider the cover I was fishing. You need the weight to take the worm down into that cover. Match the size of sinker and worm to the kind of cover and water depth you're fishing.

"Another thing that's important is to peg your sinker (with a toothpick). Pegging a sinker isn't just for flipping. You almost have to peg the sinker when you're fishing heavy cover. If you don't, the sinker is going to slide on the line and the worm is going to be suspended and it's not going to be able to reach the bottom.

"One of the most common mistakes is setting the hook too quickly and not setting the hook hard enough. An awful lot of people say that you've got to hit the fish right away when you feel him, but I believe it's better to let him eat it an extra second. You've got a much better chance of landing the fish if you do. I always make sure that he's got the worm either by making sure the line is moving off or just gently picking up on the worm a little bit to make sure he's there before I nail him.

"An old Florida fisherman once told me 'When you think you've set the hook as hard as you can, set it twice as hard on the next one.' And I do. You never know how big that fish is and if you just jerk a little, that might be fine for a little 1-pounder, but what if he's that 10-pounder? What if he's that world record bass?"

Chapter 25

An Expert's Deep-Water Approach

It was December on Georgia's West Point Lake and a week that was better suited for survival training than bass fishing.

The normal December weather patterns brought cold fronts, icy temperatures, sporadic high winds and bone-chilling, brain-dulling rain that persisted for most of the week. Even worse for the 290 bass pros competing in the 1986 Bassmaster Georgia Invitational was the instability that the 25,000-acre impoundment was experiencing.

PROfile

Eleven consecutive days of heavy rains had inundated the reservoir with muddy water, the bane of most bass anglers. Add to that a falling water level that dropped about 2 1/2 feet during the tournament week and you begin to understand that West Point was not about to provide a Disneyland-like atmosphere for its visitors.

Randy Behringer of Texas is a two-time B.A.S.S. winner and past Classic qualifier.

But in these events, the major leagues of fishing, some resourceful and often brilliant strategic mind finds a way to overcome the pending adversity and makes a lasting impression on his peers. On this week, it was Randy Behringer's turn.

Scoring big points for perseverance, the 46-year-old veteran Texas pro resorted to the tactics that usually paid off during the toughest winter times on his home lakes. Behringer struggled into his warmest clothes, stoked his inner fire with the strongest coffee available and went offshore wheremore than 46 pounds of cooperative bass awaited.

Randy Behringer went deep and, in the process, separated himself from the rest of the tournament field to fish for the only bass that could be caught in sufficient enough numbers to win the tournament. There is a lesson in that strategy for every angler.

"Deep-water fishing can be feast or famine, but, at times, it can provide you with a school of bass all to yourself," says Behringer, a two-time B.A.S.S. winner who is one of the finest open-water structure fishermen in the country. "And during the times when the fishing gets tough, deep structure fishing can be the only viable alternative.

"I don't think you can consistently catch fish year-round unless you have some knowledge and skill with deep-structure fishing. By that, I mean fishing deep points, vertical banks and other submerged structure in the middle of the lake — the stuff that Buck Perry wrote about 40 years ago. I think Buck Perry was 40 years ahead of his time. He realized the potential of deep-water structure fishing and he obviously lived in an age and time when almost no one did it. Consequently, he caught some tremendous stringers of bass. Understanding some of the statements in his book about contact points, migration routes and feeding periods was a big step for me as a fisherman.

"And it made me realize that there are schools of bass out there that haven't been caught or at least received much fishing pressure."

North Carolina's Perry is considered the father of open-water structure fishing, a highly respected fishing pioneer who once travelled the country illustrating the wealth of bass that awaits the angler who could take advantage of them.

Deep-structure fishing isn't for every bass enthusiast, though.

Most bass fishermen enjoy the visual stimulation associated with shallow-water structure fishing. Their idea of bass fishing is casting to visible shoreline targets. And, as a result, most of those areas endure a constant barrage with pressure.

The last remaining frontier in bass fishing is deep open-water structure fishing. While the rewards of mastering its techniques are obvious, it takes considerable determination and dedication to become proficient at it. It demands the patience, sensitivity and skillful interpretation of electronic depth-finding aids not required with shallow-fishing techniques.

"It all begins with the electronics," explains Behringer, who has qualified for the prestigious BASS Masters Classic on three occasions. "First of all, you have to learn to operate and interpret your electronics. This kind of fishing requires quality electronics along with properly installed transducers and literally hundreds of hours spent just idling and reading your electronics."

Through years of experience, Behringer can decipher the information supplied by his depth finder as well as most of us interpret road signs. On calm days, he can actually maneuver a lure like a jigging spoon (while watching his depthfinder) to where it will actually touch a dormant bass. He is a master at the specialized art of deep-structure fishing.

A lead jigging spoon is one of Randy Behringer's most reliable tools for probing deep structure.

Although liquid crystal display units now dominate the depth-finding market, Behringer's boat is outfitted with a paper graph and flasher on the console, along with a bow-mounted flasher. The installation and position of the transducers for these units is crucial, he claims. The transducers for his console-mounted depthfinders are drilled through the bottom of the boat (instead of mounted inside of the hull), which provides "the ultimate set-up for this kind of fishing." The transducer for his front flasher is attached to the foot of his trolling motor, which allows Behringer to position the boat directly above his underwater target — a critical factor with making a vertical presentation to the deep-water bass.

The term "deep" is relative to season, current weather conditions, the type of lake or impoundment and even personal preference. Although he remembers catching several hundred bass by dropping a jigging spoon into 85 feet of Mexico's Lake Guerrero many summers ago, Behringer's definition of deep begins at 10 feet and ends at about 30 feet.

The most productive depth range for both bass and bass fishermen is about 12 to 25 feet, Behringer believes. An abundance of largemouth bass can be found at this depth throughout the year, with the exception of the spawning season.

"Open-water structure fishing is all about pinpointing the textbook stuff that we have all read about," Behringer says. "Intersections, bends in the creek channels, spots where a channel swings up close to a road bed — textbook stuff. But, by the same token, everybody knows these textbook places, so you have to find less obvious places to be consistently successful at this game."

Deep-water fishing is at its best in the hottest and coldest times of the year. But Behringer takes a different approach to both seasons.

In the winter, the bass have a tendency to congregate on open-water structure, so Behringer relies on a vertical presentation with a jigging spoon. Using his electronic eyes, Behringer positions himself above the fish and lightly hops a 1/2- to 1-ounce Mann-O-Lure spoon up off of the bottom. Using a 6-foot-10 All Star graphite rod and 14- to 17-pound test line, Behringer uses a rhythmic pumping action to propel the spoon upward and then allows it to spiral back down.

Behringer recommends doctoring most jigging spoons by replacing the factory hook with a version that is twice as large. And he ties the line directly to the spoon. "With a snap or split ring, you will find that the bait will turn up and the treble hook will catch the line," Behringer says. "You won't have that problem nearly as much when you tie the line to the bait. And it will allow your line to twist, which is important because in the winter when the water is cold, you will catch a lot of bass by holding the spoon at a certain level — a foot or two off of the bottom. The line will twist enough to make the spoon barely turn. Everything moving around in that cold water is lethargic. So, consequently, it imitates the action of the baitfish around the bass."

While searching for wintertime bass, Behringer often casts a Little George, a heavy, shad-shaped bait that has long been considered a standard deep-structure tool. The Little George allows him to make long casts and cover considerable acreage looking for fish.

In the winter, the bass gather on the sharper, more drastic breaklines of most bottom irregularities, Behringer says. But in the summer, the bass are more likely to be scattered around the more subtle depth changes.

Behringer's summer bait choices are a jigging spoon for the rare times when the bass are concentrated on a specific piece of structure and a plastic worm. He uses a large (8- to 9-inch) Jawtec ribbon-style worm (grape with metalflake and red are his most productive colors).

Although he often utilizes a Carolina-rigged worm to entice bass that have been pinpointed, Behringer's favorite summer style involves casting a Texas-rigged version while drifting across "subtle structure like a gradually sloping point. I'm thinking of one at Lake Palestine that runs about 400 yards from land with only a 2-foot drop in depth. But that 2-foot break can be a fantastic place to fish in the summer."

Behringer emphasizes two keys to deep-water fishing that often go over-looked.

Regardless of the season, one of the most important aspects of locating deep-water bass involves finding schools of baitfish, he says. Baitfish like shad, particularly when bunched together, can point the way to aggressive bass. Also, it is important that anglers not dismiss areas where they spot one or two bass on the depth finder. "You've got to remember that in, say, 25 feet of water you will only see about 8 feet of the bottom because of the cone angle of the transducer," he explains. "If you run over a couple of fish in the space of 8 feet, it's a good bet that there are others in that area."

But, then, it is the same with deep-structure fishing in general, where the treasure is hidden from view.

Joe Thomas admires Kim Carver's trophy spotted bass caught on Arkansas' Bull Shoals Reservoir.

Chapter 26

Masters of the Spotted Bass

Their arrival has been without fanfare, but the spotted bass has quietly become a staple for bass anglers in aging reservoirs throughout the country.

Ironically, the spotted bass, also called Kentucky bass, was originally a river creature, but today it is becoming the dominant bass species in man-made impoundments from Georgia's Lake Lanier to California's Lake Perris. It is a takeover that fishermen have grown to appreciate.

PROfile

That spotted bass should begin to dominate the bass population in older reservoirs like Lanier is understandable. As a reservoir ages, its wooden structure gradually decays and disappears, making it less suitable habitat for largemouth bass. But the prolific-breeding spot is a deep-water, rock-oriented species which nicely fills the void left by the declining largemouth population.

Tom Mann, Jr., a B.A.S.S. winner and past Classic qualifier, has become an expert of patterning trophy spotted bass through years of guiding on Georgia's Lake Lanier.

Although spotted bass don't reach the size of largemouth bass — the world record is 9 pounds, 4 ounces — it is an outstanding gamefish. The consensus believes that spots are superior to both largemouth and smallmouth bass in the struggle they produce when hooked. And they can be patterned with more day-to-day predictability than their cousins, according to the experts, because this deep-water species is less affected by weather changes.

For both biological and sporting reasons, spotted bass have become the game of choice for many bass anglers, particularly in the South.

Spotted bass resemble smallmouths in both body shape and with its diminutive mouth (although they are colored more like largemouths). And like smallmouths, consistently catching spots requires a specialized gameplan that revolves around deep water, small finesse-type lures and light line.

"Spots are the world's weirdest critters," claims Mickey Bruce, a two-time Bassmaster tournament winner from Buford, Ga. "You can forget everything you know about largemouth bass when you're after spotted bass because they're entirely different creatures. There is not enough knowledge written about spotted bass to fill up the eye of a needle."

In an effort to improve that situation, here are the tactics and techniques of six excellent spotted bass anglers who have an abundance of experience and a soft spot for the oddball bass. You might call them the Masters of the Spotted Bass.

•

Although he now lives in Montgomery, Texas, Gary Klein's boyhood years were spent fishing the deep, clear waters of Lake Oroville in northern California, where spots have long been standard fare. His were lessons well learned, obviously, since he has used that knowledge to win Bassmaster tournaments on Lake Lanier and Arkansas' Bull Shoals with spots as his primary targets.

"It has become a fact of life that a competitive angler has to learn to catch spotted bass because there are times when you have to fish for them," says Klein, a perennial BASS Masters Classic qualifier and the former Angler of the Year. "If you understand spotted bass, it can be a major asset in your arsenal for bass fishing."

From his years in California, Klein has become a master at fishing deep-water bottom contour changes — the places that spots call home. He looks for spots along channel edges, bluff banks, long points, rock piles, submerged islands and other irregularities in the lake bottom. The appeal of such contour changes is heightened by the availability of any wooden structure (stumps, brushpiles or standing timber) along the contour change.

His standard tools are 6- to 8-pound test line, a light action rod, spinning reel and small, finesse lures — often called sissy baits. Through the years, Klein has developed the touch of a surgeon for fishing lures like a 4-inch straight-tail plastic worm on a 3/16-ounce sinker and 1-0 hook or light jig head; 5 1/2-inch Kalin grub on a 1/4-ounce lead head; or 1/4-ounce Garland Spider Jig.

Klein concentrates intensely when probing the depths for spots, which are infamous for their light, almost undetectable strikes. He has found that spots most often hit a lure when it is falling through the water or dragged slowly along the bottom. "As it falls, the slip sinker rides about 4 or 5 inches above the worm and it gives an appearance of the worm actually chasing the slip sinker," he explains. "I think that triggers strikes. I shake it on the fall, particularly when I reach the level that I believe the fish are suspended at. When I reach that level,

Top-notch angler Joe Hughes demonstrates the difference in markings between a spotted bass (left) and largemouth.

I stop the bait and shake it with my rod tip, which changes the direction of the fall. That allows the worm to stop and the sinker to catch up to it. When I allow it to fall again, instead of falling vertically, it spirals. As soon as I stop and change the direction of the fall, I often trigger a strike."

Although he estimates that one-third to one-half of the spotted-bass strikes he receives occurs during the fall, Klein won the Bull Shoals tournament by methodically dragging a small worm across the lake bottom behind his boat. That technique has produced for years, particularly when the spots were inactive and difficult to catch. "Dragging works because there are times when the spots are so tight to the bottom that when you catch one, it has a mud line along its side," he explains.

Klein displayed his finely-honed skills en route to winning the Bull Shoals tournament with a spotted-bass strategy that was true finesse fishing from beginning to end. First, he had located the fish along the end of main-lake bluff banks in 35 to 40 feet of water. He then caught them by dragging a Don Iovino Doodling King worm behind the boat. And he completed the ultimate finesse pattern with an innovative method of landing spots that gave him an advantage over the rest of the tournament field.

"Landing spotted bass or smallmouths without a net poses a problem," Klein says, in reference to the Bassmaster rule prohibiting the use of landing nets. "This presents a problem any time you're dealing with spotted bass or smallmouth because these fish are very hot — they fight strong and don't wear down easily. Plus, you have them on ultralight equipment and they are coming out of deep water. On top of all that, they have a tiny mouth and lipping them can be impossible.

"I started thinking that there had to be a better way to land them than trying to get your thumb in their mouth. Then I remembered my trout fishing days in the streams and how the trout didn't wiggle when I held them by the belly and took the fly out. So to land the spots, I lay on my back, lean over the boat backwards and put my right hand in the water. Using the rod in my left hand, I lead the fish into my open hand and quickly flop it into the boat. I had 100-percent success in the tournament with this method."

•

Around Lake Lanier, Mickey Bruce has become famous for his fondness for building and fishing brushpiles for spotted bass. An endless series of Bruce-signature brushpiles have helped him win numerous tournaments on Lanier, including the $100,000 top prize in the 1983 Super B.A.S.S. Tournament.

Like many older reservoirs, Lanier has lost most of its original wooden structure. But manmade brushpiles have transplanted some much needed structure in the Georgia reservoir, which has become home to a spotted bass population that makes up an estimated 80 percent of the bass in the impoundment. To concentrate spotted bass, Bruce has planted countless brushpiles in 15 to 30 feet of water in less-than-obvious locations throughout the reservoir.

"Forget about planting brush on points for spotted bass," he says. "Every big point on Lanier has several brushpiles and they get pounded every day because they are easy to find. I plant brush in places where the only way anybody can find it is by accident."

Bruce's primary weapons for fishing brushpiles are a minute ring-worm made by Zoom and a small (1/4- to 3/8-ounce) jig and pork combination. He fishes both lures vertically when possible, which allows him to maintain better contact with the lure. Contact is an important element in this type of fishing because spotted bass are notorious for their light strikes.

"Actually detecting a strike and catching a spot can be much more difficult than a largemouth," Bruce explains. "Ninety-nine percent of my strikes come on the fall — either the initial fall or after I have hopped the bait off of the bottom and it is falling back down. It is important to keep the slack out of the line and watch your line at all times."

•

On his first cast over a long, tapering point, Tom Mann Jr. was working the plug with the vigor commonly associated with Zara Spook fishing when a dark cloud suddenly surfaced beneath it. The cloud surged in response to each dart of the lure, following it in mirror-like fashion. The intensity of the moment was too much for Mann.

"Look at those spots following my Spook," he both whispered and shouted simultaneously. "Those are magnum spots. I mean full-grown spots."

Although fishing's version of jab and counter seemed to last several minutes, in reality it ended just seconds after it began as several 3-pound-plus spots battled for the plug. After two fish batted it around, a third inhaled its back treble hook and succumbed after a short, but frantic battle.

Topwater fishing for spotted bass — a time to cherish.

It is only for a period of about two weeks in the spring (late April/early May) that these deep-water creatures are shallow enough to be susceptible to a surface lure, according to Mann, a top-tournament pro and guide on Lake Lanier. During this time, the post-spawn spots have just completed the bedding ritual and have not moved back out to deeper areas where they spend most of their lives.

Mann intercepts these ultra-aggressive bass on their way out to deeper structure by using a topwater bait to quickly cover long main-lake points that feature brush, stumps or rockpiles. In the clear water of Lanier, the spots will rise from as deep as 25 feet to assault a surface lure, although they can also be as shallow as 5 feet. Mann positions his boat in 25 to 30 feet of water and casts up into shallow water (5 feet or less). He concentrates on working the topwater plug all of the way back to the boat. "With a point like this, the strike zone can be huge," Mann says.

"This is the most enjoyable spotted bass fishing there is," he adds. "I catch a lot of spots in the 3- to 5-pound range this way and the strikes are especially furious. In fact, you end up missing a lot of strikes because these big spots compete so hard against each other for your bait that they swim or jump past it a lot of times."

To take advantage of the spotted bass' competitive attitude during this time of year, Mann uses a Zara Spook on calm days and a Johnny Rattler prop bait on windy days or when boat traffic creates an artificial current. He also keeps a Fat Gitzit tubejig or a small plastic worm rigged on a jig head positioned nearby as a comeback bait for short-striking fish. "If you stop the topwater bait, pick up the other lure and quickly cast back to the same spot, you can catch almost every one of them," Mann claims.

•

For most anglers, the most difficult part about catching spotted bass is locating them. The species is most abundant in deep water and around subtle bottom contour irregularities, a combination that requires some skill with electronics. But one of Doug Youngblood's most dependable patterns revolves around a form of structure that should be obvious to all.

Marinas. The most visited Corp of Engineers lake in the country, Lake Lanier has dozens of marinas with covered boat slips to handle the recreational boating needs of water skiers and cruisers. Although many fishermen overlook these obvious places, marinas provide Youngblood with some of his hottest action from February through April.

When the water warms up to about 49 degrees, Youngblood says the spots start moving into the marina boat slips, which harbor some of the warmest water in the lake. In the early spring, the most productive docks are in or near deep water (25 to 30 feet). As the water warms later in the spring, Youngblood concentrates on shallow marinas and individual wooden docks where the spots move into spawn.

The floating docks of the marinas provide a deceptive amount of good bass cover. Most are built over deep water and although they don't have the traditional wooden pilings commonly associated with boat docks, spotted bass will align themselves with the labyrinth of cables used to secure the boat slips in place.

"I like to fish marinas and boat houses because most people aren't going to fish the ones with boats in them," says Youngblood, a past Classic qualifier, who has become a spotted bass specialist from 10 years of guiding on Lanier. "If you can skip a bait up in there, you can catch unmolested fish."

Using ultralight spinning tackle and 6- to 8-pound line, Youngblood's most productive lures are a 4- or 5-inch Texas-rigged straight-tail worm with a 3/16-ounce sinker and a 1/4- to 3/8 ounce jig with a No. 1 Uncle Josh pork chunk as a trailer. For the times when the spots are especially inactive, he relies on a 4-inch worm on a 1/32-ounce jighead fished excruciatingly slow around the structure.

"The way I approach a marina slip or boat house is to pull right up tight against it," Youngblood explains. "A lot of people stay off of it and make a long cast to the dock, but I have more success working right beside it. I pitch the bait right down the side of the dock and leave my bail open so that it can fall all of the way to the bottom, which is a key. Once it makes contact with the bottom, I engage the reel and doodle it all of the way back to the boat.

"Probably the most important element of dock fishing for spots is to really work the shady side of the dock or the boat that's moored in the slip. If you can develop enough accuracy to skip a bait well back in the shade or pitch it into tiny cracks and other places that most people can't reach, you'll catch plenty of spots."

•

Few anglers understand trophy-sized spotted bass as well as California's Dave Nollar, who Gary Klein considers one of the finest spot specialists in the country. Given the reputation of his favorite spotted bass lake, Lake Perris (which has produced a world record spot), Nollar obviously has had plenty of practice with big fish.

Nollar was among the first of the California fishermen to target big spots by discovering their affinity for holding tight to the lake bottom in deep, clear reservoirs like Perris, a 1,000-acre impoundment located about 75 miles from Los Angeles.

Although he is a master at using finesse lures to catch spots at their normal depths, Nollar has developed methods of catching the most untapped population of spotted bass of all — those in extremely deep water. Nollar actually catches spots as deep as 65 to 75 feet.

One of his most productive techniques for fishing extreme depths involves a complicated-sounding rig. Using a three-way swivel, Nollar attaches a 10- to 12-inch 6-pound test leader with a 1-ounce flat sinker on the end of it. A second leader (5 feet in length) of 8- to 10-pound monofilament is tied to the swivel and sports a floating Rapala Minnow on the opposite end.

After allowing the rig to reach the bottom, Nollar slowly drags it across the bottom, while occasionally pausing to twitch it. The unique rig allows him probe depths that are unfishable by most standards and produces some impressive trophy fish.

•

Oklahoma's Charlie Reed, the 1986 Classic champion, is a spotted-bass enthusiast who pursues the species regularly on his home lake of Broken Bow, where they are abundant.

Over the years, Reed has found the perfect tool for locating scattered spots — a 5 1/2-inch jerkbait. With the powerful wrists of a carpenter, Reed can muscle these lipped minnow-shaped lures down to about 12 feet. But he has found that he can draw spots from more than twice that depth by making a Storm Thunderstick or Bomber Long A dart and dive beneath the surface.

"When I'm after spots, I concentrate on rocky cover and avoid vegetation, because spotted bass are such heavy crawdad eaters," Reed says. "The jerkbait lets you cover a lot of territory in a hurry, like a long line of riprap, but it needs clear water to be effective. The clearer, the better."

Reed fishes a jerkbait on 8- to 10-pound line, which he believes is the perfect size for getting the optimum action out of the lure. "A lot of people don't realize it, but to get the most out of a jerkbait, you need to use the line stretch to your advantage," Reed claims. "The lighter line has just the right amount of stretch, which helps drive the bait deeper. The line stretch works like a big rubber band and as it recoils, it pulls the bait harder through the water. And the trick to that bait is getting that extra drive."

Charlie Reed, like the other Masters of the Spotted Bass, has developed a finely-tuned gameplan for taking full advantage of this emerging fishery. As our reservoirs get older, more and more of us will gladly turn our attention toward the lesser-known cousin of smallmouth and largemouth bass.

A successful vacation trip begins with plenty of advanced planning.

Chapter 27

Vacation Bass

It is a scenario that many avid bass fishermen can readily identify with.

After another year of 40-hour work weeks, it is time for that long-awaited vacation to Monster Lake, home of some of the country's biggest bass and the subject of your dreams for the past 12 months. An hour after your shift ends, you load the stationwagon, collect the kids and take off down the highway.

PROfile

Fourteen hours and four states later, you arrive at the shores of Monster Lake, check into the hotel, drop the wife and kids off at Wally World and launch the boat with the highest of expectations. It's hard to believe that you're actually fishing the renowned big-bass waters you had always heard about.

This is the life.

Three-and-a-half days later, Monster Lake has yielded three tiny, er, less-than-monstrous bass and, naturally, your expectations have fallen to about the level of the thermocline. "I could have stayed home and done better than this," you admit subconsciously. "Some vacation."

Louisiana pro Jack Hains is a guide on Toledo Bend Reservoir and past BASS Masters Classic champion.

Sound familiar?

Vacation bass fishing can be the most challenging form of the sport. Vacation time means limited time for first finding and then catching fish. At times, even a week's vacation isn't long enough when you're faced with trying to locate bass in waters radically different from your favorite lake at home.

But vacation bass trips don't have to be frustrating and unrewarding. The key is learning how to quickly read a strange lake.

According to to a panel of experienced, knowledgeable guides and tournament pros who make their living doing just that — locating bass on new lakes in a limited amount of time — there are several time-tested methods for reading and understanding a strange lake.

But the work begins before you ever leave home.

Because of the limited amount of time for locating bass on strange waters, it is important to be as prepared as possible once you arrive on Monster Lake. That means learning as much about the lake and its fishing techniques as humanly posssible before ever hitching up the boat.

"A guy who is vacationing needs to maximize his time on those waters and that means spending plenty of time planning and doing research before he ever leaves," says Steve McCadams, a respected guide on Kentucky Lake. "The absolute first step is obtaining a topographic map.

"A topo map is a necessity on any lake you plan to fish, because it shows elevations and depths, drop-offs, roadbeds and the complete bottom contour of the lake along with the names and locations of creeks. It will give you some good starting points and you'll be much better off than just going out there blind."

Maps are usually easy to obtain. A good source for larger reservoirs is the U.S. Geological Survey, Map Information Office, Reston Va., 22092. Maps of the numerous Tennessee Valley Authority reservoirs can be acquired by writing the TVA Mapping Service Branch, 200 Haney Building, Chattanooga, Tenn., 37401. State game and fish departments can also be good sources, as well as marinas and tackle shops around the lake.

"Once you've got your hands on a good map, your research has only just begun," McCadams continues. "While you are familiarizing yourself with the map and trying to conjure up a mental gameplan for a lake you're totally unfamiliar with, try to get your hands on some magazine articles about the lake.

"Go to the library and check the back issues of *BASSMASTER* and other fishing magazines for stories about the lake. Read everything you can get your hands on about that lake. You'll be surprised how well prepared you can get this way. You'll learn important things about the lake like whether its main cover is grassbeds or stick-ups or riprap. Or if it is a deep clear lake or a shallow-water lake that has mostly dingy water. That way you can prepare your tackle and tactics before you leave home. You'll know whether to bring an ultralight outfit with 4-pound test line for the clear, open water. Or 14-pound line on heavy tackle for fishing thick cover."

To make the job of researching magazine stories easier, first check your library's reference section for the Reader's Guide to Periodical Literature, an annual publication that lists the topics of stories in most major magazines during that year.

To gather enough information to ensure a good start to your vacation trip, Carle Dunn, a guide on famed Toledo Bend since 1978, recommends spending a few bucks on long-distance calls. He advises contacting marina operators and tackle shop owners to ask about local fishing techniques and areas of the lake that produce fish on a consistent basis. "Most marina owners will be happy to cooperate because they want you to be successful enough to want to come back the next year," Dunn says.

Dunn also recommends calling the local weather bureau to get information about traditional seasonal weather trends in that area. Traditional weather conditions can give you some idea of where the bass population may be positioned during that time of the year.

McCadams emphasizes the need for gaining a better understanding of man-made conditions, particularly water movement in the large reservoirs affected by power plant schedules. "In the manmade impoundments that are used for power, it's a good idea to get your hands on the schedule of when they'll be pulling water," he says. "And ask the locals how the fish generally react to the water when it's being pulled. That way, you can be sure to be on the water during the times when the fish are most active, even if it means night fishing."

"Letting this current work for you is one of the easiest ways to locate bass quickly."

Two obvious steps before leaving home: make sure that your tackle is rigged and in good shape; and take the necessary steps to ensure that your outboard is performing up to par.

Once you've learned everything possible about Monster Lake and its inhabitants, all of the guides and pros agree that your vacation time can be best spent by hiring a local guide for the first day or two.

Bill Vanderford, a guide on Georgia's Lake Lanier, says a day or so spent with a good guide will provide you with information that would take you a considerable amount of time to learn on your own. It can also help you eliminate unproductive water. Don't concentrate on catching bass during your guided trip, though. Vanderford advises paying more attention to learning to run the lake and understanding the fish-catching techniques used by the local guides and anglers.

If your budget doesn't allow the luxury of hiring a guide, there are several "rules of thumb" that the tournament pros and guides use for locating bass that might work for you.

George Medders of Holiday, Fla., a guide on Lake Tarpon and parttime tournament angler, always checks the obvious structure in an unfamiliar lake. It was a tactic that has worked for him and others in the unique format of the B.A.S.S. MegaBucks tournaments.

On the final two days of that tournament, the top 10 pros who survive the grueling four-day elimination format were placed on Little Lake Harris, a body of water that were unfamiliar with. The pros fished 10 designated spots, but are limited to an hour in each area. Considering their unfamiliarity with Little Lake

Harris and the time restraints, the pros are faced with the same dilemma that confronts thousands of vacationing bass fishermen each year.

The Megabucks finalists are forced to concentrate their efforts on the obvious structure, which included boat docks, bridge pilings, grass lines, the edges of lily pad fields and the mouths of canals that entered the lake. They simply didn't have time to scout the lake for more subtle types of structure like holes, ledges and submerged grassbeds.

"Obvious structure is a good place to start on any strange lake," Medders says. "Although obvious structure tends to get a lot of fishing pressure, those places usually hold fish."

Jack Hains, a guide on Toledo Bend, former BASS Masters Classic champion and past MegaBucks finalist, says he always approaches an unfamiliar lake by first looking for "a wood pattern. I always check for a wood pattern in places like a boat dock or fallen log or stick-up. Wooden structure is one of the most dependable places you can find to fish year-round."

Another dependable way to locate bass quickly is to understand the seasonal biological habits of the species, which positions the fish in the same type of areas each year.

Bill Phillips of Chattanooga, Tenn., one of the country's most respected fishery biologists and *BASSMASTER'S* senior writer of bass biology, says seasonal movement patterns provide good starting points for locating bass throughout the country.

His tips for each season:

SPRING. "The spawn will position the fish. If the water temperature is above 60 degrees, fish the shallows and work your way out. You may not find them in the shallows, but you'll certainly find them close (to shallow water in areas like) south-facing coves."

SUMMER: "In the summertime, I look for the thermocline (the layer of the coolest oxygenated water in a stratified lake) breakline and I concentrate on it. I use my depthfinder to locate the thermocline (which will appear on a chart recorder as a legible band) and I fish nearby structure that relates to it."

FALL: "In the fall, you have to work around the turnover period of the lake (usually during September and October in southern reservoirs), which is a time when fishing is always tough. (During the turnover period, changing water temperatures shift layers of water stratified by temperature. This results in the de-stratification of oxygen, causing the fish to become less active and harder to catch). I would talk to the local guides to try to plan my vacation before or after that turnover period. A couple of weeks after the turnover is completed, the fish can be found on normal fall structure patterns and they go on a pretty good feeding binge just before winter."

WINTER: "This is the time when I really rely on my depthfinder. I'm looking for forage (baitfish), not necessarily bass. Where I find lots of forage, I look for ambush points (around structure) at the depths that the forage is holding. Look for sheltered areas in the winter. I always look for either creek channels or river channels and where the two meet."

Guides Vanderford, Dunn and McCadams say a vacationing angler can often do well on a strange lake by applying some of the same seasonal techniques he uses on his home waters.

"A lot of fishermen seem to think that once they cross the state line, the places they find fish at home in the fall, for example, won't work on this other lake," McCadams says. "But unless you're talking about extremely different regions of the country, it's fall there, too, and the fish react very similar.

"When I go to a new lake, one of the things I automatically do is try to find something that mimics the things I have luck on at home during that particular season. If I've been catching bass off of tree-tops or blow-downs or the main river as opposed to backwater creeks and coves, those will be the first places I'll look for bass in an unfamiliar lake. If you had been catching fish on points of islands or in the back part of real small feeder creeks at home before you left for vacation, you should try those areas first. Heck, if it's April in Ohio, it's April in Alabama to the bass."

To maximize that precious vacation time, Carle Dunn recommends concentrating on one area, instead of doing a great deal of boat riding. He suggests selecting an area that has various types of cover and structure (for example: grassbeds that encircle standing timber). Another potentially productive situation would be a relatively small area that has both shallow-and deep-water structure.

Above all, says Bill Vanderford, find an area of the strange lake that you feel comfortable fishing.

"When I used to fish tournaments, we called it the confidence area," he says. "It's an area with the kind of structure and water depth that allows you to duplicate the kind of fishing style that you've done a lot of. I wouldn't try to go to a strange place and in a couple of days try to learn another man's way of fishing.

"I would try to find something similar to what I would normally fish and work hard on that area. In most cases, everywhere I went all over the country to fish tournaments, I could always find fish doing what I normally did during that time of the year on Lanier."

Vacation bass fishing doesn't have to be a humbling experience. With enough preparation and a gameplan for attacking a strange lake, the fishing vacation of your dreams can become reality.

Ken Cook's hand-operated trolling motor has been altered to enable him to manipulate it with his leg or foot.

Chapter 28

The Trolling Motor Choice

The 1988 BASS Masters Classic on Virginia's James River marked the first time that the 42 pros were given a choice between using a foot- or hand-operated trolling motor. Interestingly, that it is the same decision faced by the bass-fishing consumer.

Thirty-one pros chose a foot-operated version, while 11 preferred a hand-steered trolling motor. "That is slightly more than the national average we sell on bow mounts," according to a spokesman for MotorGuide, the official trolling motor for the '88 Classic. "Our average is 85 percent foot-operated motors."

PROfile

The reasons why the pros choose one type versus the other is intriguing and food for thought for the average angler. Even more interesting are the various alterations that the tournament warriors perform to the so-called hand-operated trolling motors to limit the amount of time they actually have to touch it with their hands.

Oklahoma pro Jimmy Houston is a two-time B.A.S.S. Angler of the Year and a 13-time Classic qualifier.

"This is the first Classic where we have a choice and I'm sure it has improved everybody's fishing," claims perennial Classic contender Jimmy Houston. "It is important to be able to fish the Classic with the type of trolling motor you are comfortable with. A foot-operated motor would be a handicap to my style of fishing, but you'll hear arguments in favor of both types."

Houston is a proponent of the hand-operated version — in his case, a MotorGuide 665, which has a foot-operated box with an on-off switch and variable speed control. But in Houston's case — like most of the pros opting for this type — the term hand-operated is a misnomer. Houston's trolling motor has a Big Foot extension that allows him to steer it with his knee or leg.

Two of Houston's main complaints with a foot-operated motor is it has more parts, making it more likely to malfunction on the water; and many versions require contact with a switch to keep them running, which can be tiresome, he says.

But the primary reason Houston uses a hand-op model is a strategic one.

"From a fishing standpoint, the hand-operated trolling motor allows you to be 18 to 20 inches closer to the front of the boat than a foot-operated motor where you're standing quite a bit farther back," he explains. "There is a real advantage to standing as far in the front of the boat as possible. Fishing is largely a matter of casting angles and the hand-op motor allows me to cast at angles up in front of the boat that can't be duplicated standing 18 to 20 inches farther back in the boat. I fish very, very close to my fish and with the angles I try to attack, I want the boat back and the cast to be slightly up in front of the boat. I personally believe this is very important."

To Houston, taking the proper casting angle means keeping a lure in the strike zone longer. Boat positioning and precise casting angles may not be important when fishing a large expanse of vegetation, but those aspects are greatly magnified when working individual objects like logs, stumps and treetops. For a spinnerbait enthusiast like Houston, casting from a position close to the bow of the boat is advantageous in those situations.

"I'll give you another example," he adds. "In this tournament, we have a lot of bright sunshine and you have to be sure to keep your shadow off of the fish. Again, if you have 18 to 20 more inches of boat between you and the fish, your shadow is going to reach your target a little quicker."

Veteran pro Basil Bacon agrees with the importance Houston places on standing as far up on the deck as possible. Renowned for his prowess at flipping, Bacon stands on a 14-inch raised deck he mounts to the very nose of his Ranger, which allows him to work well in front of the boat.

On-off and 12/24 foot switches are mounted in the deck extension and Bacon uses a hand-operated trolling motor that features an extended handle, which he steers almost subconsciously with his knee.

"I used a foot-operated trolling motor for three years and for three years I kept thinking that there had to be something better," Bacon says. "With my hand-op, I stand flat-footed all of the time. I don't have to kick one leg up and stand at an angle like you do with a foot-controlled motor. And I am as far on the front of the boat as you can go, which gives me a better position for flipping and pitching."

Shaw Grigsby prefers the foot-operated version, saying it enables him to keep both hands free and better concentrate on fishing. "It lets me steer the boat with a minimal amount of movement," Grigsby says. "And you really don't

Jimmy Houston believes a hand-controlled trolling motor keeps him in prime casting position.

have to stand on one foot. The base plate on most trolling motors allow you to put full pressure on it and I lean back against my butt seat for added stability."

Grigsby became a foot-control convert rather late in his career. MegaBucks finalist John Holley of Florida uses a hand-operated trolling motor adaptation that Grigsby designed that makes it more like a foot-operated model.

Holley's hand-operated motor does not have a handle. Instead, is is powered by a 8-inch oval- or duckbill-shaped aluminum plate that extends from the head of the motor and is supported by an L-shaped bracket that connects to the shaft. On the plate is a pressure-sensitive on-off switch that is wired straight into the head of the motor. To operate the motor, Holley keeps one foot on the nose of the boat, while the other rests on the duckbill. That foot both steers and operates the on-off switch.

"When you get used to it, the motor is super comfortable and the plate is almost strong enough to stand on," Holley explains. "This motor was made for precision casting because it puts you right up on the bow. I think it's the most efficient way to flip, pitch or make angle casts."

Ken Cook's Evinrude hand-operated trolling motor has also undergone considerable adaptation.

Cook uses a floor-mounted on-off switch and a Big-Foot extension to steer it. But what is unique about the motor is the way Cook is able to use his foot to change speeds. With his motor, like most hand-controlled versions, the handle is rotated to change speeds. To accomplish that with just the nudge of a toe, Cook has attached a 4-inch stainless steel fin to the handle using tie straps.

"That little fin sticks up and I can kick it down or up to go from one to three on the speed range," Cook says. "It makes it real easy for me to control the speed setting without ever using my hands."

Like the pros, the weekend fisherman is faced with choosing between a hand- or foot-operated trolling motor. And the pros say that is no small consideration.

"The moral of the story for the average angler is that he needs to give this some serious thought when buying a trolling motor," Jimmy Houston concludes. "Think about how you like to fish and the casting angles you use the most. If a guy likes to sit down and fish most of the time, I would recommend a foot-operated trolling motor. But you will catch more fish standing up and, I believe, that the hand-op is better suited for that type of aggressive fishing."

Chapter 29

Brushpile Condos for Bass

Georgia's Lake Sidney Lanier was no different from dozens of other aging manmade reservoirs, where the ravages of time had practically eliminated the very structure that its largemouth and spotted bass populations needed to survive.

Gone were the stump fields. Submerged tree tops, left standing when the Chattahoochee River was impounded 30 years ago, had long since disappeared. Blowdowns, as fishermen call trees that erosion and wind combine to push into the water's edge, were largely just a memory. Logjams and beaver dams had become history.

Except for piers and boat houses, wooden structure had become practically extinct on Lake Lanier.

Consequently, the bass and the bass fishing was suffering. The bass were left with a minimal number of areas that held enough wood to spawn around and provide shelter from its natural predators. The fishermen were left with the prospect of fishing deep, clear water without this valuable natural structure to concentrate the fish.

PROfile

Former Super B.A.S.S. champion Mickey Bruce won $100,000 in one tournament from his own brushpiles.

Faced with the prospect of watching the quality of fishing continue to decline, some Lanier locals, like Mickey Bruce, took matters into their own hands and began applying a little fishery CPR. They began planting brushpiles — wood pile condominiums for bass.

And it paid off. Suddenly, the impoundment's aquatic residents were finding new shelters around which to spawn and survive. In just a matter of a year or so since the first brushpiles were planted, the bass fishing improved significantly.

Brushpile farming paid off handsomely for Bruce, as well. The Buford bass pro, a past BASS Masters Classic qualifier, reeled in $100,000 worth of brushpile bass in the Super B.A.S.S.-II Tournament in 1983.

Naturally, Bruce is sold on the value of brushpiles.

"Any manmade lake that is 20 or 30 years old is going to be virtually void of structure, except for natural structure like rocks and drop-offs," Bruce says. "There is simply very little for bass to use for cover."

"But a brushpile offers everything a fish could want. It provides shelter from other fish for the fry. It provides an ambush point for adult bass to feed from. It provides cover from a bright sun or during a cold front. I believe a bass can live its entire life in a single brushpile."

After Bruce's brushpile bonanza in Super B.A.S.S.-II and subsequent similar tournament victories there, Lake Lanier underwent a complete transformation. Brushpile mania, you might call it. Where once there was not enough wooden structure in Lanier, now there is actually too much, according to Bruce and other Lanier regulars.

"When I won Super B.A.S.S., most fishermen around Lanier thought they could just throw a brushpile into the water and catch fish off of it," Bruce explains. "As a result, I challenge you to go out on Lanier with a graph or flasher and find a point that doesn't have a brushpile on it.

"There are too many brushpiles in Lanier now. The people around here have taken the lake and reversed the problem. Several years ago, a point or roadbed would have one brushpile on it and it would concentrate the fish. Rather than having to fish the whole point, you could pull up, fish that one brushpile, catch a fish or two and leave. You can't find a point on Lanier that doesn't have at least five brushpiles on one side of it and five on the other side. There too many brushpiles on Lanier today and that's almost as bad as not having any. It scatters the fish so much that it defeats the purpose of planting brush."

But that problem isn't common on most reservoirs. Although brushpiles have contributed to the resurrection of many impoundments, very few will ever suffer from brushpile mania because planting these fish attractors is hard work.

And planting brushpiles that are especially productive is anything but easy.

The best brushpiles are simply not found in obvious places like natural points, old roadbeds and creek mouths. The location of a brushpile is as important as any aspect of creating these bass condos.

"I think there's an art to planting brushpiles," says Neal Parker, a former Kentucky Lake guide and Classic qualifier who now lives in West Palm Beach, Fla. "Planting a brushpile is more than just dropping some brush in the water."

Since brushpiles are the only structure a bass angler can have all to himself — at least for a while — the experts say it is important to take some precautions.

Bernie Schultz (right), Shaw Grigsby plant part of a brushpile.

First, Shaw Grigsby advises planting the brush bundles in late evening or at night when there isn't as many fishermen on the lake.

All knowledgeable brushpile fishermen agree that brushpiles should be dropped in places where the average angler isn't going to stumble onto them.

"A point is an ideal place to plant a brushpile, but I try to put mine away from points and other places that people fish a lot," says Oklahoma's Tom Biffle, a former Classic qualifier who has about 60 brushpiles planted in Fort Gibson Lake. "Obvious places are like long points or any point that comes close to a creek channel. I look for places that are not obvious to the average fisherman."

To past Classic qualifier Rob Kilby of Royal, Ark., that means planting brush on open-water structure. His favorite and most productive brush is found at intersections of two (river or creek) channels where there is both shallow and deep water.

Three-time B.A.S.S. Top 100 Pro-Am champion Ron Shuffield of Bismarck, Ark., has planted more than 200 brushpiles in the 17,000 surface acres of Lake Degray, using one simple rule to determine where he anchors his brush. He looks for certain subtle changes in the bottom contour.

"The first thing I do is study a topographic map and concentrate on the contour lines," says Shuffield, who relied on brushpile fishing for nine years as a guide on Degray. "I try to find areas that I believe serve as feeding flats or shallow shelves located close to deeper water. Those types of areas are usually relatively void of cover, but hold fish because there is a change in the water depth.

"So instead of placing a brushpile on an obvious place like a point, I'll plant it near a drop-off. I've found that brushpiles in these places hold fish better than other locations of brushpiles because it doesn't receive nearly as much pressure as brushpiles in obvious places. Everybody fishes points or channels on a reservoir, but very few people look for the little subtle changes in the bottom contour, which is my key for selecting areas to plant a brushpile."

While Shuffield prefers relatively subtle depth changes as brushpile locations, Bruce says his most productive brushpiles are stationed along deep-water (at least 15 feet) breaklines that have a significant change in water depth. For example, the bend in an old submerged roadbed where the water drops from 20 to 30 feet would be a prime spot for a little aquatic gardening.

Veteran guide Harold Nash of Flowery Branch, Ga., who specializes in fishing Lanier, Oconee and West Point, prefers deep, open-water humps, which may be the hardest structure of all for the average angler to locate. This better assures him that his brushpile will not become public property.

While guiding on Kentucky Lake several years ago, Parker discovered something surprising about brushpile locations that he has used to his advantage since then. Instead of following one of the basic brushpile rules of planting brush near a drop-off, Parker found that brushpiles sitting in open-water flats in front of big bays and coves (but well away from significant depth changes) are surprisingly productive. "I've planted a lot of brush in the middle of the flats that are typically found between the coves and the river channel," Parker explains. "These brushpiles would be in the middle of nothing with the river channel a half-mile away. Yet, what I call off-structure brush would hold more fish than you ever would have believed, particularly during the hottest part of the year."

Regardless of where the brush is dropped, all of the experts agree on one fact: it should be planted in an area where the normal water level fluctuations of the reservoir will not leave it high and dry at certain times of the year. In addition to being practically useless during the driest portions of the year, that is an open invitation for every other angler to take advantage of your hard work.

The type of wood used to construct a brushpile will usually dictate how well (and how many) bass will be attracted to it.

All of the experts seem to agree that the small Christmas-type trees that clutter the neighborhood after each holiday season are poor choices for a brushpile that is intended to last as long as possible. In small lakes and canals in south Florida where little cover exists other than aquatic vegetation, several Christmas trees bundled together make a decent fish attractor. But they are practically useless in large reservoirs.

Oaks and other hardwoods seem to be the brush of choice among knowledgeable fishermen because they tend to be bigger and last longer. While the elements will gradually erode away any type of brushpile, the hardwoods have the greater staying power.

Cedar is a long-lasting and common material for brushpiles, but it is not a favorite of all brushpile experts. It provides excellent shade, but it is often so dense that it is difficult for a lure to penetrate. And difficult for an adult bass to position itself in.

Density of the tree limbs is an important consideration. "The most productive brushpiles have limbs that are pretty thick in terms of density," guide Nash says, "but at the same time aren't so thick that a decent-size bass can't swim in and out of it. The limbs have to be close enough to provide plenty of cover for the fish, but not really impede his movements."

The size of the fish attractor seems to be the subject of debate among brushpile fanatics. Some believe that the larger the brushpile, the more bass it will house. Others believe that bass are so territorial that the number of fish co-existing in any brushpile is limited.

Nash emphasizes that a productive brushpile will continue to produce only if it is replenished several times a year with additional brush. This helps counter the inevitable erosion that will occur.

Attention should be given to anchoring a brushpile. Most fishermen use concrete blocks and nylon rope, which will usually suffice. Others place the trunks of smaller trees inside the blocks. Roland Martin reminds us that brushpiles located in open areas of the lake are most likely to feel the brunt of the most wind and current, so they must be anchored especially well and replenished from time to time.

Just as planting brushpiles isn't as simple as it seems, taking the proper approach to fishing one of these brushy condos takes some consideration.

Since brushpiles are usually found in deep water and rarely visible from the surface, some skill with electronics is required to locate the brush. After finding the brush, knowledgeable anglers then mark it with a buoy or two. Shuffield advises not dropping the buoy directly over the brushpile, which could spook its inhabitants.

Brushpiles can be particularly productive during the coldest and hottest times of the year. But the methods of fishing it are as different as, well, winter and summer.

In the winter, most brushpile experts prefer to vertically fish the brush. The cold winter temperatures significantly slow the bass' metabolism, making it inactive.

This usually dictates using a slow up-and-down hopping retrieve with such lures as a jigging spoon, worm or jig-and-pork combination.

In the summer, the warm water changes the gameplan. The fish are much more active and likely to be moving around the brushpile, instead of holding tight as they tend to do during their sluggish winter mode. So most brushpile fishermen prefer to cast to the brush in the summer. In many manmade reservoirs, the typical clear water of summer demands casting instead of vertical jigging.

The most common lure choices for summer brushpile fishing are a plastic worm, spinnerbait and a crankbait (fished primarily around the edge of the brush). A deadly technique for catching summertime brushpile bass in relatively shallow water involves ripping a large-billed stickbait (like a Long A Bomber) across the top of the submerged brush top.

Casting to a brushpile requires the proper boat positioning. Biffle emphasizes the importance of casting to the tree from a position where you can best retrieve a lure through it. Note the position of the limbs when you plant the brushpile.

Because many brushpiles are positioned in open-water areas of the lake, brushpile fishing is often plagued by wind, the natural enemy of all bass fishermen. So the direction of the wind should be considered when approaching one of these fish attractors.

"I always try to position the boat so that I'm casting into the wind," Shuffield says. "I've always been a firm believer that fish feed facing the wind. Even if they aren't active, I think they position themselves facing the wind, regardless of the depth of the brushpile. I think that is the best way to give the fish the proper presentation and proper presentation is a key to effectively fishing a brushpile."

Tips for Planting Brush

When the brushpile craze started on reservoirs in the early 1980s, the banks soon became significantly clearer of undergrowth and fallen trees that ultimately assumed a position underwater somewhere.

Everybody got into the brushpile-planting act.

But there is much more to building brushpiles than just bundling up some branches and then dropping them overboard. Only the well-built brushpiles, constructed with considerable thought and effort, last long enough to achieve their purpose — providing shelter for bass in areas where such structure is limited.

Among the brushpile experts, the general theme is that bigger is better. The larger the brushpile, the more fish it can — and will — hold. Most say forget collecting all of the old Christmas trees in the neighborhood and tying them together in one big submerged pile.

Instead, brushpile veterans like Mickey Bruce suggest using several large trees like oaks and cedars to create a sizeable piece of structure. Most brushpile builders simply collect fallen trees from the shoreline around the lake or reservoir. Others use chainsaws to cut large trees down, but this should be discouraged since it is unethical and even illegal in some places to trespass onto a piece of property and remove a tree.

Once the trees are collected, it is advisable to remove the smaller branches, leaving the larger limbs in place. The idea is to create a piece of structure with enough limbs to provide shade and shelter, but without the smaller branches and brush that may make it difficult for the fish (and fishermen) to penetrate.

The trees should be tied together with a sizeable piece of quality rope that will not degrade with time. The rope should be bound around the trunk of each tree for added security.

Anchoring the brushpile is extremely important and the area where the most mistakes are made by well-intentioned anglers. Every brushpile should be weighted down and the most common method for anchoring is using a series of cinder blocks, which are easy to tie together and attach to the brushpiles.

There are two situations where anchoring is an especially important consideration — river systems and open-water areas. Areas that are subject to current and wind can quickly relocate a poorly-anchored brushpile. And although all brushpiles should be replenished from time to time, artificial reefs in those areas should be re-built more often than is normally necessary.

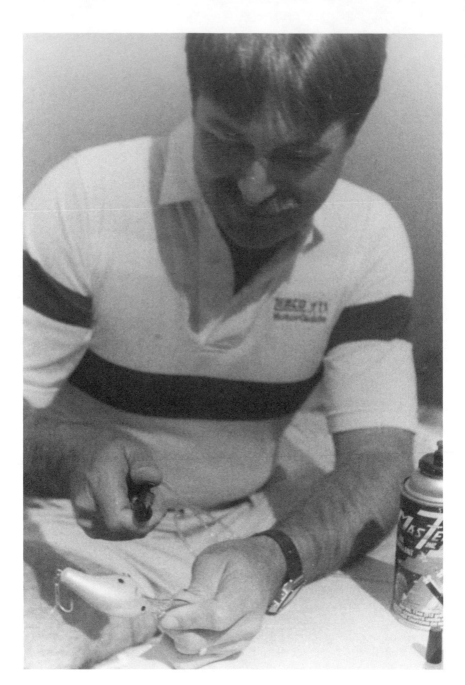

Some pros like Shaw Grigsby (above) and Zell Rowland use a portable airbrush paint system to instantly change hard lures.

Chapter 30

The Pros' Bag of Tricks

On the surface, the difference between the weekend angler and the big-league bass pro would seem enormous.

After all, the tournament pros spend most of their waking hours on the water, experiencing everything that those adaptable green fish can throw at them — while we struggle just to get a full day of fishing in during the work-week.

They travel the country in pursuit of fame and fortune and, in the process, become knowledgeable about all types of bass waters — while most of us struggle to improve our chances on our own home lake.

But, in reality, it's the little things that most separate the big-time tournament pro from the average fisherman.

"Probably the biggest difference between the pros and the weekend fishermen can be summed up in one word — resourcefulness," claims Jimmy Houston, two-time B.A.S.S. Angler of the Year and television-show host. "Through years and years of time spent on the water, we have developed tricks and back-up plans for just about any situation. Experience teaches you that stuff."

Ohio's Joe Thomas is the 1990 Red Man All-American champion and a three-time Classic qualifier.

Resourcefulness. Nowhere is that more evident than in the little ways that the pros go about their business.

Through the years, they have developed a plethora of little tricks and tactics that now translate into more consistent success. These sometimes minor efforts have a common denominator — they make the pros more efficient at their jobs.

In this case, efficiency means more time spent wisely and, in the game of tournament fishing, time is truly money.

"We all have our little tricks, things we do that make us more effective," says Ohio's Joe Thomas, a past BASS Masters Classic qualifier and winner of the 1990 Red Man All-American championship. "And we share these little tips among each other. Anything that enables you to better utilize your time on the water is important.

"I think the little things are some of the neatest aspects of our sport."

The contents of the pros' bag of tricks can be divided into three categories — boat rigging, tactical tricks and tackle tips. Individually, these tricks might seem trivial. Collectively, they can translate into hundreds of hours of time saved over the period of a year and — who knows? — be the difference between sitting at home or qualifying for the Classic.

For the tournament pros, their office is the 18 feet or so of their sleek bass boats. And, as with any type of office, they have experienced a sort of evolution that has developed some very efficient fishing machines.

All-time tournament winner Roland Martin's Ranger differs significantly from the boat that arrives from the factory. Martin uses a piece of thick plywood to build an elevated casting platform on the nose of the boat that is flush with the rail of his front deck. This carpeted platform provides him with an additional 5 inches of height, which he believes offers several advantages, including a better vantage point for spotting bass as well as allowing him to get closer to fish during the landing process.

Although it is not nearly as dramatic as re-designing his front deck, experience has taught Martin to keep an emergency system available in case of a malfunctioning livewell aerator. Martin's back-up consists of a 10-foot section of garden hose that is connected to a bilge pump. That little after-thought has saved him big bucks in past tournaments.

The trolling motor is an area where significant consideration has been given by the pros. Many of the pros have developed adaptations that enable them to better (or more conveniently) steer the boat without much conscious thought.

Oklahoma's Ken Cook is one of a segment of professional fishermen who prefer to use a hand-operated trolling motor. The hand-operated version allows the angler to stand closer to the front of the boat, where it is considerably easier to make precise angle casts.

Yet, most of these pros operate the hand-controlled trolling motor with their foot or leg. Two neat little adaptations that allow them to do that: Cook has attached a small aluminum fin (using metal strapping) to the handle of his trolling motor. To turn it off or on (as well as change speeds), he simply taps the fin with his foot — without interrupting his cast or retrieve. Tennessee's Charlie Ingram accomplishes a similar task by installing two pressure-sensitive buttons on the front deck of his Dyna-Trak. These buttons turn the motor off and on, but will not alter its speed.

Some of these modern-day alterations are changes that make so much sense that you wonder why they took so long to develop.

A prime example is Guy Eaker's unique, but common-sense trolling motor mount. The veteran North Carolina pro differs from most anglers by rigging his Stratos 295 Pro with the trolling motor directly in front of the nose of the boat. Most trolling motors sit off to the side slightly, but Eaker's motor functions from the front point of the boat.

"I never understood why they started putting the trolling motor on the side of the boat," Eaker says. "I think it's better for maneuvering the boat with it on the nose of the boat instead of off to the side. It's like the big engine on the back of the boat — it's right in the middle where it's going to operate best.

"There are two other advantages to doing it this way. If you are fishing around stick ups and heavy cover, there's always the possibility of catching a stick in a motor that's mounted on the side. With the motor mounted straight on, whatever you hit will usually glance off to the side. And with the motor mounted on the front of the boat, it reduces the wear and tear on both the trolling motor and the boat, particularly in rough water."

Eaker and many other pros are proponents of rigging a boat with a foot throttle, commonly referred to by the brand-name Hot Foot. A foot throttle enables the boat driver to keep both hands on the steering wheel, which has obvious safety advantages. And the foot throttle is more responsive to subtle changes in speeds than the typical hand throttle, which can be important when running through choppy water.

The pros give great consideration to how and where their electronics are rigged on their boat. That is perhaps the biggest area that the weekend angler overlooks.

"If you don't position your depth finders and transducers properly, you might as well not own any," explains Texan Randy Behringer, a two-time B.A.S.S. winner and deep-water specialist. "This is a shortcoming for most fishermen."

Behringer utilizes three depth finders — a bow-mounted flasher, along with an in-dash flasher and console-mounted paper graph. The transducers for the console units are drilled through the hull of the boat instead of mounted inside of the boat's bottom (the traditional method). The difference between reading the bottom unobstructed and coming through the hull of the boat is dramatic, Behringer insists.

The transducer for the bow-mounted flasher is attached to the foot of the trolling motor — standard practice among the pros. Having the transducer on the trolling motor allows the angler to position himself directly over deep-water structure, which can be crucial for vertical jigging or "doodling" a worm or tubejig.

Jimmy Houston prefers to use an in-dash flasher mounted flush into the nose of the boat. This allows him to instantly interpret its signal by simply looking down at his feet. "One thing that fishermen need to do is train themselves to watch that locator at all times," he advises. "It keeps you cognizant of where you are at all times. If you're working down a bank throwing a spinnerbait in 3 feet of water and all of a sudden you're in 7 feet, you've had something pretty dramatic happen that you need to check out — something that you could have easily missed by just glancing down at the locator from time to time."

In the interest of time and efficiency, Ken Cook mounted a leather tool belt pouch to the backside of his front deck. It holds scissors, pliers, a screwdriver and reel oil — essential tools of the trade — in a convenient location, while keeping the deck clear for fishing.

One of the most recent adaptations that is quickly gaining popularity among the pros is the use of saltwater sea anchors for freshwater applications. Florida pro Bernie Schultz, an avid saltwater flats fisherman, was among the first to see that these cloth anchors could be ideal for slowly drifting through a field of shallow submerged vegetation. The cone-shaped anchors expand and trap water inside (similar to a wind sock), slowing the movement of the boat significantly.

One area where the pros seem light-years ahead of the average angler is in emergency preparation. All of the pros keep a spare prop and trolling motor on board at all times. Many have a tool box stored below the deck and have enough knowledge of their equipment to use it in an emergency. "If anything goes wrong, I want to be in a position to fix it, rather than forfeit an entire day, which is what happened to Roland Martin and Woo Daves in the '89 Classic," says Shaw Grigsby, one of the most innovative and meticulous of the touring pros. "A tool box is a necessity. A lot of guys gamble their professions, but I won't. And it's the same with the weekend angler. If you only get to go fishing once a month, don't you want it to be a good day? This is one way to ensure that you don't have to give up and go home early."

It might surprise some fishermen to learn that an essential piece of Grigsby's fishing equipment is a microcassette tape recorder.

The Florida pro uses the recorder to make verbal notes throughout each practice day before a tournament, including where and how each strike occurred, weather conditions, temperature and so on. At the end of the day, he replays the tape, which enables him to visualize his practice period and, often, key in on important aspects that he might have overlooked. A review of his practice days often helps him recognize the best prevailing pattern and develop his strategy for the competition rounds.

After the tournament, Grigsby records information about the winning patterns and files the tapes on a lake-by-lake basis. "You don't have to be a tournament fisherman to benefit from using a tape recorder," he says. "It's basically like keeping records or a logbook. Even if you fish the same lake every weekend, an audio record can help you duplicate the ways you have caught fish previously."

California's John Bedwell believes that one aspect of fishing that separates the pros from the amateurs is the ability to utilize different types of casts for various situations. To score consistently, Bedwell emphasizes that an angler has to add an accurate back-handed cast and under-handed pitch to a typical arsenal that includes an over-handed cast and the ability to flip with some precision. "The best pros have worked hard at learning how to cast accurately with both hands," Bedwell adds. "This can come in handy when you approach a boat dock or a tree a certain way. Or when you are sharing the front deck with another tournament fisherman."

Although it doesn't take any particular skill, many of the pros put in long hours planting brushpiles in their home lakes — especially when there is a tournament on the horizon. Virginian Woo Daves spent two weeks dropping well-placed brushpiles in the James River in preparation for the 1990 Classic and those spots produced enough fish for a respectable fourth-place finish. The pros know that a strategically placed brushpile can be a bass magnet, as well as a piece of structure that they don't usually have to share with their fellow competitors.

Six-time Classic qualifier Kenneth Walker of Texas believes that the pros place considerably more importance to the art of boat positioning than the weekend warrior. Most fishermen don't take the time to plot the proper approach to a piece of cover or structure, he says. As a result, they cannot effectively work that spot and often spook its inhabitants.

"After you've fished a lot and become accustomed to operating a boat, boat positioning becomes second nature. For us, it's almost automatic," Walker says. "But most people need to be more conscious of it."

One tactic that is showing up more and more on the pro circuit is the use of a "comeback lure." When fishing a topwater plug, buzzbait or spinnerbait, pros like Californian Rich Tauber often keep a second rod rigged with either a plastic worm or tubejig. Any time that a bass misses the faster-moving lure, Tauber immediately makes a cast to the same spot with the comeback rod. "When the bass are really active and willing to chase a bait, the comeback lure works 90 percent of the time," he explains. "But not enough fishermen take advantage of that charged-up bass."

Give the tournament pros an opportunity and they will attempt to build a better mousetrap. Nowhere is that more evident than in their tackle adaptations and alterations.

Ken Cook, Charlie Ingram and others believe they have created a more efficient version of a spinning reel by removing the bail. They clip the bail off and then use a file to round off any sharp edges. "This eliminates line twist and also makes it a lot quicker," Ingram explains. "During a day's time, you get a lot more casts in because you don't have to flip the bail itself. Plus, you never have to worry about the bail-spring breaking.

"After making a cast, I catch the line with my index finger just before the lure hits the water and sit it back on the roller. It becomes an automatic movement after about 20 minutes of practice. It's just one of those little things that add up to more efficient fishing time."

Some alterations are born from discomfort. Roland Martin grew tired of bruising his stomach during a day of flipping heavy cover for big bass, so he added a piece of sponge to the butt of his flipping rod (using duct tape) — a simple, but effective solution.

Rick Clunn single-handedly changed the philosophy of many bass pros and brought the fiberglass rod back into the future several years ago. In the 1984 Classic, Clunn used an ordinary fiberglass rod to catch a record 75 pounds of Arkansas River bass in three days of competition and the fishing world took notice.

The fiberglass rod is simply a better tool for fishing fast-moving lures like crankbaits, according to Clunn, who believes that the more sensitive graphite rod actually causes the angler to respond to the strike of a fish too quickly. As a result, Clunn found himself taking the lure away from the bass before it could get it in its mouth. Many pros have followed suit and have returned to fiberglass rods for buzzbaits, spinnerbaits and crankbaits.

"I think preparation is something that separates the professional angler from ordinary fishermen and that is particularly true with tackle," claims perennial Classic qualifier Tommy Martin of Texas. "General preparation. Getting things ready. Making sure all of your tackle is functioning properly and you have back-up tackle in case you break a rod or whatever. Being fully prepared.

"Like tomorrow when I go out on the water, I will have back-up reels with the same pound test line that I plan to use in case something happens to a reel — like a bad backlash. In a tournament, I usually have about a dozen rods and reels rigged up in my rod box ready to go. I'll have a rod and reel set up for just about any situation. Flipping and pitching rods. Casting and spinning rods. Specific cranking rods. Rods designed to fish jerkbaits and small topwater plugs. I'll have something to cover every type of water and cover situation that I might encounter out on the lake."

Lures receive a great deal of attention from the pros, who never saw a bait that couldn't be altered to perform better.

Some pros like Texan Zell Rowland and Shaw Grigsby carry a portable airbrush coloring system (like the Master 7 system). These systems are easy to use and allow them to instantly change the entire color of a lure — or just alter it slightly. Its biggest advantage for the pros is its ability to instantly create a lure similar to the color that seems to be producing the best. For the weekend angler, a coloring kit could be a money-saver. Instead of owning several tackle boxes of hard baits, for example, a selection of white or pearl-colored lures can be doctored for each fishing situation.

And the pros have discovered the wonderful world of Super Glue. Florida's Steve Daniel uses the wonder glue to attach plastic trailers to spoons, spinnerbaits and jig heads. The trailer stays in place longer, which means more time fishing and less time re-rigging. And it saves money because a single grub will last for most of the day.

A final tip from Ken Cook that has enabled him to save considerable time. Cook uses a belt pouch (also referred to as a fanny pack) for storing the essentials for the type of fishing he will be doing on that particular day. For example, if he plans to fish a plastic worm, the contents of the pouch will include sinkers, hooks, beads and a handful of worms. If he is spinnerbait-fishing, extra baits, blades, skirts and trailers are stored in the pouch. "It just keeps you from having to waste time digging through a tackle box," he says.

The tournament pros and weekend anglers share a common desire — to spend their time on the water as efficiently as possible. Both know that efficiency translates into more consistent success. Armed with a few new tricks, any bass enthusiast can come closer to fishing like a pro.

SECTION THREE
PATTERNS & CONDITIONS

Large natural lakes and manmade reservoirs can be intimidating.

Chapter 31

Big-Water Shortcuts

As he steered his boat out of the Clewiston lock and through the main channel leading to Lake Okeechobee, Mark Davis' eyes began to widen, his jaws slackened.

This is Lake Okeechobee, he thought.

At 22, the Arkansas native and guide had rarely been out of the Ozarks and this was his first trip to Florida. And he had never seen anything quite like the Big O.

As he approached the open lake, Davis paused to survey the expanse of weeds and water before him. For as far as the eye could see — 730 square miles to be exact — was water and diverse vegetation. Nothing else. No islands. No trees. No brushy banks. Just a miniature ocean with lines of bulrush and peppergrass that rolled with the small open-water swells on this day.

"When I first saw Lake Okeechobee, it was overwhelming," remembers Davis, who had been brought to south Florida by the Bassmaster Tournament

Trail. "And intimidating. Here is this gigantic body of water and everything about it looks the same. It looked like it would be easy to get lost and I had this overwhelming feeling of not even knowing where to start."

Mark Davis survived the scare and did fairly well during the tournament. He went on to qualify for his first BASS Masters Classic.

Thousands of bass fishermen can identify with the emotions and thoughts that wracked Davis' mind. Whether it is a huge open-water lake filled with vegetation, a large manmade impoundment like Lake of the Ozarks or a massive, object- laden body of water like Toledo Bend, big water can be confusing to fish, at the least, and intimidating to attempt, at the most. Knowing where to start can be a major question for visiting fishermen and following the seasonal movements of resident bass can be a challenge for many regular fishermen of big-water lakes and reservoirs.

"A lot of people are intimidated by big water," claims Tommy Biffle, a veteran tournament pro from Wagoner, Okla. "But they really shouldn't be. There are ways to approach fishing big water that helps eliminate unproductive water and wasted fishing time. Those methods have really been developed by the pros who are fishing the national circuits."

The problem is time.

Few fishermen have the time it would take to thoroughly explore a major reservoir. And with big water like Okeechobee or Toledo Bend, it would take months to fish every potentially productive area. So learning to eliminate water is the first step in approaching a big-water excursion.

Experience is certainly a limiting factor in the ability to eliminate unproductive water and concentrate on the areas that hold the most potential. The tournament pros have been forced to accrue that knowledge and refine methods that will work on bass waters from Washington state to Washington, D.C. Their methods will pay off for anglers of all skill levels and living in almost any state.

Big water can be largely de-mystified before ever leaving home. Learning the lake and discovering potential starting points can be accomplished two ways before the boat is ever launched.

The more exotic way is arriving at the big lake or reservoir in time to charter a small plane for a brief flight over the water. This is particularly valuable with lakes that have aquatic vegetation and can be cheaper than hiring a local guide for a day.

"It depends on how serious you are about fishing," says Paul Elias, a past BASS Masters Classic champion from Laurel, Miss. "If two people go together, flying a lake is a pretty inexpensive way to quickly learn a lake.

"To me, flying a lake is the most effective way to form a quick opinion on how you should fish a lake. This is particularly true with a grass lake. You can see the way the grass breaks off on the channels and other key things. In the southern reservoirs that are shallow enough, I look for breaks in the grass or areas where the grass is the thickest. And you will find high spots where you can see the submerged grass from the air — spots that you might never go over if you were riding around the lake looking at your depth finder.

"The value of flying a lake isn't limited to grass lakes, though. I look for water color changes where dirty water mixes with clear water. In shallow-water

Bass waters don't get much bigger than massive Lake Okeechobee.

areas, you can often see underwater islands and humps and even the river ledge itself from the air."

A time-efficient approach to pinpoint potentially productive water that is much less expensive than taking to the air is dissecting a quality topographic map. Any knowledgeable bass angler understands the value of a good map.

There is a wide-range of maps available on most large freshwater lakes and reservoirs and their benefits are directionally proportionate to their detail and quality.

Even the least quality map has some value. Most limited detail maps at least mark navigational routes (including channels) as well as the location of creeks and other major features.

A quality topographic map can answer most questions about a large body of water by detailing lake elevations, depths, tributaries, permanent objects that potentially harbor bass (standing timber, stump fields, riprap, bridge pilings, dams and so on), main channels and bottom contour changes such as humps, submerged islands, ledges and small ditches.

Maps are like most other fishing tools — you get what you pay for.

"The first step for me is always getting my hands on a good topo map," explains successful western pro Larry Hopper of Santa Ana, Calif. "I heartily recommend spending time at home studying the map until you gain some understanding of its characteristics. Then when you get on the lake, it won't be like you're starting out on a totally foreign body of water.

"The next step is then convincing what you've learned from studying the map into a gameplan based on the time of the year."

Hopper's fishing maps are as colorful as a child's coloring book when he has completed his studying. After making a call to determine the likely lake level during his fishing trip, Hopper uses colored pens to shade in the desired seasonal depth that he plans to concentrate on. That simplifies his on-the-water map reading.

The value of map study can also vary from lake to lake. A few large body of waters have characteristics that don't lend themselves to map interpretation for locating bass. Texan Kenny Walker says "you can look at a map of Lake Okeechobee until hell freezes over and not accomplish anything. A map won't do you a bit of good on that lake because it has virtually no bottom structure change at all. But take the Thousand Islands area of New York, a vast expanse of water where a map is invaluable. You can learn more in three or four nights at home looking at a map than you would in days of riding around in a boat looking."

Somewhat surprisingly, Paul Elias insists that there is some value to map study for some veteran fishermen who know a particularly large body of water intimately. He points to Eufaula, Kentucky, Toledo Bend and several large Texas waters as massive lakes that can still harbor unpressured fish — which could be re-discovered with enough map study. "Take Eufaula, for example," Elias explains. "I think I could fish Lake Eufaula for 10 years and I could consult a map and still find places I would want to explore."

Obviously, map study will not solve all of the mysteries of approaching a large body of water in search of the mother lode of bass. Or at least, several bites a day.

To two-time B.A.S.S. Angler of the Year Jimmy Houston, the most important step is choosing a depth in which to concentrate.

"To be successful on any lake, a fisherman has to allow the lake to eliminate most of the lake for him," the Cookson, Okla., pro says. "You can let the lake eliminate the majority of the lake for you, as strange as that sounds.

"Early in his career, Bill Dance made the statement that 10 percent of the fishermen catch 90 percent of the fish and that 90 percent of the fish are in 10 percent of the water, too. I believe that's true. You can't take a 50,000- or 100,000-acre lake and fish it all. So you have to look at the lake and let the lake dictate the majority of the lake that you're not going to fish. You need to get that big water down to a workable part of the lake that you can fish.

"Most tournament fishermen eliminate much of the lake simply by a matter of the depth. That's a real simple criteria that almost anybody can use. If you catch 70 percent of your fish throughout the year in 10 feet of water or less, why spend any time fishing over 10 feet of water for that other 30 percent? Of course, the season will dictate the depth you should be fishing somewhat, but most of the time it is a good idea to fish within the depth range that you are comfortable."

Houston says that most of the successful tournament pros eliminate water over 25 feet deep and most weekend anglers concentrate their efforts in water 10 feet or shallower. "Stay within the depth that you are comfortable and don't make fishing so complicated," he advises. "If you take a spinnerbait and run it 5 feet deep, you'll catch a lot of fish. If you did that day in and day out, you would probably be about as successful as anybody. We've got some fishermen on the pro trail who do that and make the Classic every year."

Although it may be over-simplifying the approach in some cases, the pros have some valuable shortcuts for locating big-water bass.

Mark Davis recommends that fishermen look for certain areas or types of cover that they can relate to. Generally, he looks for large flats areas that have a change in water depth. It is even better if the area has a combination of structure or cover types. The water depth changes and differing structure increases the odds that the area holds a population of bass, Davis says.

Tommy Biffle agrees with that approach and often begins exploring a large body of water by starting in a creek or the river above the headwaters of the reservoir where he searches for bass by flipping a plastic worm or jig. "I like to concentrate on small, constricted areas instead of trying to cover the whole lake," he insists.

Given a limited amount of practice time in national tournaments, B.A.S.S. winner Shaw Grigsby selects a relatively small area like a major cove and explores it in search of the prevailing pattern. A cove offers a compact introduction to the most varied fishing situations usually found in a large body of water.

A major cove will likely feature primary points, secondary points, creek channels, backs of creeks and varying water depths. In essence, it can be a mini-reservoir in itself that can be thoroughly covered in a short amount of time and offers exposure to enough of the different variables that dictate existing patterns.

"The seasonal patterns will dictate which characteristics of the cove should be holding the most fish," explains Grigsby, winner of the 1988 and '90 Texas Bassmaster Invitationals. "You should systematically eliminate potential spots by starting with the shallow areas in the spring and fall and the deeper areas in the winter and summer."

Grigsby's seasonal starting points are shallow flats in the spring, creek channel edges in the summer, backs of coves and creeks in the fall and deep bends in the creeks and main river in the winter.

Paul Elias agrees with Houston's approach to eliminating water based on depth, saying "you can count on one hand the number of B.A.S.S. tournaments won by fishing deeper than 15 feet." However, Elias recommends concentrating on shallow areas adjacent to deep water, claiming that the majority of the bass in a lake or reservoir relate to deep water during most of the year. The exception is the various stages of the spawning season.

Elias believes that many bass enthusiasts would be more successful by keeping their approach to big-water bass simple.

"There are simple ways to catch fish on big water, even if you don't spend time studying a map," Elias explains. "One of the easiest ways is to fish the river channel itself.

"The river channel is marked in most areas, particularly in the southern reservoirs. You can just run the channel markers and fish the channel. You can see the bends in the channel just by watching the markers. Concentrate on the bends and fish both the inside and outside bends with a crankbait. And fish the channel markers with a worm or jig. You'll be surprised how successful you'll be just concentrating on the river channel."

Another simplistic approach Elias recommends is selecting a specific type of structure, marking them on a map and then fishing a series of those places. He cites backs of creeks, mouths of creeks, main lake points, secondary points or the rear of coves as prime examples.

Roland Martin offers this common-sense suggestion for quickly locating big-water bass: use a pair of binoculars to spot where and how the local experts are fishing.

"I'm not suggesting that you horn in on people, but it makes sense to at least know how others are catching fish," Martin says. "Use a pair of binoculars to see how they are fishing and where. If they are fishing what looks like a major point, you can then find a similar point and fish it with the same lures they are using. You may be able to duplicate their pattern in other spots."

Big water doesn't have to be intimidating. Some of the country's very best bass fishermen prove that even a simplistic approach to locating fish can tame the enormity of any lake or reservoir.

The Loran Advantage

Roland Martin was the first to apply the Loran to bass fishing.

For tournament king Roland Martin, it is just another tool that has helped him stay a step ahead of the competition.

For veteran Lake Okeechobee guide Glen Hunter, it has given him an edge against a different type of competition — consistently producing fish for his clients.

It is the Loran C navigational device, which helps the user to zero in on a spot time after time with amazing accuracy. The Loran, which has been used by ship captains and saltwater guides for years, translates signals sent out from transmitters scattered across the country into data that enables operators to navigate large expanses of water. Using coordinates that have been programmed into the device, it can be accurate to within 50 yards.

The Loran has always been considered a blue water device, but Martin believes its potential for bass fishing is greatly underestimated.

"The Loran will work on any lake where you can get more than two miles offshore," Martin explains. "It's ideal for using in the middle of Sam Rayburn Reservoir in Texas and it's an absolute necessity in the middle of Santee-Cooper (Reservoir in South Carolina). It would work well in Lake Murray in South Carolina as well as other large Florida lakes like Kissimmee and Toho. The lakes don't have to be huge for the Loran to be beneficial."

All major lakes and reservoirs harbor populations of relatively unmolested bass in the deeper, open-water areas where it takes considerable angling prowess and skill with electronics to locate and catch them. The Loran is one device that enables fishermen to return to these main-lake spots that are too far from the shoreline to allow cross triangulation with landmarks.

Martin, one of the few pros who uses a Loran unit, demonstrated the value of the device in the Florida Bassmaster Invitational on Lake Okeechobee in May of 1985. When the tournament began, almost all of the 258-man field headed for the cover that has made the Big O famous — various types of shallow-water vegetation. But Martin took an entirely different route.

In the middle of the open water in the southeastern corner of the 730-square-mile lake, Martin had located a series of unmarked holes, rock ledges and sharp drop-offs that were virtually ignored by the rest of the field. In fact, he was alone throughout most of the three-day tournament — an uncommon luxury on the tournament trail. Martin knew that low-water conditions, combined with hot temperatures would send the bass into these holes in droves.

This area had produced seven bass that weighed almost 50 pounds during his last practice day before the off-limits period and more than 50 pounds during the tournament. Located about four miles out, there were no trees or landmarks that could be used for navigational purposes. Relocating the holes and ledges would be practically impossible for his competitors, Martin believed.

But using the Loran C, Martin was able to get within 50 yards of the structure. Then he would kill the engine and use the trolling motor (and depthfinder) to locate the exact spots.

The Loran allows anglers to navigate accurately by providing such information as the direct compass course (indicating if you're veering off course to the right or left) and the distance from the programmed coordinates in nautical miles. It also computes the amount of time it should take to arrive at the desired location. A loud signal sounds once you are within a half-mile of the target.

Glen Hunter's involvement with a Loran unit is just another reason why he is one the country's most renowned bass guides. Few Lake Okeechobee guides utilize any electronics and most have never even heard of the Loran. But Hunter swears by it.

"The Loran takes me to places that are so difficult to find that they have fish that are never bothered," Hunter says. "There is very little competition for these fish. That's a big advantage."

Hunter uses the Loran for three basic purposes.

It is ideal, he says, for night fishing or running in the fog, he claims. Because Lake Okeechobee has so much vegetation it is usually impossible to run from one point straight to another. But his Loran unit will store up to 50 waypoints, which allow him to lay out a staggered course around major grasslines or spoil islands. Once he reaches a waypoint, he simply programs in the next.

The Loran makes locating both surface vegetation and submerged weedbeds in open water considerably easier. A slight chop on the water can make it impossible to see peppergrass lines that just touch the surface. But the Loran puts Hunter within 50 yards of it and, usually within sight of it. To pinpoint submerged vegetation, Hunter combines the Loran with his depthfinder.

Chapter 32

The Clear-Water Challenge

Georgia's Lake Sidney Lanier and Lake Mead in Nevada are a country apart in more ways than just geography.

Lanier is nestled in the lush, pine-tree covered hills of north Georgia. Mead, in stark contrast, is surrounded by endless miles of sheer rock canyon walls barren of vegetation, except for the pitiful weedy growth found in the deserts of the West.

PROfile

Yet, for all of the differences between the two, Lanier and Mead share a common characteristic much to the chagrin of many bass anglers. Both reservoirs are predominantly clear and that lack of water color poses the biggest challenge of all for fishermen of all skill levels.

We find ourselves faced with clear-water fishing situations across the country. The reservoirs of the West offer a crystal-clear view of the bottom as much as 70 feet deep. Older southern impoundments clear with age as the structure and cover erodes naturally. The famed smallmouth fisheries of the mid-South, particularly in Tennessee, feature deep, **Soft-spoken Pennsylvania pro Randall Romig is a six-time Classic qualifier who has mastered the deep, clear water mountain lakes in his region.**
transparent waters. And the natural mountain lakes in Pennsylvania and other parts of the Northeast have maintained the clear water that has filled them since creation.

In the bass-rich St. Lawrence River of upper state New York, you can see smallmouth relating to huge boulders 20 feet below. Sparkling clear water make the gravel banks of Arkansas' Bull Shoals Lake deceptively deep. Even in Florida, a state not usually thought of when discussing clear-water lakes, there are dozens of springs that daily pump untold amounts of the clearest, most pristine water found in North America.

So for thousands of bass fishermen, the clear-water challenge is a fact of life.

Clear-water fishing, the experts agree, is not an easy situation to overcome for the average angler. The vast majority of the bass fishermen in this country are more comfortable fishing off-colored and shallow water. Clear-water strategies usually revolve around fishing deep water, which is a whole different ballgame.

Before you can learn methods for catching bass in clear-water situations, it is important to first understand the difficulties involved.

"The biggest problem with clear water is that the fish have such high visibility, which makes them so acutely aware of anything intruding into their environment," says Dr. Loren Hill, chairman of the University of Oklahoma Department of Zoology and probably the foremost bass-fishing biologist in the country. "That high visibility and awareness can be tough on fishermen because it makes the bass a bit skittish at times. And even when the bass aren't spooky, the high visibility allows them to both see you (the angler) and get a close look at the lure you're using."

Scientific study has shown that clear-water bass depend more on sight than any other sense, much more than fish living in off-colored or even dark water (which use a combination of senses, most notably those that detect sound, vibration and smell). It is for that reason, Hill claims, that at night the clear-water bass are "more vulnerable to being caught than those in stained and muddy water."

Learning to fish clear water requires some major adjustments for many anglers. The first adjustment, says renowned bass pro Jimmy Houston, is psychological.

"The biggest obstacle is the psychological disadvantage of clear water," Houston explains. "Too many people let the thought that the water is clear and they can see the fish and the fish can see them psych them out."

Clear-water fishing usually means deep-water fishing, particularly in the manmade reservoirs.

In clear-water impoundments where most of the vegetative cover and wooden structure has eroded with time, depth becomes the only real form of cover available to the bass. The fish usually go deep enough to put a significant layer of water above them for several reasons including relief from the sun and protection from overhead, flying predators (a belief of noted big-bass expert Doug Hannon).

Since the majority of American bass anglers are more familiar with shallow-water fishing that means learning new methods for catching bass in what, for them, are uncharted waters.

Clear-water demands long casts, light line and down-sized lures.

"The hardest thing for a guy to overcome in regards to clear-water fishing, in my opinion, is the fear of fishing deep water," says three-time BASS Masters Classic qualifier Orlando Wilson of Woodstock, Ga., who grew up fishing Lake Lanier. "For instance, on a clear lake like Lanier, you'll usually have to keep your boat in 30 to 50 feet of water and cast into water no shallower than 15 feet. You lose the element of sight because you are fishing invisible cover or structure."

Deep clear-water bass are most often found relating to bottom irregularities such as humps, drop-offs, creek channel edges and bends, as well as any deep-water wooden structure a lake may have. For example, in Missouri's Truman Reservoir the bass often relate to the tops of standing trees (that top out well below the surface) in 50 to 60 feet of water.

Clear-water lakes that have vegetation are the easiest — by far to fish.

"The most frustrating type of clear lake, to me, is one that doesn't have any weed growth at all," says six-time Classic qualifier Randall Romig, who regularly fishes the deep, clear and rocky natural mountain lakes of Pennsylvania. "The fish in that situation have no escape from the sunlight other than to go deep.

"When you have a significant weed growth in a clear lake, the fish tend to relate to the weeds probably 80 percent of the time. Anytime you can find weeds growing in, say, 15 to 20 feet in a clear lake, you can almost be assured that there is going to be a certain amount of fish in it."

Deep-water eliminates several types of baits and the shallow-water techniques that the average fisherman is proficient at, Wilson explains. "There are very few baits that you can fish 15 feet and deeper, except for a plastic worm, jig-and-pig, jigging spoon and a spinnerbait — to some degree," he says.

"You've eliminated almost all of the crankbaits on the market, except for some of the new ones that sink. I think the new super-deep crankbaits like the Bagley Dredge, which is weighted, have opened up a new area for bass fishing. The other super-deep baits that claim to run 20 feet deep still require light line, the skill to make a long cast and retrieve the crankbait at the proper speed to even approach that depth."

Light line, the experts agree, is the key to scoring with clear-water bass.

Former Classic qualifier and Lake Ouachita (Ark.) guide Mark Davis is typical of most clear-water specialists. He uses light spinning tackle and 6- or 8-pound test line. The diameter of the line is under more scrutiny with clear-water bass than in other situations, so Davis emphasizes using the smallest line size possible.

Romig takes the down-sizing of line theory a step farther. He also scales down the size of his lure in clear-water situations.

"The fish have a real opportunity to get a look at the lure in clear water and, typically, the smaller baits seem to draw more strikes than larger ones," says Romig, one of the most quietly consistent pros on the Bassmaster Tournament Trail. "If you use a great big plug with a bunch of treble hooks hanging from it, the fish gets a good look at it and he can easily see that it's fake. Where as with a small, compact lure, they don't get as good a chance to eyeball it."

Small, finesse-type lures, often called sissy baits, have become standard equipment, both on the tournament trail and aging southern reservoirs where the toll of time has eroded away wooden structure such as standing timber, stump rows, blown-down trees and logs. In these impoundments where the invasion of exotic vegetation such as Eurasian milfoil and hydrilla hasn't taken place, finesse baits such as the Fat Gitzit (a hollow-bodied tube-skirted jig), small grubs and (4-inch small diameter) worms are gaining popularity.

These lures have exposed hooks, which make it, largely, impractical to fish around vegetation. But they can be limit-catchers when worked around bare bottom structure.

These light, slow-falling lures are especially productive tools for catching suspended bass, which Mark Davis says "are often a fact of life with clear-water lakes."

For situations when the bass are relating more closely to cover and, generally, more active, a slow descent is not usually productive, according to Romig.

"One of the factors that often isn't mentioned in clear-water fishing is the speed of retrieve," he explains. "Although the season of the year and the metabolism of the fish should be taken into consideration, with clear water, as

Arizona's Greg Hines knows that the plastic grub is an excellent clear-water lure.

a general rule, I think you have to fish your lure two or three times faster than you would in a dingy-water situation. That's a real key in clear water. You don't want the fish to get a good look at it, so you need to move it faster than you would in off-colored water."

Locating bass in clear lakes and reservoirs is simple, but misunderstood — just like clear-water fishing itself — claims Californian Rich Tauber, who was raised on the crystal-clear reservoirs of the West. Having grown up with clear- and deep-water fishing, Tauber says there is no mystery involved.

He even makes it sound simple.

"To me, clear water is the easiest water to fish," Tuber says. "This is why — you can see everything.

"You can see where the fish are going to be. The bass are not going to be out there in the middle of nowhere in clear water. He will be oriented to something. So what do you do when faced with a clear-water situation? You fish the biggest, most obvious cover down in the water that offers the fish shade, protection and an object to relate to. Clear water is the greatest water eliminator in the world. You can drive the lake and tell everywhere that the fish can't be."

Included in the obvious cover that Tauber looks for are weed beds, large rocks, shade pockets and over-hanging cliffs — "anything that provides an umbrella of shade for the fish."

Once the fish are located, Tauber emphasizes using light line and making long, accurate casts. It is important to stay well away from the bass in clear water, particularly on calm days when a boat is easily visible in the water from a distance.

Four-time Classic champion Rick Clunn of Montgomery, Texas, has won two national tournaments in the clear water of Lake Mead, primarily, on the strength of shallow-water fish. He is a walking contradiction that clear water automatically dictates deep-water tactics.

"It is a fallacy that you have to fish deep to catch bass in clear water," Clunn says. "There are resident shallow-water fish in clear lakes year-round. There are certain times of the year when there will be less fish shallow than other times.

"There's no doubt that the majority of the fish in a lake like Mead are deep, probably 80 percent of them. You just have to evaluate in your own mind — 'Am I more efficient at catching that 20 percent that is shallow or that 80 percent that are deep?' In my case, I'm better at catching the 20 percent that are shallow, even though 80 percent are deep. No doubt, the average guy is more efficient in shallow water, too."

Both Clunn and Houston agree that the key to catching clear-water bass in shallow sections is the amount of wind blowing into that area. The wind acts as cover of sorts, refracting the sunlight to the point that the surface of the water is a jumble of wavy lines that makes seeing a boat in the distance practically impossible.

Wind will also sometimes move baitfish into an area and keep them piled up against the shoreline. That will move the bass shallower, making them more accessible.

Houston calls wind "one of the premier covers for clear water" and says that without the disruption of the wind, "the fish can see you so well that you almost can't get back far enough and still be able to cast to them."

On calm days, Houston resorts to a ridiculous-sounding trick that has paid major dividends for him in Lake Mead. He will pull into a small cove (that he believes is holding fish) and then run in a circle four or five times in the middle of it. While his man-made waves swamp the shoreline, Houston quickly grabs a rod and begins to fish it. "In other words, create your own wave action," he says. "I've done it quite a bit and it definitely works.

"It works for the same reason that some areas of a clear lake will produce more fish just because there is more weekend boat traffic that creates waves."

Catching a limit of resident shallow-water fish in a clear lake may require covering a great deal of water to execute what Clunn calls an individual fish pattern. According to his 80-percent-deep/20-percent-shallow theory, there will usually be a limited number of bass holding in shallow areas. In lakes like Lanier, you can find individual bass relating to the same shallow structure, such as boat docks. But Clunn emphasizes that you will have to burn some gas to collect a limit. "You can't go in one area and stay all day long," he says. "You don't have that luxury with resident shallow fish in clear water."

There is certainly a challenge to catching bass that you can see — and that can see you. But clear water is a fact of life in a growing number of states. So it is becoming increasingly important to learn more about what it takes to catch fish in a visual situation.

Years of experience on lakes throughout the country has enabled Woo Daves to catch bass under the toughest conditions.

Chapter 33

Scoring When It's Tough

With enough practice, casting accuracy can become simply an afterthought. With enough experience, boat positioning is easily mastered.

The ability to read a topographical map and the reliability of a personal fishing log will point you toward the area of a lake or reservoir with the most potential during that particular season. Today's high-quality electronics help the angler keep his lure in the strike zone at all times. Lifelike artificial lures fool bass like never before. And paying attention to meticulous detail (sharpening hooks, changing line regularly, re-tying often and so on) will eliminate most mistakes once a bass strikes.

PROfile

Florida's Steve Daniel, a transplanted Tennessean, is a three-time BASS Masters Classic qualifier.

The sport of bass fishing has never been so much under control, right?

That is a good theory with a serious flaw — weather, the one aspect of bass fishing that is completely beyond any control.

Weather. Fishermen rarely see weather that they like. It's either too warm or too cold or too bright or too overcast or too windy or not windy enough. Bass anglers are certainly picky when it comes to the elements.

And then there are the most severe weather conditions, times when bass fishing becomes more survival than sport. There are certain conditions — both natural weather acts and manmade water-level manipulation — when bass fishing is at its challenging best and frustrating worst.

These are the times when most anglers head for shore. Only the most dedicated fishermen endure these periods when the odds, for the most part, are blatantly against catching a decent stringer. But these bass enthusiasts know that bass can be caught under any circumstances.

The nation's tournament pros are a prime example of this. The vagabond pros don't have the choice of when they fish and, with their livelihood on the line, must persevere through the worst possible conditions. And it is through this forced process that the pros have discovered the best methods for combatting the worst that weather can throw at them and still bring fish to the scales.

There is a great deal that we can learn from the techniques they rely on for Scoring When It's Tough. Here are the toughest times for catching bass and the methods that will increase your odds of succeeding.

It has happened to all of us.

Arriving at the launch ramp, you discover that several days of relentless rain has transformed your local lake into a sea of brown soup. Just the sight of muddy water is enough for most anglers to simply put the boat back on its trailer and head for home. After all, muddy water means that the bass will not be able to utilize their most powerful sense — vision.

"But muddy water isn't all bad," claims Rick Clunn. "Muddy water doesn't mean that your chances of catching fish are over. Fishing muddy water just means that you have to change your approach."

Clunn prefers off-colored water — muddy, murky or stained — over a clear-water situation. Muddy water actually provides the angler with some advantages over other types of water clarity, he claims: it positions bass at a predictable depth; the fish tend to be less spooky; and dark-water bass are more likely to attack a lure invading their territory than those who can examine it in clear water.

When faced with muddy water, a rule of thumb is to fish in 2 to 5 feet of water and stay near the bank. Bass in muddy water will almost always be positioned shallow. Since muddy-water bass depend almost entirely on hearing sound and detecting vibration, Clunn prefers to use bulkier lures that displace water, creating more vibration. His muddy-water choices are a big, shallow-diving crankbait, large-bladed spinnerbait, bulky jig-and-pork combination, buzzbait and fat plastic worms like the Ditto Gator Tail.

The only times when muddy water is almost impossible to overcome is when it is cold (below 50 degrees) or freshly churned up (suspended particles in the water affect the food chain and confuse a bass' senses). Fish the shallowest, sunny banks to find the warmest water. And when the lake is in the process of becoming muddy, concentrate your efforts around large beds of aquatic vegetation, which help strain the floating particles in the water.

No two words are more despised among the bass-fishing fraternity than "cold front."

The usual foreboding of its appearance occurs late in the afternoon when the wind starts to build and the barometric pressure begins to plummet. The temperature drops 10 to 15 degrees during the night as the wind continues to howl. The next morning finds the clouds beginning to break-up and dissipate. The barometer soars to announce the coming of the worst part of a cold front's passage — bright, clear skies often referred to as "bluebird days." The barometric pressure then stabilizes high.

And the bass in the area become different creatures. The barometric pressure affects the fish's metabolism, according to biologists, making them sluggish and inactive.

"A lot of fishermen simply give up and throw in the towel when a cold front passes through," says Ken Cook, a highly successful tournament pro and former fisheries biologist in Meers, Okla. "While it may not be the best condition for fishing, there are ways to catch bass under these circumstances."

The first step toward scoring under cold-front conditions, the pros agree, is making a mental adjustment. They recommend adjusting your attitude to accept the fact that the conditions will yield a limited number of strikes, which makes concentration and execution especially critical.

To locate cold-front bass, the experts agree that deep-water (15 feet and deeper) fish are less affected by a frontal passage than those holding in shallow water. Shallow-water bass will usually move to the thickest cover in the area or, if no cover is readily available, to a nearby breakline (like a drop-off along a creek channel). Big-bass expert Doug Hannon says the key to re-locating bass that move in response to the effects of a cold front is noting their position before the weather front arrived. With that knowledge, you then look to the nearest cover or drop off.

There are several tried-and-true tactics that will score best when the bass are least cooperative. First, concentrate your efforts around the densest vegetation, brush or other structure with accurate casts and precise lure presentations tight to the cover. Secondly, light line and small baits seem to produce best. And, finally, slow down. Cold-front bass will not aggressively pursue a baitfish — alive or artificial.

The key to catching bass, for most of us, is the fact that largemouth, smallmouth and Kentucky spotted bass are structure-oriented creatures. We target bass by fishing the most likely structure that could provide shelter for fish.

When bass suspend, the entire game changes. When some type of unusual condition drastically alters the bass' world, it often responds by moving away from cover or structure and seemingly positions itself with no relationship to any part of its habitat.

It's important to understand the reasons why bass suspend: low metabolism — the temperature extremes of winter and summer most often trigger the suspending instinct, according to Dr. Loren Hill, a renowned bass biologist; cold fronts — some bass often lose contact with the shoreline or bottom during its passage; baitfish movements — bass will often suspend under a school of baitfish, regardless of the submerged terrain below them; drawdowns — bass often respond to a severe water-level drop by suspending in open water; fishing pressure — Hill believes that bass in certain heavily-pressured lakes and reservoirs behave differently on the weekends when the water is most crowded.

"Suspended bass are less likely to bite because they aren't object-oriented," explains Rich Tauber, one of the most successful western bass pros. "They're not using the cover or structure for a point where they can ambush something. They're out in the open water and not in an ambushing position. You almost have to bump your lure right into the fish's nose to get a reaction strike."

The first step toward scoring on suspended bass is determining the exact depth at which the bass are staged, according to Joe Thomas, the 1990 Red Man All American champion who studied fisheries biology in college. He utilizes his electronic eyes to get a general idea of the depth and then uses a crankbait to pinpoint it even further. A single strike can lock Thomas in on the exact depth and signals him to slowly work that level with a finesse lure like a plastic worm or small jig with a tiny pork trailer.

With suspended bass, it is important to use a lure that allows you to probe the exact depth of the fish. That task eliminates some baits. Standard suspended-bass lures are a lead spoon, plastic grub, rubber-skirted jig, tubejig and small diameter worm. These lures can be fished on light-line (which is especially important with suspended bass) and presented vertically to the sluggish fish.

There is a love-hate relationship that exists between reservoir fishermen and those who control its water level. Bass anglers love it when those in control pull water for industrial (usually electrical power) uses because the moving water seems to make fish more active. But let the water level drop drastically over a short period of time and the anglers turn on them with the aggression of a pit bull.

Few anglers understand the difficulty that falling water causes as well as Gary Klein. Although the top tournament pro now lives in Texas, he was raised on California's Lake Oroville, which fluctuates as much as 92 feet vertically over the course of the year. Klein has watched the reservoir rise as much as 24 feet over a 24-hour period and the bottom fall out overnight.

"Rising water isn't really much of a problem," Klein explains. "Rising water puts fish shallower and they are easy to figure out.

"But falling water can create a tough situation, particularly on certain types of impoundments at certain times of the year. The difficulty, obviously, with falling water is re-locating the fish. The dropping water will move them off of the obvious places where they have been and you have to hunt them."

Chet Douthit, an accomplished tournament fisherman and former guide on Missouri's Truman Reservoir, emphasizes that re-locating falling-water bass is just Part One of a two-part dilemma. "Bass in a falling-water situation just aren't active for a while," he says. "They will be disoriented for a while until the lake level stabilizes somewhat. At that point, my best advice is to move to the nearest deep structure to where they had been holding before the water began falling and fish slowly."

Douthit's most effective weapon during this treacherous time is a jig-and-pork combination. It is a lure that can be presented vertically, which is important with these bass, which tend to be suspended.

Fishermen of all types complain about the wind more than any element of the weather. A bass angler has never met a wind that he liked. Usually, the complaint centers around the strength of the wind, which makes it difficult to maintain boat positioning, make accurate casts and sustain contact with a lure. But there is an even worse consideration with the wind, according to Steve Daniel.

"Probably the toughest time to catch bass is on real calm days," claims Daniel, a three-time Classic qualifier and guide on Florida's massive Lake Okeechobee. "When you have enough wind to put a chop on the water, the fish are going to be a little more active. The water will be a little darker and the fish will roam around a little more. The days when the wind doesn't blow at all affect shallow fish especially.

"I think bass are a little more light-sensitive than we realize and the lack of wind will allow the sunlight to penetrate the water better. Shallow bass just won't roam as much. They will feed early in the morning when the light is low, but that's about the only time. Ninety percent of this game is being around feeding fish. Anybody can catch them if they're feeding. But if they're not feeding, it's hard to catch them. That's when you have to pull out all of the tricks you've learned over the years — and sometimes nothing works."

Daniel's most effective way to combat calm days is to concentrate on scattered patches of vegetation with a fast-moving lure like a topwater plug or vibrating, shallow running crankbait like Rat-L-Trap or Cordell Spot. These lures allow him to cover a considerable amount of water in search of fish and can trigger a reactionary strike. That is important with bass that are not actively feeding.

Butch Ray witnesses the same scenario every weekend.

Ray is a guide on Texas' Lake Fork Reservoir, which may be the best big-bass lake in America. Located less than 90 miles from metropolitan Dallas, Lake Fork gets an enormous amount of fishing pressure every weekend. And the bass respond to that increased fishing pressure.

"Amazingly, these fish adjust to the weekend pressure," Ray says. "On Friday at mid-day when the boats start arriving, the fish stop biting. Period. In the spring time when they're on the beds, they move off. When Monday morning arrives, it's as if you had set an alarm clock. They'll be back in position and feeding again. There is no question in my mind that these fish behave differently when the weekend pressure arrives."

From extensive tracking studies of bass living in reservoirs that are heavily utilized, Dr. Loren Hill firmly believes that bass behave differently on the weekend, as a result of increased fishing pressure and surface commotion. Using telemetry units implanted inside of bass, Hill has noticed that the fish tend to move off and suspend more on the weekends.

"When the boat traffic elevates, their behavior changed (in the studies)," Hill adds. "They moved out down to here on Friday and then on late Sunday or Monday, they would come back up and have a different pattern — move around in a different manner. It's amazing how much their basic (behavioral) patterns changed when the weekend arrived."

How can the anglers who share these waters succeed on the weekends, which may be their only time to fish? Be different.

The key to scoring in such a pressured situation is twofold. First, fish areas that the crowd overlooks. This could include secondary structure on a point or the submerged outside edge of a weed bed. These pressured bass will move off to some type of cover or structure adjacent to their usual lair. Secondly, use a different lure or technique from the majority of the fishermen. If most of the anglers are flipping big baits on heavy line, try making long casts with finesse lures on light line.

If it is impossible to escape the crowds, use a different lure and take a varied approach. In other words, mix up your casting position and angle of retrieve. This will provide the bass with a new look and might just trigger a reactionary strike.

You can catch bass in a crowd — and under almost any condition, no matter how difficult. Armed with these tips, there is rarely an excuse to surrender.

Chapter 34

Timely Tips for Tidewater

When the Bass Anglers Sportsman Society tournament trail made an unusual stop at the Hudson River in late 1984, the world discovered what Roland Martin had learned early in life as a young man growing up in eastern Maryland.

PROfile

When the tournament produced more than 2 1/2 tons of bass and set a B.A.S.S. record with 308 limits, it was hailed as the rebirth of a great old river, the Miracle of the Hudson. Local anglers bemoaned the fact that their secret was revealed. But it was no surprise to Martin that he won the tournament with ease, catching 15 bass that weighed an impressive 50 pounds, 2 ounces and outdistancing Ohio's Larry Williams by almost 13 pounds.

All-time tournament winner Roland Martin was raised on the tidal waters of eastern Maryland.

Roland Martin has known for quite a while now just how good fishing tidal rivers like the Hudson can be.

"The Hudson River was the epitome of good tidal fishing," Martin says.

"Tidal fishing can be some of the finest fishing you'll ever experience and it can be a very predictable type of fishing," he continues. "One reason tidewater bass aren't hard to catch is they simply don't get heavy pressure.

"I can't stress enough how many acres of good bass waters there are in tide creeks compared to the small percentage of bass fishermen you'll find there."

But with performances like Martin's, that should change somewhat in the future.

One factor about fishing tidal conditions rarely changes — the predictability of its patterns.

"There is a pretty good degree of consistency with this kind of fishing," Martin says. "The main patterns really seem to hold up well. When you find a tidewater pattern, you treat it differently than you would in a lake. To me, a tide pattern is a more positive thing. You can really work it. You might find a beautiful boat dock in a lake and catch a lot of fish and think you can duplicate that pattern at other boat docks in the lake. But you might not be able to. It's much more difficult to duplicate a pattern in a lake situation. A river just doesn't change much.

"But to take advantage of it, you have to understand that this kind of fishing has a lot of changes that occur quickly. You can't be fooling around. With tide fishing, you have to know your tide tables well and the speed of that fill-in (incoming tide) and, boy, you have to move quickly. You have to be ready to go."

The key to tidal fishing, most pros agree, is being in likely spots during the changing tide. Martin particularly likes an incoming tide that moves water into the main river or channel. And he took full advantage of that piece of predictability during the Hudson River tournament.

"The secret to tidewater fishing is running the tide," Martin says. "Whatever pattern you find that works, then you can run the tide and basically duplicate any pattern for a period of time by running in front of the tide.

"I developed this gameplan 20 years ago. What people don't realize is that the tide doesn't arrive, say, at 10 o'clock throughout the whole tidal river. It's not all high at 10 o'clock. Say you have a 80- or 100-mile tidal system. It's going to take many hours for the tide to get to the upper end.

"With the advent of today's fast boats, you can run ahead of the tide and keep duplicating your pattern throughout the tidal system. Back in the '60s when I first learned this way of duplicating a tidewater pattern, we didn't have boats that ran 60 miles an hour, so we couldn't beat the tide as well as we can today. But we did our best to stay out in front of the tide as long as possible.

"Today, we're able to run down river on a falling tide — as the tide falls — and keep going in front of it and keep taking advantage of it. If you run fast enough, you can maybe make three or four stops at the same tide level and fish for three hours or so."

During the Hudson tournament, Martin ran 60 miles south each day to get into position to fish beds of milfoil, an exotic vegetation, during the tidal change, which creates current and makes bass more active. By calculating the tide tables and the speed in which the tide changed, Martin put together a stop-and-go pattern of running and fishing that put him in position to cast to the best types of structure at the right time and water level.

Successful tidal fishing involves running the tide, according to Martin.

"I would run to a spot, fish it during the tide change and when I sensed it was about over and the water had gotten too high for my pattern, I would then crank up the big motor and move along the river to another spot where the tide change was beginning to occur," Martin explains.

"That hectic pace of fishing a while and running to another spot kept me fishing during the tide change all along the river.

"It put me in the ideal position for tidal fishing, because the fish move and bite with the tide change and that's definitely the key to catching a lot of bass on tidal rivers like the Hudson."

While Martin insists that a variety of lures will work during the tidal change, his tournament success came on the strength of his prowess with a willow-leaf spinnerbait.

"On the surface, tidal fishing might look difficult," he says. "After all, you're dealing with a body of water where the water level fluctuates a great deal twice a day.

"But it doesn't have to be. There are a couple of simple patterns and techniques that can make it a lot easier. First of all, I prefer fishing the lower ends of these tidal river systems and using a falling tide pattern and moving a lot.

"A very simple pattern is fishing when the water is pouring into the river. On the lower end of these tidal systems, characteristically, you have a marsh system that surrounds the main river or creek. On a falling tide, the main river is lower than this bulrush-type swamp which will drain into the river as the tide goes out.

"So you have all of these little sloughs and drains pouring into the river, little, small tidal tributaries. The marsh has countless little channels that funnel together that are too small to navigate, but finally come into the main tide creek. When the water falls, these huge marshes drain into little feeders and cuts, so all of the fish are moved into these little waterways that empty into the main tide creek.

"These little entrances are usually very small and where they enter the river is real structure. A good tide creek might have 10 or 15 feet of water, while the marsh on the outside might be only 2 feet deep during high water. And these little feeder creeks are maybe 4 or 5 feet deep when they enter the river. So you always have a little ledge there where the incoming water drops into the main river."

"By positioning your boat correctly, Martin says it's easy to cast to the entire mouth of these little tributaries and the underwater ledge created by this influx of higher water into the lower main river. "Cast up into these little openings and the lure will float down like the baitfish do," Martin adds. "And you're going to catch fish."

For this falling tide pattern and working the mouth of these small feeders, Martin says most types of lures will produce fish. That ranges from deep-running crankbaits to plastic worms because you're dealing with bass that will usually be actively feeding.

By calculating the speed of the tidal stage and learning the tables, you can be in this position during the ideal changing tide throughout the lower portion of the river system. "In some cases, you're talking about running and fishing 20 and 30 miles of the lower tidal system and duplicating the pattern as you go along," Martin adds.

Understanding the characteristics of tidal systems is the key to consistent success, Martin insists.

"If you learn something about tide rivers and creeks in general, you'll be ahead of the game," he continues. "For example, the farther north you go, the higher tide you'll have. In New York, you'll have 6 and 8 feet of tide. In Florida, you'll only have a foot or two of tide.

"In a place like Maine, there are gigantic cranberry marshes that on a full moon can produce a 15-foot tide. But a real high tide condition like that is not too good for bass. That's just too much tide. It seems like your good bass tidal waters are places like the Chesapeake area or Currituck Sound in North Carolina where you're dealing with tide of about 2 feet.

"On the Hudson, you deal with 5- or 6-foot tides. That's the highest tidal fluctuation I've ever attempted to fish. That's a lot of flow."

When calculating the tide change and speed of the flow, Martin suggests taking the speed and direction of the wind into consideration.

"An important thing you have to remember about fishing tidal conditions is that wind will influence the system," he explains. "If a strong wind is blowing up the tide river, that will back everything up and hold this water up, so that it wouldn't drop as much. If there's an opposite wind blowing in the direction of the flow or out towards the main river, it would increase this flow."

Martin offers two other important tips about fishing tidal systems. "Every tidewater river I've ever fished had its biggest fish on the lower end of it," he says. "That's a correct statement about tidewater fishing wherever the river is located.

"Another thing to remember when fishing the tidal rivers of the northern rivers is that when the water gets cold (below 55 degrees), the fish will seek noncurrent places like up in the feeder creeks. They don't like to fight current in the winter. But they love current in the summer. Summer fish in tidewater areas will seek out points where the current is ripping. Keep that in mind."

Armed with Martin's insight into fishing tidal conditions, the mystery has been reduced somewhat for the average angler. It basically boils down to putting yourself in the right place at the right time.

Texas pro David Wharton has found that a jigging spoon can be the cure for post-spawn bass.

Chapter 35

David Wharton's
Post-Spawn Solution

For many bass fishermen, the post-spawn period is a time of frustration and defeat.

During this time, the bass have recently left the beds and are making their way toward their deeper summer lairs where they will ride out the hottest temperatures of the year. As a result of the bedding activity, the fish are stressed out and, often, not as aggressive as usual. And they can be difficult to locate during this shallow-to-deep migration in the late spring.

But veteran Texas pro and Sam Rayburn Reservoir guide David Wharton has a post-spawn solution that is a little unorthodox in both its form and results. Wharton intercepts the bass on their migration routes and uses an unusual method to coax them into biting.

PROfile

B.A.S.S. winner David Wharton is a guide on Sam Rayburn Reservoir and an eight-time Classic qualifier.

"Many people make the mistake of continuing to look for the fish to still be shallow near the end of April and the beginning of May, but the bass are long-gone," explains Wharton, a eight-time BASS Masters Classic qualifier. "But most people feel more comfortable fishing shallow, so they hesitate to move deeper.

"It has been my experience that post-spawn fish are usually easy to locate. The key to finding them is to concentrate on the closest structure to the traditional spawning areas. That can be a creek channel or main-lake point. The fish will be on a definite breakline, which makes them easier to locate."

Using his depthfinder, Wharton scours water in the 15- to 22-foot range for any structure that has a well-defined edge. Surprisingly, he most often finds post-spawn bass suspended over breaklines that are void of cover. A clean, barren drop-off edge is usually more productive, Wharton insists, than one that features stumps or brush.

Although the bass often suspend, they will usually be concentrated, which Wharton believes makes them considerably easier to catch during this time of year.

The tool that Wharton uses to score consistently on post-spawn bass may surprise some — a jigging spoon.

"I have always considered spoon-fishing to be an excellent numbers technique," Wharton says. "When the bass are schooled up, there is no bait — period — that will catch more fish.

"But I don't think most people use a jigging spoon as much as they should. A spoon is considered strictly a cold-water, wintertime bait. But in certain situations, it will catch fish year-round. And I think it's the perfect lure for catching post-spawn bass."

There are several natural factors that make a jigging spoon a prime lure for enticing post-spawn bass into striking.

First, it is an excellent deep-structure bait and perfectly suited for working the bare drop-offs. And it is a productive tool for suspended bass because its depth can be regulated with pinpoint accuracy. "Another reason why it catches fish so well during this time of year is that it matches the size and appearance of shad as well as any lure made and shad are what the bass will be usually be feeding on," Wharton adds. "Plus, you can cover a lot of water with a spoon in a hurry."

Wharton uses a 3/4-ounce Hopkin's spoon on 14- to 20-pound test line and a light-action graphite rod that sports a relatively quick tip. He modifies the lure by exchanging the factory treble for a wide-throat VMC hook and inserting a split ring in the eye of the bait. The factory-stamped hole is often jagged enough to cut monofilament. And he occasionally adds a white or yellow bucktail to give the lure a little extra appeal. Unlike some anglers, Wharton does not use a swivel above the spoon, believing that it hampers the action of the bait.

In somewhat of a break from tradition, Wharton casts the spoon as well as vertically jigs it. Most fishermen assume that the only way to use these small steel slabs is to work them in an up-and-down motion from directly above the structure. But that will significantly limit your success, Wharton says, particularly on post-spawn bass.

Wharton vertically jigs a spoon during the times when he has pinpointed the fish with his electronic eyes, but abandons that slower method when looking for bass. "Casting and retrieving a spoon is a new technique to most people," Wharton continues. "But it's the most effective way to cover a lot of water in search of these post-spawn fish. It will surprise most people to find that you can cover a lot of water by casting and retrieving a jigging spoon.

"Casting a spoon can also be a dynamite way to catch suspended bass. I've caught a ton of them this way. Since you are fishing water without a lot of cover, you can cast a spoon without staying hung up. The idea is to let it sink to the bottom and use a slow-to-medium retrieve — depending on the reel — to make it kind of wobble back and forth. That wobble is the key. If you go too slow, the spoon is going to drag the bottom. If you go too fast, it will twist your line. If your line is twisting, you need to make an adjustment in your presentation."

Post-spawn bass don't have to be a mystery to locate and catch. Armed with David Wharton's insight, productive fishing doesn't have to disappear once the bass leave shallow water.

Canals provide excellent habitat for bass, particularly in the spring.

Chapter 36

An Overlooked Home for Bass

You know the names.

Okeechobee. Kissimmee. Rodman. Tohopekaliga. St. Johns. George. Orange. Lochloosa. Seminole. All have been outstanding bass waters for years. All are large, heavily pressured areas, the result of their reputation.

But some of the finest bass fishing in Florida is found in waters with names like L-28 and C-42. Or have no names. And these no-name bodies of water combine to form an extensive fishery that harbors an impressive quality of bass as well as a largely unmolested population of fish.

"Canals are the most overlooked fishery in Florida, yet they are still one of the few places where you can catch 100 bass in a day on occasion," claims Roland Martin, a 12-year resident of Clewiston, located on the southern shore of famed Lake Okeechobee. "When they think of bass fishing in Florida, most people think of the big lakes. But there is some outstanding fishing in the canals that is easily available to just about every person.

PROfile

Floridian Jim Bitter has won two major events — MegaBucks and the Golden Blend Championship — and came within 2 ounces of winning the 1990 Classic.

"People just don't realize what's in their own backyard. In Florida, there's a canal near everybody and these canals have some of the best bass fishing to be found in Florida. It's also the most accessible fishing there is, yet people don't seem to be taking advantage of these places."

One angler who has taken advantage of this largely untapped fishery is Charlie Frederick of Boynton Beach. Although he lives less than an hour east of Lake Okeechobee, Frederick prefers to explore the large canal system near his home that connects with several small lakes.

Frederick became hooked on canal fishing in 1971 and spends about 75 days a year on those waters. Since that time, Frederick, a meticulous record keeper, has caught about 2,200 bass from Boynton Beach area canals (releasing about 90 percent of the fish), including several that topped the 9-pound mark. In 1987, for example, his home canal system produced 31 bass that topped the 5-pound mark, including six over 8 pounds.

Those numbers are remarkable when you consider that the canal system he fishes is less than 10 miles in length and snakes through a heavily-populated urban area.

"It's a misconception that to catch big bass, you've got to go somewhere like Okeechobee," Frederick says. "There are plenty of big bass to be caught in these canals close to home.

"It takes me over an hour to get to Okeechobee and an hour to get back, where here I can be fishing in less than a half-hour. And to fish a place like Okeechobee, you've got to be over there regularly and know the fish, because the fish move a lot and you've got to know the lake real well. Here in these canals almost in my backyard, I have fished them so much that I know the good spots and I enjoy consistently good fishing and catch some big fish as well."

In an effort to drain the swamp and wetlands that were early Florida, developers and state and federal officials spent untold millions of dollars building endless miles of drainage canals throughout Florida, particularly in the central and southern portions of the state. The canals range from huge, fast-water ditches to small, but deep waterways that you can cast across. Many provide a quality form of urban fishing, while others offer the solitude of wilderness fishing. Many connect to a larger body of water.

In the process, they developed some of the best bass habitat in Florida, canals where good water flow breeds a healthy fishery by providing an abundance of fresh oxygen and forage.

Most Florida canal fishing is the perfect sport for anglers afoot. Most have easy access from major roadways and can easily be covered on foot. And almost any type of bass tackle will suffice, making it an inexpensive fishing venture.

Top pro Shaw Grigsby of Gainesville grew up canal fishing, getting his earliest fishing education in the narrow confines of north Florida's artificial waterways that serve as tributaries for large lakes. Some of his largest stringers have come from canals, a lesson that he has not forgotten since becoming a big-time touring pro and four-time national tournament winner.

"Canals are greatly overlooked, except in the springtime," says Grigsby, a former Red Man All-American Championship winner. "Everybody wants to fish them in the spring, but they never think of fishing them any other time —

even the advanced fishermen. To them, it's a migratory spot, a place where fish move into spawn in the spring and then move back out into the lake in the summertime.

"One reason I love canal fishing is that there are resident fish in the canals at all times, although few people seem to realize it. I fish them all year long because of those resident fish. For years, they were a completely untapped resource that I had all to myself."

Florida's canals get the most pressure in the spring when the impressive numbers of bass move into these ditches to spawn. Canals provide the perfect spawning habitat. Many have a sandy bottom and all provide protection from the elements. Generally, canals are harbor the warmest water in a lake system.

But canals can provide ideal bass habitat, which is why many house large resident populations of fish. Again, they offer shelter from wind and many have enough depth and cover that bass can quite ably live their entire lives within its confines.

The better canals are a microcosm of a small lake, providing varying degrees of depth, cover and even water flow in a condensed area.

Depth is a determining factor of whether a canal will have a significant population of resident bass. A canal that has 5 to 10 feet of water is "similar to a creek," Grigsby says. "It's almost identical because there are always fish in the backs of creeks and along the creek channels regardless of the time of year — even the dead of winter."

The deeper the canal, the more consistent the fishing will be, believes Missouri's Denny Brauer, who has become a canal convert from fishing numerous tournaments in Florida. The shallower it is, the more sporadic the fishing will be.

Although the size of Florida's canals can range from a 300-foot landlocked ditch to a 100-mile waterway that dumps part of Lake Okeechobee into the Atlantic Ocean, Jim Bitter believes that the width of a canal is more important. The wider the canal, the more range of depth it is likely to have, says Bitter, one of Florida's top tournament pros and a guide on the Harris Chain of Lakes.

In Florida, aquatic vegetation is a crucial element separating the most productive canals from other ditches. While Bitter prefers lily pads in canal systems, any type of emergent or floating native or exotic vegetation provides canal bass with the shelter, ambush cover and congregation points for baitfish.

Floating vegetation, such as hyacinths and uprooted hydrilla, can provide the best bass action of all. The floating vegetation provides a surface mat with an open-water cavern beneath it, a combination that attracts significant numbers of fish. Although most anglers flip a worm or jig through this horizontal mat, Brauer has enjoyed good success with big bass by ripping a Bomber Long A along the edge of such places. "That bait allows you to cover a lot of water, which is important because a lot of the canals are so long that you need to cover a bunch of water in a hurry," he says.

The sheer design of a canal simplifies the normal problems posed with locating bass. That should appeal to anglers of all skill levels.

"It's real easy to locate fish in canals because there aren't a lot of places they can be," Grigsby explains. "The narrow confines of a canal works in your favor. They're either going to be in the middle or on the edge. And the amount of cover in most canals will be fairly limited, whether it be visible or a little bit of underwater cover. It's very easy to pinpoint where the bass should be positioned."

Brauer, the 1987 B.A.S.S. Angler of the Year whose success in Florida canals has prompted him to explore similar situations in residential areas adjacent to Missouri's Lake of the Ozarks and the James River system in Virginia, stresses the importance of analyzing the cover in relation to the seasonal patterns of bass.

"Each canal is different, so you have to analyze the cover in that canal along with the season of the year to try to put the percentages in your favor," Brauer explains. "Don't be afraid to look at the total picture of a canal and don't concentrate completely on any one thing — like vegetation.

"Canals can have a lot of cover options, including underwater structure like intersections and bottom irregularities where the dragline stopped or turned around. There is always wooden cover in the form of docks and pilings. And a lot of the canals are along heavy-traffic areas, so they'll have riprap. Analyze what cover is available and then decide where the bass are likely to be based on the time of the year and the water temperature."

There are some general rules of canal fishing that usually pay off.

Although bass are often located in the deeper, middle sections of a canal, Jim Bitter always fishes the banks first, saying the shoreline usually harbors the most cover, clear water and baitfish. Pinpointing his approach a step farther, Bitter always begins with aquatic vegetation, if available. But he recommends making a few casts to the edge of sections of the bank that are without cover, either with a shallow-diving crankbait or plastic worm.

Although Brauer agrees with this "grass-first" approach, he emphasizes that the lower the water temperature, the more the bass will relate to wooden structure in both canals and lakes. In canals, Brauer believes the larger bass relate to docks and pilings.

Intersections in canals, which are abundant in waterfront residential areas, are always worth checking, Brauer says, because they are similar to secondary points on a lake or reservoir. Concentrate on the four corners formed by the intersection and use the direction of the wind to determine where the bass should be positioned for ambushing baitfish.

In Florida, concrete and wooden seawalls are quickly replacing the natural shoreline cover that often borders a canal. Surprisingly, most canal-fishing enthusiasts say seawalls enhance the fishing.

"Seawalls are beneficial and the fishing around them can be excellent," Brauer claims. "They stabilize the bank, keeping it from silting in and the water from going bad. Bass love to hold right up next to a seawall, because it will normally have at least 2 or 3 feet of depth right against it. And a seawall offers shade for part of the day and extra warmth when the water is cold."

Bass will also bed close to a seawall, taking advantage of its protection from heavy winds as well as the added warmth of the water.

To take advantage of seawalls, most canal fishermen use a crankbait, either paralleling it or making quartering casts toward the wall. The key is keeping the lure as close to the wall as possible.

Considering the close-quarters type of fishing that canals provide, one would assume that these artificial waterways could suffer fatally from fishing pressure. But that, generally, isn't true.

"Canals aren't as overlooked today as they once were," Jim Bitter says. "But there is still one thing working in my favor and others who fish canals. People won't usually stay in a canal long enough to hurt it. If it isn't hot enough to where they can catch five or six fish fairly quickly, they'll make a pass through the canal and leave. But you can go into that same canal right after other people have gone through it and still do pretty well if you will just slow down and concentrate."

It may not have the reputation of the big-lake big-bass fisheries, but canals remain quiet, consistent producers of quality fishing that can be easy to conquer and just as satisfying as any day spent working the big water.

Rich Tauber with proof that cold-front bass can be cooperative.

Chapter 37

Confronting Cold-Front Bass

The anatomy of a bass fisherman's nightmare:

Late in the afternoon, the wind begins to build and the barometric pressure starts to plummet, triggering an all-too-brief feeding frenzy among the hyper-active bass. During the night, the temperature drops 10 or 15 degrees and the wind howls.

PROfile

The next morning, the clouds have started to break up and dissipate, while the barometric pressure soars. The fishing is still decent, while the early-morning clouds provide some overcast. But as the afternoon arrives, the clouds have disappeared, leaving bright, clear skies. Bluebird days, anglers call them. The barometric pressure stabilizes high.

And the fishing is tough.

The anatomy of a cold front, an all-too-common occurrence during the winter and spring. The recipe for frustration.

Cold fronts, bluebird days and inactive bass are a fact of life, the formula for fishless day and forgetable outings. Nothing depresses fishermen as much or inflicts fish with such a severe case of lockjaw as the appearance of a cold front.

Texan Tommy Martin, a former Classic champion, is practically an institution on the national tournament circuit.

By definition, a cold front is the leading edge of a mass of cooler air moving into a concentration of warmer air. The temperature between the two colliding air masses usually produces cold temperatures, wind, rain and sometimes snow.

It is a well-documented fact that atmospheric conditions affect all living creatures and the impact of a passing cold front on a resident bass population can be attested to by frustrated fishermen from coast to coast.

But cold fronts don't have to signal the end of all hopes of a successful fishing trip. There are ways to catch these high-pressure bass, methods for confronting a cold front. No one knows that better than the nation's travelling bass pros who get plenty of practice battling cold fronts during tournaments throughout the country.

"A lot of fishermen simply give up and throw in the towel when a cold front passes through," says Ken Cook of Meers, Okla., a highly-successful tournament pro and former fisheries biologist. "While it may not be the best conditions for fishing, there are ways to catch bass under these circumstances,"

While cold fronts can be a year-round problem, winter and spring are prime-time for these frontal passages. "Cold fronts don't seem to affect fish as negatively in the summer and in the fall," Cook explains. "In the winter and particularly in the spring, it really tends to hurt the fish, which can be attributed not only to the barometric pressure, but the temperature changes as well,"

Former BASS Masters Classic champion and perennial Classic qualifier Tommy Martin of Hemphill, Texas, agrees that cold fronts affect bass to different degrees, depending on the time of year. "When I talk about cold fronts, I automatically break it down into seasonal categories," he says. "In my opinion, spring is the worst season for cold fronts, the season when cold fronts most affect the bass and your ability to catch them. They just clam up,"

Clamming up is a common occurrence during a cold front, no matter what the season. The exact causal effect between bass and cold fronts has never been sufficiently documented by the scientific community. But biologists and the top pros all believe that barometric pressures (which run the gamut during a cold front), water temperature changes, wind and the cloudless sunshine all play a role in creating the most inactive bass of all.

To understand the intricacies of a cold front and put together a plan for combatting it, Cook and others agree that it is important to pay attention to its various stages. Most use barometric pressure to gauge how active the bass are likely to be.

"I relate to a cold front in terms of barometric pressure," Cook explains. "As a cold front approaches, the barometric pressure drops off pretty rapidly and during this period of time, fishing is usually pretty good. The fish are usually fairly shallow and up on the feeding ledges.

"As a cold front passes through and the clouds break up and move on South, generally, the pressure gets higher. It increases into the 30s, usually, and during that period, the fishing is still pretty good as long as some clouds are still around providing some cloud cover. Then the clouds start breaking up and the barometric pressure starts to rise more. When the clouds move completely out and the barometric pressure is at its peak, that's when the fishing is toughest.

"I think the barometric pressure, along with the water temperature, will give you some idea of how active the bass are likely to be and you should adjust how fast you fish and where you fish according to those two factors,"

After a severe cold front, the bass sometimes don't feed actively for several days. But with the proper gameplan, you can often prompt a reactionary strike from a bass that is not in a feeding mode.

The first step toward combatting cold-front bass is all mental, according to Rick Clunn.

"Before you even step in the boat, you have to prepare yourself mentally," he says. "By that, I mean adjust your attitude to accept the fact that you're probably only going to get a handful of bites all day. You have to accept that and then concentrate extra hard to be in a position to take full advantage of those few strikes you do manage to get during the day."

With that in mind, the next step is locating bass, which will make some predictable moves during a cold front.

As a rule of thumb, the bass pros agree that a deep-water bass (generally, 15 feet and deeper) is less affected by a frontal passage than fish holding in shallower water. Shallower fish will usually take one of two routes: if there is thick cover nearby, the bass will often move to some type of vegetation or brush; if no decent cover is around, the fish will often move to a nearby breakline, like the dropoff of a creek channel (especially if there is some type of structure on the break).

But, according to pros like Martin, bass rarely make a radical move from shallow to extremely deep water if it means travelling any distance.

Burying up in thick cover like hydrilla, milfoil or buck brushes is probably the move that most of the country's bass anglers will encounter during a cold front. The bright, cloudless sky after a front passes through provides a relentless sun that usually sends bass looking for shade.

And the fish will often wrap themselves in the midst of the thickest cover imaginable. Divers have reported seeing bass buried so far into the vegetation that only their tail was visible.

In many lakes and rivers, bass often stack up close to bridges and boat dock pilings during a frontal passage. Intelligent anglers will often maltune a crankbait to run off to one side so that they can work extremely close to the pilings, which is crucial for catching these fish.

"To catch fish under the worst cold-front conditions, it's usually a matter of doing two things," Ken Cook says. "The biggest thing is to slow down because the fish are inactive and not likely to chase down a lure and, secondly, fish real tight into the cover where you had caught fish before the cold front.

"If you had been catching fish in a certain area before the cold front and the high pressure, the fish normally won't leave that area if there's good cover. I've found that if there are good bushes or logs or any good overhead cover where the fish have been, they won't leave it when a cold front arrives. If you've been catching fish on a gravel bar or on a rock ledge where there's no overhead cover, they'll generally move away from that shallow cover and find some deeper water nearby that has some type of overhead cover on it.

"So you have to concentrate on the thickest, interior portions of the cover in areas near where you had been catching fish before the cold front. And you really have to work it thoroughly,"

Because of the inactive nature of the bass, good lure presentation and accurate casting is important. That's why most pros automatically start flipping.

That inactive mood also dictates slowing down the actual lure presentation. Pros like 1987 B.A.S.S. MegaBucks champion Lonnie Stanley of Huntingdon, Texas, down-size the sizes of the worm or jig being used. With a jig, a pork trailer will provide buoyancy, which slows the fall.

Former Classic qualifier and syndicated television show host Jimmy Rogers of Lakeland, Fla., has a cold-front cure that involves down-sizing to an ultralight crankbait like the Bagley Honey B and fishing it slowly in a stop-and-go manner.

The ideal lure presentation is one that slowly drifts down in front of the bass, close enough to draw a reactionary strike, an impulse strike. But because these fish are inactive, their bite is often subtle, so it is important to watch your line at all times. Many pros finger the line near the reel to detect even the slightest strike.

Even for the best fishermen, cold fronts are a challenge to solve.

Ironically, though, fishermen utilizing warm power-plant lakes report that cold fronts can trigger outstanding fishing throughout the entire weather passage — just the opposite of its usual effect.

Veteran pro Kenneth Walker of Round Rock, Texas, regularly fishes several warm-water power lakes and reports incredible success during frontal passages

"Normally, on any manmade reservoir anywhere in the country, when you have a cold front, the fishing gets tough, but not these power-plant lakes," he says. "On these power-plant lakes, we often wait until the worst front of the year shows up and go out and freeze to death, but really catch some good strings of largemouths.

"On those lakes, a cold front really turns the fish on. The fish are so active you can catch them by fishing a crankbait fast or swimming a jig. I can't explain it, but I've seen it consistently happen year after year on those lakes,"

But these electrically warmed power-plant lakes are the exception. The vast majority of American bass anglers simply must face the fact that cold fronts mean tough fishing that calls for tough tactics.

"It comes down to a mental test of fortitude because you begin to wonder if there are any fish there at all," Ken Cook says. "Confidence and concentration is the key. Have confidence in your ability to catch fish under even the worst circumstances and concentrate hard on the job at hand."

Cold-Front Tips

Doug Hannon's underwater observations offer an insight that bass fishermen can utilize:

√ Bass prefer to go shallow and bury up in heavy cover instead of going deep. Moving to deep-water is usually an alternative bass take when no shallow-water cover is nearby. "A big reason why they prefer to go shallow instead of deep is that going deeper forces a readjustment of their bladder to attain buoyancy," Hannon explains. "That keeps them from being able to quickly move up into shallower water and immediately return to feeding."

√ Bass will move deeper only if there is no adjacent shallow-water cover. In that case, the fish will usually drop below 12 feet in depth and use the layer of water between it and the surface as a form of cover.

√ Thick overhead cover is essential for the fish that stay shallow, offering protection from predators like ospreys and herons. "They'll go to the deepest, darkest cover that is the closest," Hannon says.

√ The metabolism of the bass slows greatly to conserve energy. So, to catch this inactive fish, you have to present slow-moving baits as closely as possible to it.

√ "The secret to cold fronts is knowing where the fish were before the front came in because they move as little as they have to with definitely predictable preferences," Hannon says. "If you're good at that, you can find them during a cold front."

Manuel Spencer, a B.A.S.S. winner, is an excellent grass fisherman.

Chapter 38

On Reading Weeds

Every bass enthusiast worth his plastic playthings knows that aquatic vegetation provides outstanding cover and habitat for the species they crave.

Vegetation, whether it be floating weeds, rooted plants, or emergent grass, furnishes everything that bass need to survive and thrive. The vegetation serves as protection from predators for bass fry and ambush cover for adult fish. Its very being congregates the food chain, beginning with microscopic plankton that feeds off of the plant, which attracts baitfish and other food sources of the bass. And vegetation can provide cooler temperatures in the summer and warmer water in the winter, while offering shade and protection from overhead predators like birds.

PROfile

Texan Harold Allen has qualified for an impressive 10 BASS Masters Classic appearances.

Aquatic vegetation, both the exotic invaders and our native neighbors, are the wave of the present and the future — and likely the battleground of controversy in years to come as governmental agencies fight to control its spread.

Even the novice angler understands the allure of vegetation to fish, particularly the largemouth bass. It is as much a magnet for fishermen as it is for fish. But there is a real art to taking full advantage of the predictability that aquatic weeds provide. And the curriculum for that art includes understanding the basics of eliminating unproductive vegetation, pinpointing exact fish positioning in the grass and applying the proper tools for specific types of vegetation.

"Weeds have become the dominant bass cover in lakes and reservoirs throughout the country and will play an even bigger role in the years to come," says Shaw Grigsby, a two-time Bassmaster tournament winner who learned the intricacies of fishing vegetation in Florida. "But there is more to fishing vegetation than just blindly fishing it. Grass fishing requires as much of a detailed gameplan as any type of structure fishing."

ELIMINATING UNPRODUCTIVE VEGETATION

Almost all of the more than 500 10-pound-plus bass that have fallen victim to Doug Hannon were winched from the grasp of aquatic vegetation. As a result, few anglers understand the complexities of fishing grass of all types.

Most fishermen make the mistake of approaching vegetation differently than other types of bass structure, Hannon claims.

"The main thing about reading vegetation is to look at it in terms of the total structure of a weed bed," he explains. "You should approach a weed bed the way you would select a creek or cove — use similar criteria.

"The first thing I try to do is pick out a weed bed that would be large enough to hold several bass. It is for that reason that I prefer large weed beds, rather than small isolated patches of grass. That is the starting point. Then I move in and examine the grass more closely to weigh whether or not it is likely to hold a good school of bass."

Hannon uses a three-step approach to eliminate unproductive vegetation. First, he examines a weed bed in its entirety to determine how attractive it might be to schools of bass. That is determined by the number of structural options it provides the fish in terms of depth, cover types, ambush points and more. Is the weed bed adjacent to a channel with deeper water? Does it have a point where baitfish might collect? Are there bottom irregularities under or near the grass?

Secondly, Hannon analyzes the ecology of the weed bed to determine its current health, which will indicate its viability as bass habitat. He looks for fresh, green growth, which is an obvious indication of the weed's health. Although Hannon often measures the oxygen content in the vegetation, he emphasizes that you can tell a great deal about the health of the grass by using a lure like a buzzbait or large topwater plug that creates a commotion as it comes through the grass. "If that causes baitfish to spook, that's great because you know that you've got the presence of food in the weed bed, which is an ecological necessity," Hannon adds. "That will also tell you that the weeds are viable and producing oxygen and food."

It is also important to examine aquatic vegetation closely to determine if it has been poisoned by governmental agencies and is in a state of decline. "It's become a fact of life today that you've got to distinguish which grass beds have been sprayed and poisoned," claims David Yarbrough, a veteran Alabama tournament pro who lives on Lake Guntersville, one of the most controversial sites of the continuing nuclear war on vegetation. "The fish will leave the areas that have been sprayed and move to the closest milfoil beds that have not been poisoned and won't return for three to seven days. It is easy to tell whether an area has been sprayed by simply pulling up a piece of grass. You will either smell the poison or see where it has turned brown."

The third step used by Hannon to pinpoint productive weed beds involves areas that have different types of vegetation intermingled. Different types of plants provide bass with more options for adjusting to changing weather conditions, along with greater ambush opportunities.

"I always prefer to fish weed beds that provide a stable habitat that has been there a while," Hannon says. "This is far superior to something that has just blown in and could float away with a change in the wind direction."

One rule of thumb that has worked for Grigsby in lakes and reservoirs throughout the country is to concentrate on the thickest patches of grass that are located adjacent to deep water, such as a creek or river channel.

Like most pros, Tennessee's Charlie Ingram takes a seasonal approach to selecting productive sections of vegetation and eliminating unproductive areas.

"Using seasonal tendencies and habits is no different with fishing weeds as it is with any other kind of structure," Ingram explains. "In the early spring, you look for the warmest grass pockets you can find, which is where the bass will spawn first. Once summer arrives, most of the fish move out to the main-lake grass flats close to deep water. They'll hold in those same areas into the fall, but the grass will be topped out, so you have to use different lures to catch them. In the winter, you'll find bass in grass that is out of the current. And because the grass retains the heat somewhat, you can catch fish just as long as you can keep the ice out of your guides."

PINPOINTING BASS IN WEEDS

Once you have selected the vegetation patches with the most potential, successful grass fishing gets even more complicated.

"Pinpointing exactly where the bass are located takes hard work," world champion Rick Clunn advises. "The bottom line with weeds to me and the toughest aspect of fishing weeds for most people, is that you literally have to drop your trolling motor and cover miles of vegetation.

"The strange thing about weeds is that you can hit a stretch that's loaded with fish and then you can duplicate that stretch and not get a strike. With weed beds, there are areas that year in and year out hold fish and there are areas that year in and year out don't produce many. Yet, they look identical. That can be frustrating. But I think that's also the neat thing about weeds, too. It forces you to be a fisherman. It forces you to work. You can't simply decide that the bass are holding on points and just run from point to point."

Most pros would agree that it takes time and effort to dissect large weedy areas and pinpoint the fish. But over the years, they have developed a few shortcuts that can give the average angler a starting point for probing grass.

Seasonal habits and movements of bass can help you position them in vegetation, according to veteran Georgia pro Tom Mann, Jr. In addition to pinpointing the most productive areas, seasonal conditions often indicate where bass will most likely be hiding in the weed bed itself. For example, in the spring, the bass can usually be found in the shallow pockets and flats that are better suited for spawning. In the early and late portions of spring, Mann recommends searching the slightly deeper and thicker patches of grass adjacent to the spawning areas — logical places for pre- and post-spawn bass to hold. In the summer, the bass will likely be on the deeper edges of the vegetation where the slightly cooler water exists (Florida is an exception. The fish will often hide in the middle of the thickest weed beds). As the water cools in the fall, the bass will be shallower and aggressively hunting along the edge of grass lines. And winter will find the fish in the deepest and heaviest portions of the vegetation — away from any current.

Like most fishermen, former BASS Masters Classic champion Stanley Mitchell routinely starts on the outside edges of the grass beds and works inward to locate bass. That, according to Doug Hannon, is a logical and sound approach, since bass are "edge creatures" and will most often relate to some type of border area (when the conditions allow it).

One method of quickly pinpointing grass bass is to concentrate on any irregularities — or unusual physical features — along a weed line.

"I look for things that are a little different than normal," Shaw Grigsby explains. "That is true with any kind of fishing, but grass is especially susceptible to that. Over the years, my bigger bass have come from places where you have some type of irregularity — a pothole in the grass, a dip or curve in the grass line, a spot where the channel runs close to it, an especially thick section of grass, a sand bottom in the middle of a big bed of grass or spots where two types of vegetation meet."

Wind and current direction can also indicate spots where bass could be positioning, according to Mann. Bass, generally, will hold on the downstream side of either natural or a wind-driven current, while facing the flowing water. With that in mind, Mann then concentrates on the points of grass and outer edges that allow such positioning.

"Reading weeds to pinpoint bass is like reading any other kind of structure," Mann reminds us. "Structure is structure, whether it be weeds, a boathouse, brushpile, stump, rock or whatever."

Rick Clunn emphasizes that submerged grass is much more difficult to both analyze and fish. First, it often takes considerable skill at reading electronics to pinpoint the exact positioning of the grass and any irregularities. And submerged vegetation limits the options of a fisherman, such as flipping.

Areas where different types of vegetation like lily pads and hyacinths mix can be a bonanza situation.

SELECTING THE PROPER TOOLS

"You could just about equip a whole tackle box with nothing but different lures for different grass applications," claims Harold Allen, a Texan with 10 Classic appearances to his credit. "There are different lures that are best suited for different types of grass and the different stages of their growth. The fisherman who takes the time to learn to use more than just a couple of lures around grass will certainly catch more fish."

The physical characteristics of different types of vegetation will eliminate some artificial lures, which would seem quite obvious. But it is common to see anglers trying to make their favorite lure work in weedy situations where it is not the best tool for the job.

For standing, rooted vegetation like reeds and bulrushes, a spinnerbait and plastic worm can be worked the most efficiently — although you can fish the outer edges of such plants with other baits. For less rigid vertical weeds like hydrilla and milfoil (that has not topped out on the surface), those lures can be used, along with a plastic frog, weedless spoon and in-line buzzbait. With matted, floating vegetation like hyacinths and water lettuce, your options are significantly limited. Experienced fishermen in Florida (where this type of cover is most often found) rely almost exclusively on a plastic worm.

Almost as limiting is vegetation like hydrilla and milfoil that has completed the growth cycle and thickens at the surface. A plastic worm, weedless spoon and rubber rat or frog are the only real choices in this situation.

For fishing submerged vegetation with a layer of water above it, a variety of lures will work, depending on the depth and water clarity: jerkbaits, worms, spinnerbaits, crankbaits, spoons, buzzbaits and topwater plugs.

In that situation, Clunn prefers to use a lure that will attract bass, rather than a finesse-type bait that requires precise presentation. His first choice is a Rat-L-Trap, a lipless, vibrating crankbait that has a sound and action that attracts bass from the interior portions of submerged grass.

"I think the most underrated grass bait is the jig-and-pig," Shaw Grigsby says. "Most people will throw a jig in grass a few times, get hung up and get frustrated. So they put it down and use a plastic worm or a bait that will come across the top of the water instead. But the jig-and-pig catches some of the biggest bass in grass beds. It may be a little harder to work, but it's the bait to use."

In the last few years, Florida fishermen have discovered the allure of the jig-and-pork chunk. Kentuckian Corbin Dyer opened some eyes with a six-fish, 31-pound-plus stringer caught on a jig-and-pig during a B.A.S.S. stop in Lake Okeechobee. Tennessee transplant and Big O guide Steve Daniel caught three bass that topped the 9-pound mark in a single day on the bait and Grigsby has a 10-pound jig victim to his credit.

The art of fishing vegetation involves much more than covering large expanses of water and hoping to stumble onto a school of fish. The real grass experts are part biologist and part tactician, a combination that allows them to take full advantage of the greatness of aquatic grass.

Chapter 39

Fast-Water Bass

One of the most basic lessons in the ABCs of a bass fisherman's education is that largemouth and smallmouth bass are attracted to current.

Current brings all of the comforts known to bass past its watery lair — oxygen, cooler temperatures and food. It is for that reason that bass positioned into current are usually more active, more aggressive feeders, whether they live in California or Connecticut.

But there comes a point where the current — both natural and artificial — is so swift that it becomes difficult to figure out and fish for some anglers. But that swift current harbors bass with the same aggressive characteristics found in more subtle flowages. Fast-water bass can be a challenge to fish for, but the experts say they are usually more than willing to bite.

The first step is understanding the characteristics of fast-water bass and how their habitat dictates their behavior.

Former Classic champion George Cochran of Arkansas has been the model of consistency with nine Classic appearances.

"Fast water, to me, means a lot of river movement and lots of turbidity," says Dr. Loren Hill, prominent fisheries biologist and fishing tackle innovator. "Fast-water fish are completely different in their habits than bass in a pool or lake because they are normally restricted in their movements. They will establish a home range that is much smaller than a lake bass.

"We've radio telemetry-monitored lake fish and discovered that many of them have a wide movement over a six-month period. The opposite is true with river fish. Their home range is very small. That's because they are always encountering these currents and the turbidity in them."

Hill emphasizes that bass living in fast-water situations are typically easy to pinpoint, by following one simple rule: although bass are attracted to the edge of the swift water because of what it supplies, they will avoid positioning directly in the current. Bass will usually seek small eddy pockets of calm water behind some large object (primarily rock, but often logs, stumps, even a bridge or boat dock piling).

"If there is a rock big enough to create an eddy on the backside, the fish are obviously going to be there," Hill explains. "Whether you're fishing the Ohio River or the Mississippi River, a fisherman should know pretty much where to be fishing — areas that minimize the amount of current.

"That's the first key, even if you're fishing for smallmouth bass. A smallmouth bass is built differently from a largemouth and they are stronger swimmers. But still, they seek out these quiet eddy places as much as possible."

The term "fast water" doesn't refer to normal river current. It can apply to a number of different swift-water situations (which will be discussed later).

Regardless of the fast-water situation, bass fishermen face two major problems: difficult lure presentation and boat positioning.

"I think the biggest problem with fast-water fishing for most fishermen is that even if they know where the fish are, they don't know how to present a lure to them properly," claims 1987 BASS Masters Classic champion George Cochran of N. Little Rock, Ark., a river-fishing specialist. "Basically, what happens is that the fish get tight to rocks and big logs where they don't have to fight the current.

"And you are faced with having to present a lure real close to the structure, with the baits going with the current. Those fish are not going to go a foot the wrong way to catch something when there is so much baitfish available. Presenting your lure tight to the structure just right is crucial."

When the spring rains make the Arkansas River swell and swift, Cochran has little trouble making near-perfect presentations with his bait, regardless of the type. But the only advice he can give others is to fish in these fast-water situations enough that repetition creates accuracy. With enough practice, most skilled anglers will be able to correctly gauge where and when to place a lure so that the current enables it to hug a piece of structure where a bass might be holding.

If finessing a lure past a rock or stump in swift water is a problem, controlling a boat can be even more difficult.

Guy Eaker, a perennial Classic contender from Cherryville, N.C., has as much fast-water experience as almost any pro. His approach to boat positioning in swift water may seem a little unorthodox to some.

"When I get into real fast water, I always back down the river," Eaker explains. "People don't realize that the better fish will get up against the bank and they won't be out fighting the current. So you have to fish the bank.

"By backing down the river, I mean pointing the bow of the boat upstream and using my trolling motor on high 24 to fight the current. That allows me to present my lure upstream and let it drift right toward the bass in the direction he will likely be facing. This is one the few times when fishing out of the back of the boat is actually advantageous. I've won several tournaments in North Carolina this way because as you back down the river, the man in the front of the boat will usually only have time to get in one cast before he is washed past the spot. The guy in the back of the boat may have time to make two or three underhanded pitches before the current forces the boat past it."

Bass fishermen in different regions of the country can encounter fast-water situations in many different forms and during any season, although most occur in the spring. Here are four swift-water situations that often occur.

Above most major reservoirs, far above the headwaters that create it, lies a bass-fishing haven that relatively few anglers ever experience. It is a fast-water situation that hides perhaps the most underfished and untapped source of bass left in America.

As you leave the reservoir and motor into the headwaters, the river is usually wide, deep and navigable. But keep heading against the flow and you will finally find an environment that seems almost impenetrable. This is particularly true in the fall of the year when the upper 5 miles or so of the river system that was navigable in the spring, now resembles a patchwork of swift, shallow water and rocky shoals. Few fishermen get this far and fewer will attempt to go any farther.

Two men who have conquered the navigation dilemma and subsequently enjoyed the outstanding fall fishing existing quietly there are Roland Martin and Pat McEvoy. Martin is perhaps America's best-known bass angler and McEvoy, according to Martin, is the country's best river fisherman. Martin gives McEvoy, who lives in Atlanta, Ga., much of the credit for his upper-river bass-fishing education. Together, they have experienced the pleasures associated with being modern-day explorers and catching almost virgin bass.

McEvoy uses a jetboat to skim over the shallow water and shoals, while Martin has used everything from a two-man miniboat to a full-sized fiberglass bass boat. The jetboat is one of McEvoy's most guarded secrets.

"The problem with this fast-water situation is that the average bass-boat guy never goes to this type of fast water," Martin says. "It's super-shallow and full of riffles and rocks and stuff. Out of 100 guys that own a $15,000 bass boat, only one or two would take their boat to the kinds of places they need to be fishing. Only a couple will take the chance of bouncing across a gravel bar and up into the fast little creeks to ever fish there.

"It's a hidden fishery that requires some real effort to get to. You're going to knock some gellcoat off and ding your prop and maybe even bend the trolling motor shaft while careening down the river half out of control. These are certainly not easy places to get to or to fish. But, believe me, it is worth all of the trouble."

Despite the fast water, Martin rarely anchors his boat, preferring to cover as much water as possible, using fast-moving lures, like crankbaits and spinner-baits. Once the swift water carries him through a particularly productive pool, he simply cranks up his outboard and heads upstream to make another drift. At times, Martin has used two trolling motors to help slow the drift.

This type of river fishing is rewarding, but very challenging. Martin emphasizes that it calls for fast, accurate casting to spots behind rocks and stumps as well as beneath overhanging vegetation. The speed of the water beneath the boat only amplifies the difficulty involved.

John Bedwell's favorite fishing area is neither easy to fish nor close to his Stockton, Calif., home.

Located 80 miles away lies the San Francisco Bay delta, where four major rivers converge and create a marshland of peat bog islands and more than 1,000 miles of brackish water sloughs. Although it gets practically no fishing pressure, the delta is home to some of California's most outstanding bass fishing.

The delta region is difficult to learn because it all looks similar and is heavily influenced by San Francisco Bay tides, which can drop the water level 6 feet in a matter of a few hours. It also creates a tidal rush that sweeps the water through the narrow slough channels and around the islands at an alarming pace.

Some of Bedwell's greatest success has come on a falling (outgoing) tide that created a 10-knot current through his best backwater spots.

"I love it when the water is really moving," says Bedwell, one of the West's most successful tournament pros. "That makes the fishing the easiest. That fast water moving down the bank makes it so easy to read where the fish is going to be versus a calm-water situation.

"If you were fishing a shoreline where everything looks the same, you know that fish will be relating to the cover — somewhere on that shoreline. But when you've got a lot of current going by, you can see the sheltered places where the bass are going to be. It makes it real easy to determine where to put your lure. Instead of casting every 2 feet, you might only cast every 30 feet."

As with other fast-water situations, Bedwell concentrates his efforts on calm-water areas that are less affected by the current. In addition to eddies formed by objects in the water, the power of the current and the tidal shift creates large undercuts beneath the edge of the islands, which often hold fish

Bedwell is particularly fond of narrow sloughs that funnel the fast water past islands located in the middle of the swift stream.

His primary weapons are small-diameter 4-inch plastic worms fished on a 5/16th- or 3/8th-ounce weight and a 3/4-ounce rubber jig when the current is particularly strong.

The super-swift current sometimes dictates how he positions his boat, though. Usually, Bedwell uses his trolling motor to slow a drift through a slough, but often has to find an eddy area to hold his boat during those 10-knot tidal days. The soft bottom composition eliminates anchoring as an option.

A veteran guide on Georgia's Lanier, Oconee and West Point Lake, Harold Nash knows something about current, particularly artificial current created by the generation of water to produce electricity.

Nash knows well how current affects bass behavior.

"As soon as that current appears, the fish immediately get active," he says. "It has a direct effect on bass."

Over the years, Nash has noted that bass seem to move to places where the current is most intensified. His most dependable areas are places where the riprap foundation of bridges channel the water flow through a relatively small area, which speeds up the flowage. This is often a limit situation, he says.

"The majority of the bass will move to that heavy current," Nash believes. "Rather than be somewhere mid-way along the riprap, they'll be right off the edge of the channel and on the points of the riprap where the current is greatest. Or holding behind the pilings."

Nash agrees with the common belief that bass in this situation, as with most fast-water situations, can be found adjacent to the current flow, seeking a little shelter beside any object that deflects the flowage somewhat.

No discussion of fast-water bass would be complete without the mention of tailrace fishing.

Tailrace waters are extremely strong currents created by water rushing through the turbine generators of large dams built to house major southern reservoirs. Although this current is artificially created, it attracts bass for the same reasons that a river flow does. Since the water is usually drawn from the bottom of the lake, it is cooler and provides an abundance of oxygen. The dam also blocks the migration of baitfish, concentrating and disorienting an easy meal for predators like bass.

Anglers have long known how productive tailrace waters can be, particularly for smallmouth bass. Structures like Alabama's Wheeler Dam have produced numerous smallmouths in the 7- to 10-pound range. The Wheeler Dam tailrace has long provided a reliable fishing grounds for smallmouth king Billy Westmoreland of Celina, Tenn.

"I like fishing swift water for smallmouths," says Westmoreland, who has caught an amazing number of trophy smallmouth bass in his lifetime. "Swift water usually makes the fish really active."

In his tailrace-fishing system, Westmoreland drifts with the current instead of trying to hold his position with the trolling motor. Once he completes a drift, he motors back to the beginning of the tailrace.

Tailrace bass, Westmoreland says, will seek a break in the current, like most fast-water fish. But these bass will usually be positioned near the bottom, so he uses weighted jigs and grubs, which are allowed to sink and drift with the current while approaching a submerged rock or other object.

"You've got to be in total control of any lure you're fishing before you can catch fish in a tailrace," Westmoreland explains. "What I do is drift with the current and throw at an angle above the boat toward whatever the structure is. If you can get the lure in close to the bottom as it approaches the structure, more than likely you're going get a strike."

Tailrace veterans like Westmoreland are emphatic about concentrating on safety as much as fishing when it comes to this swift-water situation. Strong currents and sudden surges can make this type of fishing very dangerous so wearing a quality personal flotation device and avoiding generator outflow areas is essential. Also, small, unstable boats should not be used.

With enough respect for the power of the water flow, tailrace fishing, like most fast-water situations, can be particularly rewarding.

Chapter 40

pH and Bass Fishing

When the first pH meter specifically targeted for bass fishermen entered the marketplace, most anglers aligned themselves with three basic positions.

The soon to be disenchanted. The gadget-minded fisherman rushed right out and bought still another electronic device for his boat. But failing to understand the principals behind the instrument, he soon became disillusioned with it. It was not the magical meter he thought it would be.

PROfile

The confused. The back-to-basics fisherman never understood how it could work and never bothered to buy one.

The eternal skeptic. Here is another device that was built to catch fishermen, not fish, he believed.

Largely missing from that lineup was Mr. Satisfied, who had learned the limitations of the meter and how to best put it to use. He has definitely been in the minority.

Perhaps the times are changing.

Those who understand the biological principals behind the role of pH in bass behavior believe that it

Former fisheries biologist Ken Cook has won five B.A.S.S. events and qualified for the Classic on 10 occasions.

is an important — even essential — consideration for eliminating water. Those who understand its intracacies, like pH Meter inventor Dr. Loren Hill, believe that the pH level can even tell fishermen what lures to use.

All agree that checking the pH in any lake, reservoir or river system should be an integral part of a thinking-fisherman's gameplan.

"If you aren't checking the pH regularly, you're missing out on an advantage you have over the fish," claims Ken Cook of Meers, Okla., a former fisheries biologist and one of the top pros on the Bassmaster Tournament Trail. "I believe pH plays a significant role in bass behavior based on the research I have read and my own experience. Both have been too conclusive to ignore."

"Its is often difficult for fishermen to understand and comprehend the pH factor," adds Hill, perhaps the foremost bass behavioralist in the country. "This is normal because pH is so intangible. We cannot see it, touch it or taste it. However, the pH factor has an absolutely incredible influence on fish including their distribution within lakes, ponds and rivers, their habitat selection and their physiology or function within aquatic environments."

A little biology lesson is in order.

The term pH refers to the level of acidity and alkalinity in bodies of fresh water. The pH level will be the highest on the surface and becomes progressively lower as the water deepens. This is because of the diminishing light penetration that progressively limits the process of photosynthesis leaving organic material on the bottom to decompose, releasing carbon dioxide. The carbon dioxide leads to acidic conditions.

The pH scale reads from 0 to 14, with 7 considered the level of neutrality. Any water below 7 is considered acidic and water above that level has an alkaline condition. Biologists tell us that the ideal pH level is between 7 and 9.

What does that mean? It means that pH in the 7 to 9 range is the most comfortable zone for bass and other gamefish. Bass in that range tend to be the most aggressive. Fish in water outside of that zone tend to be less active because the pH level translates into degrees of difficulty in extracting oxygen from the water.

"I relate it to indigestion in humans," Cook explains. "The bass can't get enough oxygen in their system to digest the food properly, so they tend not to feed. When we have indigestion, we don't eat.

"Bass don't act normal. When a bass is acting normal, it is very reactive and very opportunistic. When something falls in front of them, they bite it because that don't want to waste energy. But if the pH level is such that they don't feel normal, you have to make it even more easier for them to eat. That means slowing down and using small baits, which you have to leave in front of them for a long time."

Or simply avoiding those areas and those fish.

Perhaps the most beneficial use of a pH meter is eliminating water. When possible, Cook and others simply avoid fishing water that has a significantly high or low pH level.

Former BASS Masters Classic qualifier Joe Thomas, an Ohio pro who studied fisheries biology in college, shuns areas that have a radical change in pH. "Not only does a bad pH level affect bass," he says, "I believe it affects the whole ecosystem in that area — the entire food chain."

With his scientific background, Ken Cook probably understands the principals involved better than his fellow pros. In the 1988 Classic on the James River in Virginia, Cook even used the pH readings to dictate where he fished on a per cast basis.

Cook was pitching a grub into shoreline cover that included fallen trees, stumps and rocks. Unfortunately, Cook's best area was also among the river's busiest and the boat traffic continually disturbed the bottom sediment, which changed the pH. Taking regular readings with his Multi-C-Lector, Cook concentrated his efforts on the depth along the shoreline that had the most favorable pH. In other words, he would fish the shallower points of the cover until the pH level there became poor. He would then fish a little deeper.

"The measurements I took tended to support that pH was the major factor and not the color of the water in that case," adds Cook, who finished third in the Classic.

Hill believes that the pH level can even indicate what type of lure to use. "For example, since the pH is normally highest on the surface and decreases with depth, whenever you encounter pH values of 9 on the surface of the water, that tells you something you would otherwise never know or believe — do not use a surface bait," Hill explains. "Isn't it incredible that a lake can tell you what kind of bait to fish or not to fish?"

For those who allow pH to play a role in their fishing, the degree of its influence varies with each season. Spring and summer are the times when the pH level is most influential. Here is a seasonal breakdown, according to the experts:

WINTER: The most stable pH conditions occur during the winter when there is very little variation under natural conditions. But man-induced pollutants can occasionally play havoc with it.

FALL: Joe Thomas believes it is important to check the pH in the fall because of the usual vegetation die-off that can create acidic conditions. If he pulls into a creek or cover and finds the surface of the water littered with leaves, Thomas lowers the pH meter probe and often finds the water is too acidic for his (and the bass') taste.

SPRING: During this time of year, Cook combines pH and water temperature readings to indicate areas where bass are spawning or about to spawn. He looks for the warmest water in the lake, which is where the bass will spawn first. But then Cook checks the pH level in that water to be sure that it is in or near the comfort range to enhance the spawning ritual. Runoff from spring rains often create a pH that is too low.

SUMMER: During the hottest times of the year, Cook checks the pH in an effort to find vertical changes in its level. Lakes typically stratify in the summer, creating both a thermocline and pH breakline. Those two conditions can provide deadly accurate information for locating bass.

"A recent B.A.S.S. tournament on Bull Shoals was a prime example," Cook says, in reference to an unseasonably warm fall tournament on the Arkansas reservoir. "It was a textbook example of how pH works and the value of taking measurements. During that tournament, there was a very distinct pH breakline at 41 feet and virtually all of the fish were at 38 to 40 feet throughout the lake. By taking a few readings, I figured it out in 15 minutes and some guys didn't figure it out in six days."

In the summer, the pH can change drastically from day to day as the sunlight level fluctuates (due to weather fronts or summer storms). The key to consistent summer fishing, Cook claims, is staying on top of those pH changes, which is easier than it sounds. Any change in the water color could indicate a change in the light penetration (which dictates the degree of photosynthesis). Cook simply takes a new reading when he notices a different look to the water color.

Although the ideal pH level is said to be 7 to 9, Cook emphasizes that fishermen should not to be locked into those levels. The comfort level for bass may differ somewhat from region to region.

For example, lakes from western Oklahoma to California tend to be more alkaline than their eastern counterparts and often have a high pH level. But the bass in those lakes are more active at the higher pH level than those in eastern waters, Cook says. In contrast, lakes in the New England region tend to be more acidic, but the bass are accustomed to the slightly lower pH.

"Like everything else, pH isn't a magic wand for finding bass," Ken Cook emphasizes. "But it is a tool that, when used properly and during certain times of the year, can point you toward the more aggressive fish in that lake. And that can be a big advantage."

Special Bonus Section

SECTION FOUR
RICK CLUNN'S
SEASONAL SYSTEM
FOR LOCATING BASS

EDITOR'S NOTE: In 1988, I had the pleasure of collaborating with past BASS Masters Classic champion Rick Clunn on what I consider to be one of the most worthwhile editorial projects I've ever been involved in. The result of that collaboration was a three-part series that appeared in *BASSMASTER* Magazine, with excellent illustrations by Bernie Schultz. It is an approach that any angler can use to locate more bass.

Rick Clunn has practically eliminated luck as a factor in bass fishing.

Chapter 41

The Seasonal Advantage: The Concept

By Rick Clunn With Tim Tucker

It is sometimes a little painful when I look back to the end of my bass club days and the beginning of my professional tournament fishing career. I can easily remember how primitive I was then and how far the entire sport has advanced since.

But it was that ignorance about certain aspects of bass fishing that proved to be the impetus for my entire approach to locating and catching bass today — my seasonal approach to bass fishing.

As I left the comfort of Texas and my bass club days behind and headed out on the vagabond bass circuit that took me to unfamiliar states and foreign bodies of water, it became quickly apparent to me that the first problem I faced was also my biggest problem — knowing where to start looking for bass. Here I was in South Carolina on Santee-Cooper Reservoir and before me lies this massive lake that I've never seen before. It was intimidating.

With just three days of practice, I found myself running around the lake like a chicken with its head cut off. I'd stop in one place, but the mystique of what was around the next point would call and I'd take off for that next point. That's a vicious cycle that you struggle through and at the end of your practice time, you haven't accomplished anything toward establishing a pattern.

I knew there had to be a better way.

It was early in my career that I began to devise a systematic approach to locating bass that I've refined over the last decade through fishing lakes, reservoirs and rivers from the Nevada desert to upper state New York. It is a system that will work for fishermen of any skill level in any geographic region of the country.

My system centers around utilizing the seasonal behavior and movement patterns of bass, which are universal. It is a very simple system, although a lot of people don't believe in the universality of things. They don't believe that a bass is a bass even though he's in New York and not in Florida. But it is the same creature with the same biological habits — the same predictability that we, as fishermen, can take advantage of.

This chapter outlines my seasonal approach system to locating and then catching bass in natural lakes, manmade reservoirs and rivers anywhere that bass are found. In this segment, we will explore what seasonal patterns consist of, compiling the kind of records that help you detect seasonal patterns before ever leaving home and planning your time on the water. Chapter 42 will get more specific, discussing patterns to look for on a season-by-season basis. And Chapter 43 concludes with applying seasonal patterns and determining the specific current patterns that will catch fish.

Seasonal patterns will put you in the ballpark before you ever leave home. They will eliminate two-thirds to three-fourths of the lake before you ever see it. It's a lot less intimidating, not to mention time efficient, to arrive on a lake with only one-third or one-fourth of the lake left to explore once you arrive.

The first thing you have to understand is what seasonal patterns do for you. Whether you are a tournament angler like myself or a weekend fisherman, the biggest problem you have is a limited amount of time. If you go out on a strange lake or even a body of water you know well, that limited amount of time is a problem unless it is a pond that is small enough that you can completely fish it in a few hours. The problem lies with a large impoundment of 10,000 acres or more, which you simply can't cover thoroughly in a limited amount of time.

The weekend fisherman is often in the same boat as the tournament pro. Just as we have limited practice time before a tournament, the average angler gets off from work on Friday afternoon, drives to the lake, where he spends all day Saturday and part of Sunday. Then it's time to go back home. That's not much time even on lakes you know intimately.

Yet, by understanding the value of taking a seasonal approach and keeping records, seasonal patterns will point you to the area of the lake that you should concentrate on.

I have been a record-keeper since I first fished an organized tournament. I began keeping notes on my fishing since my bass club days in 1969. But I probably wasn't taking full advantage of the seasonal trends that my records were indicating for several years.

The BASS Masters Classic is what really keyed me in on the value and reliability of seasonal patterns.

Record seasonal pattern information for each trip or tournament on index cards.

Back when I first started qualifying for the Classic, the writers and even some of the fishermen believed that winning the Classic was primarily luck. B.A.S.S. officials would take us on an airplane and wait until we were at 30,000 feet before announcing what body of water would serve as the Classic site. We went into the early Classics completely blind, which led many people to believe that winning the Classic was just a matter of who was lucky enough to pull into the right cove.

I didn't like the idea of luck being involved and I just knew there had to be a way to approach the Classic instead of just passing it off as luck. Then one day I was reading through the old Classic publications and all of a sudden it hit me like a ton of bricks — all of the Classics had been won in the same area of the lake. That was no small realization.

At that point, all of the Classics had been held in October on manmade lakes and all had been won in the backs of the creeks. The first year I fished the Classic, that is exactly where it was won. The following year, I qualified for the Classic, but the event was held on a natural lake (Currituck Sound), which threw a wrench into it and produced a totally different winning pattern. But the Classic was held on Alabama's Lake Guntersville the next year (another manmade reservoir) and I simply applied the pattern that had won the previous Classics held on impoundments. I picked out the largest creeks in the lake and all but four of my fish were caught in the rear of those creeks.

This very simple strategy enabled me to win my first BASS Masters Classic and has played a role in my other three world championships, not to mention all of my national tournament victories.

In my seasonal system, I divide both the lake and the creeks into sections. Taking an overview of the main lake, (see diagram) I divide it into thirds. The lower section (beginning at the dam in a manmade reservoir) is designated as Section 1. This is the area that will usually have the deepest and clearest water.

Section 3 includes the headwater areas, which tend to be shallower and have more color to the water. Section 2 is located in the middle and features a blend of water depths and clarity.

I use the same system to mark off a creek. Section 1 is the deepest area — the closest to the main lake. Section 2 is the mid-section of the creek. And Section 3 is the back of the creek, which will be the shallowest area. I will sometimes include a Section 4 with a creek that has a small tributary leading from the rear of it.

Sectionalizing a lake map is a critical first step toward applying seasonal patterns to any body of water.

You now want to review any records you can obtain about that particular lake, whether it be your own notes, a guide's logbook, magazine stories or tournament results. This information can be organized and applied, according to season, to the various sections of the lake. I kept notes during my bass club days, but I really got serious about it after understanding the repeatable seasonal result I was seeing with the Classic each October.

As I began really researching it by digging through books and magazines, it soon became even more obvious how universal seasonal patterns were. Today, I have filed the results of more than 500 tournaments, which I access through my computer. I need to emphasize that the computer is just a tool for accessing information. The computer gives me no real advantage, other than the quick availability of the information stored inside.

The average guy reading this article is saying "Well, it's great that Rick Clunn has a whole library of magazines and now he has all of this information in his computer, but how do I go about collecting enough information to find seasonal patterns?" The way I and other people started was reviewing records we had been keeping of our fishing trips.

Organize those notes if you have them and start keeping records if you don't. If you're in a bass club and even if you don't catch any fish in a tournament, talk to your buddies and they'll usually tell you their pattern and the general area of the lake where they were fishing. They may not tell you the specific lure or the specific spot, but that doesn't have anything to do with seasonal patterns anyway.

When your local newspaper reports on a tournament, record the results and where the winning catch (and runner-up's bass) was caught.

Probably the best source for accumulating this type of information are the tournament organizations that have magazines. On some cold winter day, go to the library and look through the back issues of *BASSMASTER Magazine*, concentrating on the tournament results. Concentrate on what area of the lake the tournament's top finishers fished. Was it in the backs of the creeks, up the river or down by the dam? To me, that is the most valuable piece of information available.

At the conclusion of tournaments you have either competed in or watched as a spectator, listen carefully to the top finishers. I have found that fishermen are not very reliable except after they have won a tournament when they tend to spill their guts during their moment in the spotlight. And don't be afraid to question them. I have made it a point of personally congratulating each tournament winner and politely asking them about their pattern. They'll usually tell you every thing.

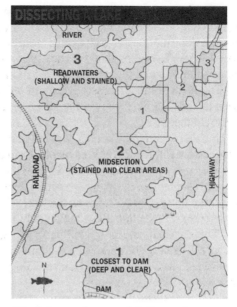

You'll be surprised at how quickly you can begin compiling data that will be important in the future. You don't have to have the results of 500 tournaments like I do to gain enough information to start detecting seasonal patterns on a particular lake. You can do pretty well with the results of 20 to 50 events. With a minimum of five years worth of events, you can start seeing some reliable seasonal patterns. Obviously, the more data you accumulate, the more accurate the seasonal patterns will be.

It is important to arrange your record-keeping under three headings — natural lakes, manmade reservoirs and rivers.

The differences in seasonal patterns between natural and manmade lakes will be subtle. The differences between those types of lakes and rivers can vary significantly. The universality of the patterns varies somewhat when you start mixing records from unlike bodies of water, so I recommend making those distinctions.

The neat thing about compiling records is that the more information you obtain, the more prepared you can be to fish that lake. With enough data, you can not only pick out seasonal patterns more quickly, but a secondary pattern will also emerge.

And even a third pattern. By the time you get to the lake, you have the patterns that you're going to be looking for. And that gives you some alternatives if you arrive to find that recent rains have muddied the backs of the creeks, which was your primary seasonal pattern.

An obvious question is how many seasonal patterns should you concern yourself with?

If you know three patterns in every season of the year, you will be ahead of 90 percent of the fishermen. You don't have to know 10 patterns for every season. For example, if I print out the month of October on a certain lake, I look for only three or four patterns. Those patterns will tell me, basically, the general area of the lake and the type of water I should be concentrating on.

The most dominant seasonal pattern will often be the only pattern you'll need to consider once you get on the water. Let's use the October Classics to illustrate that point.

Upon examining the results, we find that 80 to 90 percent of all of the fish caught in these Classics (held on manmade impoundments) came from the back of the creeks — Sections 3 and 4. So now if I'm going to any lake in the fall of the year (September through November), I will automatically look at a map and select the three largest creeks on that lake. Then I will start right at the rear of those creeks, forgetting about the rest of the lake.

The data puts me in the ballpark. My work is far from over, however, because I've still got to develop the current (prevailing) pattern and exactly position the bass. But I know I am spending my limited amount of time in the area with the greatest potential.

Chapter 42

Probable Patterns
For Each Season

The average weekend angler and the tournament pro share a common dilemma — time.

Our practice time is limited, meaning we have just three days to find enough bass to have a shot at winning. Although the monetary stakes aren't as high, the weekend fisherman's valuable fishing time is usually limited to a day-and-a-half or so on the weekend. So he has to locate fish quickly as well,

And we all know how difficult that can be, even on a lake you know well.

The answer, as we discussed in the last chapter, is to take advantage of the seasonal movements and behavior of bass, nature's way of patterning the fish for us. By keeping notes and records, both unfamiliar bodies of water and our home lake focus into a clearer picture when we have seasonal patterns that show us where the bass are usually positioned during each season of the year.

Seasonal patterns give you a starting point on any natural lake, manmade reservoir or river in America. The differences in seasonal patterns between natural and impounded lakes are subtle, while rivers can be such unstable environments that they will have patterns that vary greatly from lakes. We will discuss the differences in these three water types a little later.

Since obtaining data is a chore that will take some time to accomplish, I will attempt to give you a head-start on any upcoming fishing trip by outlining seasonal patterns to look for. Utilizing my experience on the national tournament trails and what the results of more than 500 tournaments have shown me, I will attempt to offer the most generic starting points for locating bass on a season-by-season basis. This information should be valid on natural lakes and impounded reservoirs in any geographic region of the country.

Keep in mind that, for sake of clarity, we have dissected the lakes into three sections. Section 1 is the lower portion of the main lake (beginning at the dam on an impoundment), where the water is usually the deepest and clearest. Section 3 begins at the headwaters and tends to be the shallowest and more off-colored section. Section 2 is the area between the two where you have a mixing of water depths and clarity.

In my system, I also sectionalize the major creeks. Section 1 is the part of the creek closest to the main lake, which is where the clearest water will usually be found. Section 2 is the middle part of the creek and Section 3 is the rear, where the shallowest (and often most off-colored) water is located. On creeks that have a tributary leading from the back of it, I designate that as Section 4.

With that diagramming in mind, I'll attempt to guide you on a seasonal tour to locating bass, using seasonal patterns as my compass.

Based on past experience and my seasonal records, the first pattern I would look for in the fall is the backs of the creeks. Sound simple enough?

But if you are fishing a massive body of water like Toledo Bend that has 35 major creeks, you can't possibly check all of them in a limited amount of

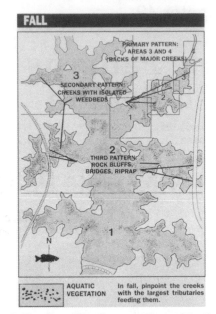

In fall, pinpoint the creeks with the largest tributaries feeding them.

In fall, pinpoint the creeks with the largest tributaries feeding them.

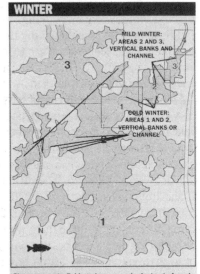

Clunn suggests fishing clearer creeks instead of murky ones in cold weather and most importantly, "Think Vertical."

Clunn suggests fishing cleaner creeks instead of murky ones in cold weather and most importantly "think vertical."

time. At this point, you basically have to select the best creeks. I use two methods for this.

First, examining a map, I pinpoint the creeks that have the largest tributaries feeding them. These will be the creeks that will be most fertile and have the most cover. That means these creeks are most likely to harbor the largest populations of bass, as well as the bigger fish. The smaller secondary (feeder) creeks that extend up into the country side will not be as fertile, which means the amount of baitfish that lives there will be limited. Consequently, the number of bass (particularly big bass) will be limited as well.

The second step I take to select the creeks that I should concentrate on is to fly the lake. This is really an inexpensive way to learn a lake — much cheaper than hiring a guide or even the gas you would spend running all over the lake. You and a friend can spend an hour flying over the lake for $35 to $50 each and easily pinpoint the creeks with the most potential.

After that, I select two or three creeks for each of my three practice days and go directly to the final third of it (sections 3 and 4). That's where I start in the fall on lakes from New York to Texas.

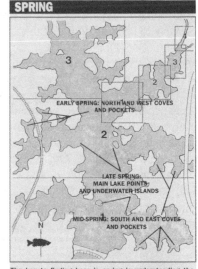

SPRING

EARLY SPRING: NORTH AND WEST COVES AND POCKETS

LATE SPRING: MAIN LAKE POINTS AND UNDERWATER ISLANDS

MID-SPRING: SOUTH AND EAST COVES AND POCKETS

The key to finding bass in spring is understanding the heating cycle in your own lake — knowing which areas heat up earliest. Illustrations: Bernie Schultz

Understanding the heating cycle in your own lake is important in the spring.

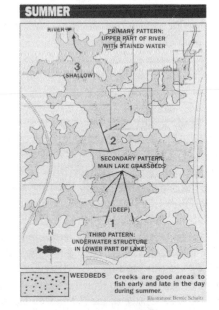

SUMMER

RIVER

PRIMARY PATTERN: UPPER PART OF RIVER WITH STAINED WATER

(SHALLOW)

SECONDARY PATTERN: MAIN LAKE GRASSBEDS

(DEEP)

THIRD PATTERN: UNDERWATER STRUCTURE IN LOWER PART OF LAKE

WEEDBEDS — Creeks are good areas to fish early and late in the day during summer. Illustrations: Bernie Schultz

Creeks are good areas to fish early and late in the day during the summer.

My secondary fall pattern revolves around aquatic vegetation.

You have to keep in mind that the vegetation will be declining during the fall, depending on the month. The grass will be in various stages of breaking up and disappearing. I actually look for vegetation that has broken up considerably, which is the center of my secondary fall pattern.

Let's say you are fishing Alabama's Lake Guntersville in October. You pull into a creek where there are thousands of acres of vegetation that is still extremely thick. But in the next creek, the vegetation is about half of what it was during the summer. The vegetation is broken up and not quite as thick as the grass in the previous creek. This is where I concentrate my efforts. There is probably an equal population of bass in both creeks, but the fish in this creek are likely to be more concentrated and easier to locate. In the previous creek, the abundance of lush vegetation would create a greater challenge (not to mention more work) because it would spread the bass throughout.

I find isolated weedbeds to be especially productive during this time of year.

The third fall pattern I always look for centers around broken rock, either manmade or natural. A lot of people will automatically think of rock bluffs or bridges on the main lake. But I look for these small bluff banks or bridges crossing Sections 3 and 4 of a creek where vegetation is also present. This would be what I would consider a bonanza-type area — where all three of my fall patterns exist in the same locale.

My approach to locating bass in the winter is extremely simple. I start with my best fall pattern (the shallow water in sections 3 and 4 of the creeks) and work my way out.

It is also important to think vertical when looking for wintertime bass. The fish are going to align themselves on something vertical, whether it is the vertical outside edge of a weedline in shallow water or the vertical back of a cove in 80 feet of water in a deep canyon lake. They will be on the more vertical sides of the points as opposed to the sloping sides.

Think vertical. That is why the creek channels are such a key during this time of year. The bass were in Sections 3 and 4 at the beginning of the winter, but they will start to relate to that channel more and more as the season progresses. In the middle of winter, they may be in Section 2 of the creeks. And if it is a brutal winter, the fish can often be located along the channel in Section 1, the area closest to the main lake.

You can follow bass in the winter by taking into consideration the severity of the weather. If it has been a mild winter, they could be in the back of the creeks (Sections 3 and 4) instead of out on the channel. With the passing of cold fronts, they will move out on the channel. If it has been a harsh winter, they may move along the edge of the channel to the mouth of the creek. It's just a matter of following them along this vertical edge which most of the fish are going to relate to in the winter months.

Winter is a simple time for locating bass. But it will usually be either feast or famine because the fish tend to be more concentrated, whether it be a natural lake, manmade impoundment or river.

Springtime bass will always be positioned in relation to the stages of the spawning cycle — pre-spawn, spawn and post-spawn.

Although many anglers enjoy fishing for bedding bass during the spring, I do not. These fish can be too unpredictable, especially when you are dealing with a limited amount of time, such as a tournament situation. To me, the easiest bass to catch are pre-spawn fish, so I concentrate on fish in this phase.

The key to spring is understanding the heating cycle within your own lake — knowing which areas traditionally heat up the earliest and the latest. And then following that heating cycle around the lake.

The first bass that will move up to spawn will probably be on the northern and western portions of the lake, the areas that will warm up the earliest. Or in certain protected areas on the lake like marinas and some coves. These are the areas I will concentrate on because they will be 4 or 5 degrees warmer than other portions of the lake. And the bass will be most active here.

As the bass in these areas go on the beds, I'll then leave them and move to the southern and eastern banks. By now, these banks are beginning to warm and their inhabitants are getting more active as they enter the pre-spawn mode.

I tend to chase the pre-spawn bass all around the lake. The last pre-spawn fish will have led me out to the middle of the lake. Obviously, the deepest part of the lake will be the last to warm. The bass will move up on underwater islands and long main lake points. These resident fish, which don't travel all of the way to the backs of the coves to bed, will be some of the last bass to spawn in the entire lake.

Once I have finished fishing the final pre-spawn bass in a lake, I then return to the northern banks where the fish have completed spawning and have just begun to enter their early summer pattern. This way I avoid having to fish for spawning bass. But a guy who enjoys chasing bedding bass could follow the same cycle all over the lake.

Post-spawn bass are, traditionally, difficult to catch, because they tend to be so transitional. They come off of the nests and move, I believe, to deep water and into their summer pattern almost overnight. And they tend to be in a deteriorated state, which makes them tentative and finicky. They tend to suspend a great deal because the bottom of the deeper portions of the lake hasn't warmed.

I've had the greatest success — by far — with concentrating on pre-spawn bass during the spring.

The summer months can be approached from two directions — fishing for either deep or shallow bass.

In most lakes, you usually have a situation where 80 percent of the fish will be deep and only 20 percent will be shallow. So you have to make the mental decision to do what you are most efficient at as a fisherman. In the summer months, the bass have more options than any other season. They can be shallow or deep. Or the fish can be shallow early and move off deep in the middle of the day. That means you have a wide range of territory to consider.

What I try to do with the limited amount of time I usually have available is eliminate several of the options for the bass. That's why my prime summer pattern takes place up the river in Section 3 of the main lake. By going there, I remove the deep option. I go up the river where he is a resident shallow-water fish year-round and the only deep water he relates to is the edge of the river channel.

In the summer, these bass will relate to the edge of the river channel, which usually means a depth of less than 15 feet. That is my No. 1 choice because I am more efficient at catching the 20 percent of the lake's bass population that will be shallow.

If you are good with electronics and fishing invisible structure is your game (and you have the time to spend probing the depths), you might want to stay down in Section 1 of the main lake and fish for the 80 percent that are resident.

The second summer pattern I always look for involves aquatic vegetation, which will hold shallow-water bass throughout the year. The most productive summer vegetation is found in the main lake, where it is exposed to the wind. The wind can really be beneficial because it offsets any problem you might have with too much water clarity.

The grassbeds along the main lake can be productive throughout the day during the summer, while the vegetation found in the creeks will usually only yield fish during the early and late hours. Once the sun gets high and the creek heats up, the oxygen gets depleted in tributaries with very little flow. And the bass get sluggish. But the main lake vegetation doesn't have that problem, because of its proximity to deep water, which has a cooling effect.

The third summer pattern I always consider centers around broken rock, such as riprap. But this is another early-and-late pattern unless you have wind blowing into the rocks. It is strictly a game of accessibility in this case. The wind allows the fish to move up shallow, making them more accessible to you. Otherwise, the bass will be deep and, for most fishermen, out of their level of efficiency.

That is my short-course in using seasonal patterns to pinpoint the areas with the greatest potential for holding large numbers of fish. I need to emphasize that these are not the only patterns that exist. These are the successful patterns that the seasonal tendencies have produced for me over the years.

Chapter 43

The Final Steps

Now that you understand the concept of using seasonal patterns to locate bass and even have some insight into my favorite patterns for each season, you are half-way home. But the work is far from over.

Seasonal patterns allow you to take advantage of the biological predictability of the bass, so that you have a good starting point when attempting to locate fish in a limited amount of time. Understanding the universality of the seasonal patterns and using them to produce a gameplan before ever leaving home is the major step in my approach to locating bass.

But there are two final steps that the top-notch fishermen have mastered — determining the current (prevailing) pattern on that body of water and then fine-tuning that pattern.

Establishing the current pattern means spending the necessary time to determine exactly where the bass are positioned. The seasonal patterns indicate the areas of the lake where the bass should be most abundant and the current pattern positions them with the accuracy you need to be able to fish for them.

With confidence that the seasonal patterns have directed you to the area or areas with the greatest potential for harboring fish, you arrive in Lake X. What do you do next?

Let's say you are going to concentrate on Section 3, the backs of the creeks. That could be an area of 5 acres or 2,000 acres, depending on the size of the lake. Regardless of the size of the area, you've got to be able to establish the current pattern. That means applying the prevailing weather conditions and variables as well as the lake conditions to pinpoint the position of the bass.

I use a simplified approach. I go into an area and mentally shut out the rest of the lake, concentrating only on the section or sections that the seasonal patterns have pointed me toward. I approach this section the way I would work a small farm pond. When you walk along the edge of a farm pond, the first thing you do is identify the visible alternatives where the bass could be, which might be old dead standing timber in the back surrounded by lily pads or a few stumps on the opposite shoreline. That gives me three visible alternatives where the bass could be. And there is probably some invisible structure, like a couple of brushpiles that the farmer pushed in with his bulldozer.

In this pond, we have five alternatives where the bass could be — three visible and two invisible. Bass are such object-oriented creatures that 99 percent of the fish you catch in that farm pond are going to be relating to one of those alternatives.

The neat thing about applying that same approach to a section of a lake or reservoir — regardless of size — is that there are always less than six alternatives where you will find bass. It is not like you have a massive amount of structure and cover to eliminate.

Once you identify those alternatives in the backs of the creeks, for example, you've got to systematically eliminate the places where the bass could be positioned. As a rule of thumb, I eliminate the easiest alternatives first, which include the shallow and visible cover, which is what most anglers are most efficient at fishing. If the bass are on the shoreline structure or shallow-water cover, you don't have to even concern yourself with the more difficult types of structure to locate found in deep water.

A question that often arises at this point is how long should you fish various alternatives in an area before eliminating them? That can vary. But don't be in a rush. For example, if you are fishing lily pads in a cove, check out more than one set. I'll fish the pads in the back of the cove and then those found on the points. I'll then fish the pads on the calm side of the cove as well as those on the windy side. If you spend two or three hours concentrating on lily pads in various situations without much success, it is probably time to switch to a different type of cover or structure.

There is no substitute for spending sufficient time during this elimination process. You should not run around hurriedly, spending 15 minutes here and then running across the lake to another spot.

If you systematically work your way from the shoreline out, you will have accomplished something at the end of the day — even if you haven't caught a fish. You have eliminated some of the alternatives where the bass could be holding. That's enough to get me excited, because I know there are only two or three alternatives remaining that the bass can be relating to.

So we've eliminated the shallow cover on the first day. Today, we're going to move out a little deeper. I decide to try running a crankbait down a creek channel, when suddenly I catch a fish. Then I miss one and have a couple of bass follow it to the boat. Then I catch another one. After that kind of action, I decide that the bass are out on the creek channels in 5 to 10 feet.

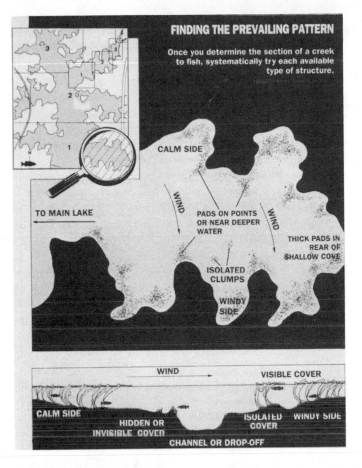

FINDING THE PREVAILING PATTERN

Once you determine the section of a creek to fish, systematically try each available type of structure.

CALM SIDE

TO MAIN LAKE

WIND

WIND

PADS ON POINTS OR NEAR DEEPER WATER

THICK PADS IN REAR OF SHALLOW COVE

ISOLATED CLUMPS

WINDY SIDE

WIND

VISIBLE COVER

CALM SIDE

HIDDEN OR INVISIBLE COVER

ISOLATED COVER

WINDY SIDE

CHANNEL OR DROP-OFF

What we have done is establish the prevailing pattern by systematically eliminating the alternatives available to the bass. People try to make pattern fishing so much more complicated than it really is.

Now is the time for take the prevailing pattern we've found a step farther.

Because I've missed a couple of fish, I begin to wonder if the crankbait I'm using is too big. So I tie on a smaller one in an attempt to improve my strike-per-catch ratio. I catch a couple bass on that bait. Then I have to consider if there is another lure that will catch more or maybe larger bass. So I go back through the area with a jig or a plastic worm.

This is the beginning of the fine-tuning process that transforms the current pattern into the specific pattern.

Establishing the specific pattern — the exact positioning of the bass to the structure or cover — is the final step to my seasonal approach to bass fishing.

To illustrate this, let's say you've determined that the fish are on fallen trees that have been cut down by beavers or dumped by erosion. It's about 10 a.m.

and you haven't had a strike all morning. The sun has risen above the trees and the light is getting bright. So you toss a spinnerbait down the shaded side of the fallen tree. This produces your first bass, which makes you suspect that you may be onto the specific pattern. You approach another tree the same way and pull another fish out of the shade. But that is not enough to be the specific pattern, in my opinion.

Take it a step farther. You know the bass are relating to the shady side of the fallen trees, but examine it closer. Which limbs are the bass on? Determine what part of the object the fish are using.

Very few of even the best tournament pros are adept at pinpointing the specific pattern. The first guys to become efficient at flipping were the first anglers to really concentrate on the specific pattern, because they actually got inside the whole structure and broke it down into major limbs. They also took note of what water depth the fish came out of along the larger tree falls.

You will be surprised how many times the bass will come from the same area of the tree fall. This isn't anything magical. It is just the environment positioning the fish, a fact of nature. A prime example is in the fall when the reservoirs are being lowered. The bass tend to position themselves toward the end of the fallen tree to avoid that super-shallow water at the base of the tree (near the bank). In the spring when the lakes and reservoirs typically rise, the fish will usually be in the new water, the shallow sections of the tree fall.

Or if there is current present, you might find small eddy pockets along a fallen tree. That will usually hold fish because a bass will tend to avoid having to battle the current.

Be conscious of the exact water depth along that tree fall where you caught a fish. If it is spring and you pitch a jig along the tree and it sinks about a foot before a bass nails it, that should tell you that he is suspended near the surface — warming himself like a snake or turtle. That should tell you not to waste time by letting your lure fish deep. In the summer, though, you might have to fish that jig deep around that fallen tree.

The idea is to try to be as in tune with the bass' environment as possible. Pay attention and be alert because the first bass you catch will often tell you exactly how the second, third and fourth fish are going to be positioned. If you were watching some girl water-skiing down the lake or slapping at a fly and you suddenly caught a bass, you probably wouldn't notice that your bait had fallen a little deeper just before the strike. You might have missed the most important clue of the day.

That's why I don't like to carry on a conversation while I'm fishing. Fishing to me is almost like this huge play that is taking place on the water and you're part of the act. You are just awaiting your cue to get involved in the play. If you miss your cue, you miss the whole play. On the water, you've got to always be looking for your cue to get involved in this natural act that is taking place.

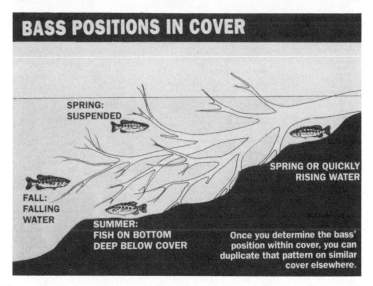

BASS POSITIONS IN COVER

SPRING:
SUSPENDED

SPRING OR QUICKLY
RISING WATER

FALL:
FALLING
WATER

SUMMER:
FISH ON BOTTOM
DEEP BELOW COVER

Once you determine the bass'
position within cover, you can
duplicate that pattern on similar
cover elsewhere.

After enough time spent concentrating on the water, you will finally realize that there is a natural reason for where the fish is positioned, an environmental reason for his behavior. And what is affecting him is probably affecting the next fish you come across in the same area during the same time frame. That is what is so neat about it. With enough experience, you will become part of the whole scheme of things and, all of a sudden, you will realize why that bass is sitting there. Then it is almost electric because you know where the next fish is going to come from. You throw your bait in there and you know when he's going to hit it.

Reaching this point is not that hard. But for some reason, it's almost like we've got blinders on and few of us really pay the kind of attention it takes to detect nature's cue.

HOT OFF OF THE PRESS!

Secrets
of
America's
Best Bass Pros

Every angler knows that the key to becoming a top fisherman is spending enough time on the water to experience all that bass fishing has to offer. But even the most serious weekend angler cannot afford to spend the number of hours that the nation's tournament pros put in each year.

The Pro Advantage

With the recent publication of the new book **Secrets of America's Best Bass Pros,** you can take advantage of their years of experience. In this impressive new book, the biggest names in fishing share their innermost secrets with Bassmaster Magazine Senior Writer Tim Tucker. Every aspect of consistently locating and catching bass is explored in this fully illustrated new book.

To Order:
Send a check or money order for $10.95 (plus $2 for postage and handling) to Tim Tucker Outdoor Productions, Rt.. 2, Box 177, Micanopy, FL 32667.

Name _____

Address _____

City_____ State/Zip _____

Roland Martin

Rick Clunn

Larry Nixon

Bill Dance

Guido Hibdon

Hank Parker

Gary Klein

Shaw Grigsby

Doug Hannon

Tommy Martin

Ken Cook

Jimmy Houston

Denny Brauer

Joe Thomas

Charlie Ingram

Paul Elias

Guy Eaker

George Cochran

Charlie Reed

Jim Bitter

Rich Tauber

Woo Daves

Dave Gliebe

Greg Hines

Learn From the Pros

In the comfort of your home . . .
While driving to the lake . . .
Or sitting in traffic . . .
Or fishing your favorite bass hole!

High-quality instructional audio cassettes — a unique way to improve your skills as a bass angler!

"*The Bass Sessions tapes will become among the most valuable learning tools available to bass fishermen from the novice to the most serious angler.*" — Shaw Grigsby

"The Bass Sessions series of instructional audio cassettes are designed to allow the country's top bass pros to share their insight into various aspects of bass fishing in a conversational forum that bass enthusiasts like myself can take advantage of at their convenience. In the Bass Sessions tapes, which are about 30 minutes in length, I go one-on-one with top bass pros with real credentials. And they willingly share their innermost secrets.

"You have my personal guarantee that the Bass Sessions series will make you a better fisherman!"

Tim Tucker

The Bass Sessions Lineup

☐ **Trophy Hunting for Bass** $8.95

Roland Martin, Doug Hannon and Guido Hibdon discuss the habits and habitats of *big* bass.

☐ **Championship Worm Tactics** $8.95

Get an insight into fishing plastic worms from the experts — Shaw Grigsby, Jim Bitter and Bernie Schultz.

☐ **Tubejig Trickery** $8.95

The three best tubejig fishermen in America — Guido Hibdon, Shaw Grigsby and Roland Martin — share their secrets of finesse fishing.

☐ **Surface Fishing Secrets** $8.95

Learn to get more out of topwater lures from veteran surface-fishing pros Jim Bitter, Steve Daniel and Larry Lazoen.

☐ **Heavy Cover Tactics** $8.95

Big bass live in some *bad* places. Shaw Grigsby, Roland Martin and Guido Hibdon reveal their most effective tactics.

☐ **River Fishing Simplified** $8.95

River fishing is a whole new ballgame from lake fishing. Experts Doug Hannon, Bernie Schultz and Pete Thliveros remove the mystery associated with fishing moving water.

☐ **Advanced Shiner Fishing Techniques** $8.95

The wild shiner is the best big-bass bait known to man and no one knows more about fishing shiners than Doug Hannon, Glen Hunter and Dan Thurmond.

Special Offer!

Order all seven tapes and receive a bonus tape *Pro Bait Modifications* absolutely free!

☐ I want to receive the tapes checked above and enclose $8.95 for each, along with $1 for each to cover postage and handling

☐ I want to receive the entire Bass Sessions Series. Enclosed is $65, which includes the cost of shipping. Send my free bonus tape.

Send check or money order to Tim Tucker Outdoor Productions, Rt. 2, Box 177, Micanopy, Fla., 32667. Visa and MasterCard orders can call 904-466-0808.